Therapeutic Residential Care for Children and Young People

Therapeutic Residential Care for Children and Young People

An Attachment and Trauma-Informed Model for Practice

Susan Barton, Rudy Gonzalez
and Patrick Tomlinson

Foreword by Brian Burdekin

Jessica Kingsley *Publishers*
London and Philadelphia

Extracts from Hannon, Wood and Bazalgette 2010 are reproduced
by permission of Louise Bazalgette, Demos.
Figure 1 from Prilleltensky, Peirson and Nelson 2001 on p.23 is
reproduced by permission of Isaac Prilleltensky.
Figure 10.1 from Friedman 2005 on p.242 is reproduced by permission of Trafford Publishing.
Figure A2.1 from Prilleltensky 2006 on p.260 is reproduced by permission of Isaac Prilletensky.

First published in 2012
by Jessica Kingsley Publishers
116 Pentonville Road
London N1 9JB, UK
and
400 Market Street, Suite 400
Philadelphia, PA 19106, USA

www.jkp.com

Library of Congress Cataloging in Publication Data
Barton, Susan, 1951-
   Therapeutic residential care for children and young people : an attachment
and trauma-informed model for practice / Susan Barton, Rudy Gonzalez, and
Patrick Tomlinson ; foreword by Brian Burdekin.
       p. ; cm.
   Includes bibliographical references and index.
   ISBN 978-1-84905-255-9 (alk. paper)
   1. Child psychotherapy--Residential treatment. 2. Adolescent psychotherapy-
-Residential treatment. I. Gonzalez, Rudy, 1973- II. Tomlinson, Patrick,
1962- III. Title.
   [DNLM: 1. Stress Disorders, Traumatic--therapy. 2. Adolescent. 3. Child
Abuse--therapy. 4. Child. 5. Residential Facilities. WM 172.5]
   RJ504.5.B38 2012
   618.92'89--dc23
                            2011017938

British Library Cataloguing in Publication Data
A CIP catalogue record for this book is available from the British Library

ISBN 978 1 84905 255 9

Printed and bound in Great Britain

Dedication

This book has been inspired by the love that we have for our own children and the children that we work with. Who constantly inspire us to lead from the heart. We hope that this book inspires the community to respond to every child in a way that fills them with a sense of love and belonging.

Rudy

To Patricia, Lucas, Thalia and Giselle for your love and support. To my parents for instilling in me the importance of family and community and a belief in the value of education.

Susan

To my beloved grandchildren Sienna, Tahnee, Maia, Isaiah, Asher, Ethan, Jedd, Yasmin, Anastasia, Eloise, Otelia and to my grandchildren yet to be born to our family. Good enough reasons to change the world. I am thankful knowing that you belong to such devoted and loving parents. I long for each moment with you. How blessed I am to have you all in my life. Remember to always lead from the heart.

Patrick

To my daughter and son, Patsy and Daniel.

Contents

Foreword

More than two decades ago, as Federal Human Rights Commissioner of Australia, I chaired the National Inquiry into Homeless Children. We recommended specific strategies for a co-ordinated and effective national policy to protect the most vulnerable and disadvantaged young people in our community. The government responded with a $100 million package of various initiatives – and the wider community could no longer ignore the issue.

However, notwithstanding Australia's wealth, outstanding work by several individuals and community groups, further government initiatives, and mounting evidence of what works in practice, thousands of vulnerable children still receive sub-standard care and the number of homeless young people has increased. In 1989 we estimated that 25,000 children and young people under the age of eighteen were homeless; in 2011 it is estimated that there are 50,000. In 1989 there were 14,000 children and young people in state care; by 2006 there were 27,000; by 2009, 34,000; and by 2010 there were 35,895.

We continue to see high levels of complex trauma experienced by many of these children, due to their abuse and neglect, and we continue to see 35 per cent of children in state care enter homelessness within the first twelve months of 'leaving care'. These figures are a national disgrace. In many cases the basic human rights of these children are still being violated – or simply ignored.

The authors of this book clearly demonstrate that 'trauma-informed' approaches, focusing on community reintegration and providing meaningful attachments for children and young people, have positive outcomes and can end the cycle of abuse, neglect and homelessness. Their approach and, more importantly, their results give real meaning to the rights all children should enjoy.

The book provides a theoretical as well as practical understanding of all the elements involved in a successful model of care for traumatized children. The authors, with over 70 years of relevant work between them, relate their extensive personal experiences, those of other professionals working with traumatized children, and the stories of children themselves who have successfully recovered from childhood trauma. The result is a comprehensive account of what actually works, which could potentially provide a blueprint for both governments and communities working with homeless and at-risk young people.

This book clearly sets out the Lighthouse therapeutic approach to working with traumatized children in 'out of home care' and homelessness. It promotes something close to my own heart: the critical importance of 'family' and a sense of community in healing trauma and providing a better future for our most vulnerable children and young people. The authors have my thanks – and, I hope, your attention.

Professor Brian Burdekin BA LLD LLM,
International Human Rights Adviser,
former Federal Human Rights Commissioner of Australia

Acknowledgements

To the young people who shared their stories for this book, and all the children and young people who have trusted us to share their stories over the years, and have given us the gift of being part of their lives.

We wish to pay special tribute to Vicki Vidor. Vicki has been our staunchest supporter and lifelong friend, who from the beginning realized the importance of the young people's stories being told and of providing a voice to the many children around the world who have experienced abuse and neglect. She knew that homelessness was more than a lack of shelter but also included a lack of family, social and material supports that most of us take for granted. Her concern matched our own – she knew that more needed to be done. Vicki became intimately involved in our dream and through her unwavering support of our Therapeutic Family Model of Care we have been able to advocate for a more loving response to those who have missed out on the love and care of a parent. Your support and encouragement to write this book creates further opportunities to share our approach with others throughout the world. Vicki, we will never have the words to describe the depth of gratitude that we have for you and your support of our work with abused and traumatized children. You can be assured that your gift to humanity has been large and meaningful and has provided children with their fundamental right to live in a safe and loving home. You continually give of yourself wholeheartedly and for that the Lighthouse community has been blessed. The world is a better place for having you in it. We hope that our appreciation of what you contribute to these children sings through these pages. Your family must be proud of you – as we are.

To all the countless people who have supported us over the years with love and inspiration and expanded our horizons, our heartfelt gratitude. To all the members of the Lighthouse community: our young people, carers, direct and indirect care teams, volunteers, community committees, corporate partners, trusts and foundations, community partner organizations and board of directors.

And especially to our beloved families who over the years have contributed to our understanding of the need for love and the importance of family: Trish, Giselle, Lucas, Thalia, Mirta and Adalberto, Cardoso and Gonzalez family,

Brett, Cooper and Deb, Chandima, Renee and Kane B, Kane and Diana, LaToya and Chris, Jacob and Letetia, Michael and Terrie, Mark and Paul.

To the many teachers, mentors and colleagues that we have had in our years of study and work who have inspired and have expected more of us and encouraged our passion for our work. We are sorry we can't list everyone's names, but all of you deserve our gratitude. We will name those who have been pivotal in our professional development including: Dr Jo Grimwade, Dr Isaac Prilleltensky, Heather Gridley, Dr Renzo Vittorino, Dr Denise Charman, Dr Alison Griffiths, Dr Adrian Fisher, Greg Lolas, Dr Sarah Crome, Dr Colin Riess, Kane Bowden, Leo Maher, Cynthia Johnson, Lilly Cabrillo, Bernie Durkin, Tymur Hussein, Les Terry, Emma Sampson, Briony Kercheval, Helena Culbertson, Margot Cairns, Jane Jordon, Jim and Suzanne Fizdale, John Whitwell, Chris Knight, Adrian Ward, Olya Khaleelee, Clive Firman, Paul van Heeswyk, Mary Walsh, Dr Linda Hoyle, Dr Neil Thompson and Quinn Street Philosophical Society.

And to those who read the manuscript and provided much valuable feedback and support: Patricia, Cheyne, Jorge, Jo, Kane, Kristen and Sarah.

Our literary and legal support team which has included Jason Watson and Hayley Sher at FAL Lawyers, Mark Krenzer and Dr Lisa Symonds at Clayton UTZ, Anne O'Donovan and Brian Doyle.

Jessica Kingsley Publishers, for their belief in the book and their commitment to supporting the publication. In particular, Stephen Jones, Caroline Walton and Alexandra Higson.

We wish to acknowledge each other, for the bond that we have developed through the journey writing this book and which will last a lifetime. The collaboration to put into words so elegantly what we feel and value about the way we care for the most vulnerable children in our community is a true gift.

Authors' Note

The stories in this book are true and in order to ensure anonymity and protect privacy we have altered identifying details. The children's names have been changed as have the names of carers.

The stories provided are a small number of the many that we have heard over the past thirty-five years. Collectively we have worked with over a thousand children and adults who have endured severe neglect and abuse in their childhood at the hands of those who should have loved and protected them. We hope that the courage and resilience of the children whose stories we have told, and the many others who have similar stories, shine through in this book.

Introduction

A child's life is like a piece of paper, on which every passer-by leaves a mark.

Ancient Chinese proverb

The aim of this book is to provide an understanding of childhood trauma, how it impacts on child development, and how we might work with traumatized children to facilitate recovery. The book is specifically about working with children in the entirety of day-to-day life. For children who have been severely traumatized by abuse and neglect, often from infancy onwards, every aspect of their life needs to be considered. Every event in everyday life is an opportunity to encourage therapeutic change. The authors have over seventy-five years' experience between them of working with traumatized children and young people. This experience has informed the approaches and beliefs expressed in this book.

In particular, the authors refer extensively to our work at the Lighthouse Foundation, which Susan Barton founded in 1991, after sixteen years of working with traumatized children in her own home as a foster carer. However, in doing so, it is our intention to highlight theory and practice which is universal and can be used or adapted by anyone working with children in therapeutic residential care and other settings, such as foster care.

We have developed a 'trauma-informed' approach that influences every aspect of our work: the work with individual children; the work in groups; the way we organize the home environment and daily routine; the way we run our organization; and our relationship with the wider community. Our theoretical approach is particularly influenced by community psychology, psychodynamic, attachment and neurobiological trauma theories. Therefore we take account of the individual psyche, the social and the biological to create a holistic and integrated approach to care and treatment.

We draw upon some of the concepts developed in therapeutic communities over the last fifty years or more and combine this with contemporary neurobiological research on child development. We believe it is necessary for an organization, like the Lighthouse Foundation, that provides therapeutic residential care and treatment to have a coherent theoretical model. This enables the whole team and organization to have a shared understanding of trauma and the approaches used; use the same language; and provide the consistency that is so important for traumatized children. It is particularly important that the organizational culture, processes, leadership and style of management are compatible with the therapeutic approach.

Throughout the book we talk of the traumatized 'child' and 'children', whilst the work we are talking about is often with teenagers who we normally call 'young people', we have used the words 'child' and 'children' for a number of reasons. The words are commonly used internationally and therefore it makes for consistent and easier reading.

Often we are talking about trauma that has occurred in early childhood and infancy; so much of what we have to say about the treatment of trauma is also relevant to younger children. We also draw on the experience of the authors in working therapeutically with younger children. We refer to 'looked-after children' and children in 'out of home care'. There are different definitions of these terms in different countries. For example, when talking about children in out of home care in Australia, it refers to children who are in the care of the state. In this book we have used the term more broadly, referring to children who are unable to be cared for by their families of origin, and are now residing in other care environments – foster care, kinship care, residential care, therapeutic residential care, homelessness services and other forms of care.

The term 'carer' is also used extensively in the book. We understand there are people that provide care to children who may not refer to themselves, and are not referred to, as carers, for example residential youth workers, youth workers, social workers, child care workers, and various other roles. When we refer to carers we are talking about those who provide care to children as an alternative to the parents of origin. This book is as relevant to foster carers and professional carers as it is to other workers who provide care to children in out of home care. Finally, throughout the book we tend to use specific gender, he or she, for ease of reading rather than continually using 'he/she'. Usually the role or person we refer to could equally be male or female and we are not intending to be exclusive in any way.

In writing this book there are three specific dilemmas we would like to draw attention to. First, as we are particularly focused on trauma, its impact on child development, and how to treat it, there is a danger that we give a slanted view of the child. Whilst the children we work with have all suffered significant trauma, we are aware that it is important not to label the child and attribute all aspects of his or her personality and behaviour to trauma. Labels can become like a mask that binds the person in and prevents us from seeing the whole person. For instance, a fifteen-year old child who has been traumatized and is in a withdrawn state, as he begins to recover may develop into a difficult and challenging adolescent. The difficult behaviour may be healthy but it would be easy for us to respond as if it is entirely related to the child's trauma. In this sense the label of trauma can become difficult for the child to move on from. The same has been said about working with sexually abused children. It is easy to focus on the abuse and lose sight of the child.

We aim in our work, to create thoughtfulness about children and to work hard at not making too many assumptions. Tomlinson describes how the holistic approach aims to avoid labelling:

> This is where we see the child as her problem or as the sum of her problems rather than as a child first and foremost. It doesn't let us see Lucy, only the self-harmer; it doesn't picture Tom but only the sexually aggressive 10-year-old. It is also a kind of labelling which focuses on the child's deficits rather than her strengths, that sees her as passive, rather than someone who, with help, can participate in her own recovery. (Tomlinson 2008, p.90)

This brings us to our second dilemma. We have attempted to provide the reader with an understanding of the issues we write about and to offer some practical guidance of what we and others in the field have found to work. However, this is done within the spirit of encouraging a certain kind of thinking and sensitivity rather than a prescriptive approach. As Turner, McFarlane and van der Kolk (2007, p.537) pointed out, 'Helping people who develop Post Traumatic Stress Disorder (PTSD) in the aftermath of a traumatic experience is a complex process that cannot simply be described like a cookbook recipe.' Recovery is a process rather than an event and there is no perfect recovery. Thompson (2000) also talked about the 'notion of uncertainty, of no security and no guarantees' as being important for practice. There is a messiness about dealing with human beings that demands a flexibility, which is integral to the idea of working with uncertainty. We may seek evidence to support the way we work, but that should not be taken to mean that there are formulaic solutions to people's problems.

Dockar-Drysdale (1993) referred to 'the toleration of doubt' and the need to recognize 'the inadequacy of knowledge'. Every child, situation, worker, organization and cultural context is unique. So on the one hand, our theories and what we have learnt from experience can be reassuring and helpful in dealing with a new and challenging situation, while on the other hand, we need to keep an open mind and be careful not to 'jump to conclusions' before we have had time to fully digest what's happening. Tomlinson (2004, p.17) argues that, 'There is not a simple solution to recovery from trauma. It cannot be prescribed, but needs an environment where it is safe to think about the trauma, experience feelings about it and make reliable provision to heal it.'

This type of environment has been referred to as a 'holding environment' and Winnicott explains the essence of it:

> it has as its aim not a directing of the individual's life or development, but an enabling of the tendencies which are at work within the individual, leading to a natural evolution based on growth. It is emotional growth that has been delayed and perhaps distorted, and under proper conditions the forces that would have led to growth now led to a disentanglement of the knot. (Winnicott 1990, p.228)

As with ordinary childhood, work with traumatized children involves many paradoxes. For example, a parent might be worried that a baby cries too much or too little, or that an adolescent is too compliant or too challenging. We want our children to be safe but we also want them to take risks. We want them to do well and get things right but not at the expense of being afraid to make mistakes. We want them to be protected from negative external influences, but we also want them to explore and learn how to manage themselves in the world.

Along similar lines, the child psychotherapist, Phillips (2009), in his paper 'In praise of difficult children', said that, 'The upshot of all this is that adults who look after adolescents have both to want them to behave badly, and to try and stop them.' At Lighthouse we understand that it is part of adolescent development to challenge boundaries, but it is also the role of a parent to provide appropriate and consistent boundaries. We feel hopeful when we start to see the challenging aspects of a child's behaviour, as it is part of the recovery process. We start to see the 'true' rather than 'false' self (Winnicott 1960).

It is also an opportunity to start to do the real work that is necessary, and for the carer to be the 'good enough' parent. Winnicott (1990, p.148), made the distinction between true and false self, 'The spontaneous gesture is the True Self in action. Only the True Self can be creative and only the True Self can feel real. Whereas a True Self feels real, the existence of a False Self results in a feeling unreal or a sense futility.' The false self typically hides and protects the vulnerable true self. Whilst feeling unreal, a child who has developed a false self can be seductive. They have learnt how to comply and please, whilst keeping an emotional distance.

One of the reasons why these dilemmas can worry us is that we don't actually know how things are going to turn out. We aren't in control and at some level we probably wonder whether we are helping or not. We are also faced with our own experiences of childhood and these inevitably influence and sometimes cloud our thinking. As child psychotherapist, van Heeswyk states,

> Typically views held by adults in regard to adolescents are, to say the least, ambivalent. We see them as vulnerable victims, or as young sadists who inflict terrible damage on others; we fear them as posing grave danger to our cars, property, jobs, morals and way of life, or fear for them as an endangered species requiring special protection; we envy their freedom and hopefulness, or cling to them as the only hope for ourselves and the planet; we curse and constrain their wild impulsivity, or seek to facilitate and encourage their escape from the repressive convention that constrains the school-children that they were and the adults they will become. (van Heeswyk 1997, p.3)

These potentially worrisome dilemmas or paradoxes can cause us considerable anxiety and if we aren't careful we are likely to project too much of this onto the children. Our deep care for our children and our concern about being a good caregiver, coupled with the uncertainty involved are challenging for us to manage. As with parenting, the same applies in work with traumatized children. In many ways the day-to-day uncertainty is more extreme and difficult to contain.

Our third dilemma has been how to combine an emphasis on the individual as well as the group, organization and community. It is probably true to say that many books can be found on each of these subjects. It is far less common to find a book that recognizes the importance of all four and attempts to integrate them in a coherent way. It would be easier to write one book that was purely for those working directly with children and another that was for those that manage and lead organizations, policy makers and politicians.

Some argue that practitioners are not interested in reading about the wider and macro issues and that leaders, managers and policy makers don't want to read about the detail of practice. We believe this is misguided and not necessarily true. Just as parents recognize that their parenting doesn't take place in isolation, effective practitioners and managers also recognize that they are mutually interdependent. An understanding of each other's perspective helps to strengthen their collaboration. Therefore, we argue, it is helpful to encourage practitioners and managers to spend some time considering each other's primary domain. This will also diminish the tendency towards the kind of splitting, which is common in our work, where managers and practitioners sit on different sides of the fence, neither understanding each other's work, and both blaming each other for any difficulties.

We also believe that effective practice must have an orientation that equally considers the importance of the individual, the group, the organization and the community. It is striking the right balance that is critical. For example, some programmes provide high quality individual treatment but pay little attention to the relationship with the community. This can cause major difficulties once the treatment has ended and the young person is on their own in the community. Some residential environments have placed an emphasis on group order and discipline and neglected the need for individual treatment. This has resulted in many young people becoming severely institutionalized. Dockar-Drysdale, as far back as 1961, discussed 'the problem of making adaptation to the needs of the individual child in the group' (p.167) and the importance and difficulty of getting the balance right.

This balance between the individualistic and collective approaches is evident from Susan's story about the beginnings of the Lighthouse Foundation (see Appendix 1).

As a young woman Susan experienced the unnecessary death of an infant who was malnourished and died with no family around him. She recognized this not only as an individual tragedy but also as a sad reflection on our society. In her attempt to do something, she first of all started fostering and helped children individually. She kept in mind the need for a wider solution and began the development of Lighthouse. As she did this, she intuitively knew the importance of developing an approach that recognized the importance of the individual, 'family' group, organization and wider community. As the model has grown, all these aspects have become embedded into the organization's culture. Needs are met on individual and group levels, the sense of 'family' is central, the organization is trauma-informed, and links with local communities are strong and collaborative.

Referring generically to social work, Ward (2010, p.196) states that, 'Social work is a multifaceted profession, and the practice extends through many layers – individual, family, group and organization, community – and this can all be interpreted in many different ways.' It could be argued that the political context is a final and containing layer. Lighthouse is now in a position where it can consider its influence, however small, on this context, which can move forward the way we think about and tackle collectively the problem of child abuse and deprivation. These layers are captured well by Prilleltensky, Nelson and Peirson (2001) in Figure 1.

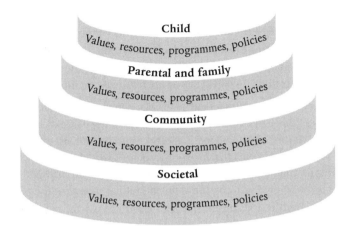

Figure 1 The ecological and hierarchical structure of wellness (Prilleltensky, Peirson and Nelson 2001)

The kind of dilemmas we have mentioned are implicit in much of what we write about in this book. For instance, we discuss the need for a consistent and predictable environment, whilst also providing space for spontaneity, idling, exploring, following an interest, and so on; for adults and leaders to take responsibility, but also of the need to not take so much that children don't have the opportunity to become responsible; to protect children and ensure they are safe, and yet one of the strengths of the Lighthouse model is the way children are supported to become fully involved in all aspects of community life; to pay full attention to the individual needs of children but in a way that also recognizes the importance of the group and community. In reality these are not 'either or' issues. It is the way we go about them and grapple with the dilemmas that is important. Probably the most important thing we can do in our work is to strive to keep the child in mind, so that she can begin to experience feeling emotionally held and thought about rather than forgotten.

WHAT IS CHILD ABUSE AND NEGLECT?

Despite our preoccupations with 'stranger danger' we know that the majority of abuse and neglect that children suffer occurs within their own families. In the worst cases, some of the parents and other caregivers involved commit the most appalling crimes.

However, it is important to acknowledge that there are a variety of factors that can contribute to a parent becoming abusive or neglectful of their own children. For example, the parents may have any, or a combination, of the following: mental health problems, drug addiction, socio-economic difficulties, lack of support and an emotional inability to understand the needs of an infant – perhaps related to their own childhood experiences. As Belsky explains,

> Although most child maltreatment takes place in the family and thus 'behind closed doors,' this immediate and even developmental context of maltreatment itself needs to be contextualized. Cultural attitudes, values, and practices, as well as the economic circumstances of a society and its cultural history, play an important role in the etiology of child maltreatment. It is important to bear this in mind when we focus on the more individual aspects of the parent–child relationship. (Belsky 1993, p.423)

Child abuse and neglect happens within a context where those responsible fail to provide the children under their care with the experiences necessary for healthy development. This can be unintentional or intentional on the part of the 'parents'. Neglect often takes place because the parents do not have the competence or are unable to provide appropriately for their own children. Abuse is normally more intentional than neglect on behalf of the parent or other adults, and can include sexual, physical and emotional abuse. The adult exploits his or her position of power to use the child for his or her own gratification. Sexual and physical abuse tends to be clearly defined and classified in law. However, there are cultural differences as to what constitutes abuse. This is especially apparent in relation to physical abuse.

Some cultures and societies have legally defined corporal punishment as abusive and illegal. Others see it as an appropriate form of discipline and an essential part of parenting. However, even in these cultures and societies there is usually a line drawn whereby physical punishment is deemed to be excessive and harmful. Emotional abuse and neglect are more difficult to define clearly. In most cases the evaluation is related to the emotional safety of the child that impacts on development, characterized by other evidence such as psychological problems, failure to thrive and physical illness.

Child abuse and neglect often co-exist together. Abuse often involves a combination of different forms and is cumulative. It can be difficult to determine which form has had the greatest impact. For example, sexual abuse often takes place within a general context of neglect and inadequate parenting. And as Tomlinson states, a parent's cumulative neglect and lack of attunement to an infant can be equally devastating:

The infant's reaching out may not be noticed, so the infant may perceive the world around him as unresponsive, uncaring or even hostile and attacking. This can happen within a context that does not appear to be an explicitly abusive or turbulent environment. To the infant, repeated failure to respond appropriately to his needs can be a catastrophic breakdown. He has no internal resource to manage this failure or even experience it. At the worst extreme the child may become completely shut off and appear 'emotionally frozen'. (Tomlinson 2008, p.17)

Whilst the child may be 'labelled' as sexually abused, it can be misguided to consider that the abuse has been the most harmful aspect of their experience and the only thing that needs treating. Often the child will have a multitude of difficulties that need addressing. Issues related to neglect may need addressing first of all, so the child can feel safe that basic needs will be met.

Lamont (2010, p.2) defined chronic abuse and neglect as 'recurrent incidents of maltreatment over a prolonged period of time'. Experiencing abuse over an extended time period has a significant impact on developmental milestones. This has a profound and compounding effect on the child's life, which impacts on the emotional and physical growth of the developing child. Contemporary researchers, including Perry and Szalavitz (2006), have shown how experiences of abuse and neglect literally injure and damage children neurologically, emotionally and physically. Infants who are neglected aren't sufficiently soothed and so experience persistently high levels of stress hormones, which restricts the growth of brain cells. Cameron and Maginn state that,

The experience of a prolonged insecure attachment, whatever the cause, has long been suspected of producing 'invisible damage'. New methods of measurement in neuro-psychology and neuro-biology have been able to quantify this damage in terms of brain growth and activity (Gerhardt 2004). In short, we now know that parental rejection, abuse and neglect not only cause grievous developmental harm, but also grievous *bodily* harm. (Cameron and Maginn 2008, p.1159)

The developing brain is damaged by these experiences to the extent that the brain of a severely neglected child, by the age of three can be seen to be physically smaller and underdeveloped compared to the brain of a healthy child (Perry and Szalavitz 2006). If the abuse and neglect is prolonged, the child can become locked into a traumatized state, where their development becomes frozen and/or severely distorted. Dockar-Drysdale (1958, p.17) referred to these children as 'frozen' children. She explains her preference for the term 'frozen' rather than 'affectionless' because 'affectionless' sounds final, but a thaw can follow a frost'. We now know that it is the excessive production of stress hormones that can literally freeze the growth of the developing brain.

The potential consequences of chronic abuse and neglect include attachment difficulties, physical health problems, trauma and psychological problems, learning and developmental difficulties, behavioural problems, youth suicide, eating disorders, drug and alcohol abuse, aggression and violence (Lamont 2010). Children who are abused have a higher risk as adults of becoming violent criminals; entering prostitution; committing suicide and serious self-harm such as starvation, cutting and self-mutilation; or being abused and becoming victims of rape.

A recent review of the children in the Lighthouse programme highlighted the following: 86 per cent had a diagnosable mental illness; 60 per cent had a history of substance abuse; 60 per cent had been sexually abused; 68 per cent had been physically abused; 48 per cent had attempted suicide; and 82 per cent had been exposed to family violence. This highlights the impact of abuse on the developing child and adolescent, as well as the complex nature of the therapeutic task.

THE COST OF ABUSE

Levels of child abuse in countries such as Australia, Canada, USA and the UK appear to be escalating and putting a huge strain on our capacity to provide an adequate response. van der Kolk and McFarlane (2007, p.5) state that, 'A random survey of 1,245 American adolescents showed that 23% had been the victim of physical or sexual assaults, as well as witnesses of violence against others. One out of five of the exposed adolescents developed Post Traumatic Stress Disorder (PTSD). This suggests that approximately 1.07 million U.S. teenagers currently suffer from PTSD.' Putnam (2004, p.ix) claimed that, 'child maltreatment is the single most costly public health problem in the United States today'. It has been shown that untreated trauma significantly increases the use of and further strains the financial resources of health care and behavioural health services; decreases productivity in the workplace; increases reliance on public welfare; and increases incarceration rates. The economic costs of untreated trauma-related alcohol and drug abuse alone were estimated at $160.7 billion in the USA in 2000. The estimated cost to USA society of child abuse and neglect is $94 billion per year, or $258 million per day. For child abuse survivors, long-term psychiatric and medical health care costs are estimated at $100 billion per year (Witness Justice 2011).

According to Mitchell (Tucci, Mitchell and Goddard 2010, p.5), in Australia, more than 60 per cent of children coming into state care met the criteria for at least one major psychiatric diagnosis. Most commonly, these are Post Traumatic Stress Disorder and adjustment disorders. The cost to society both in the present and future is immense. Some of the costs include: treatment for victims; imprisonment; unemployment; hospitalization and poor health; homelessness; police and emergency services; criminal justice systems; and the general harm caused to the wellbeing of communities and individuals (Bromfield, Gillingham and Higgins, in Lamont 2010, p.2).

In Australia in 2007, the estimated annual cost of child abuse and neglect for all people ever abused was $4 billion. The cost of the burden of disease (a measure of lifetime costs of fear, mental anguish and pain relating to child abuse and neglect) represented a further $6.7 billion. The estimated lifetime costs for the population of children reportedly abused for the first time in 2007 would be $6 billion, with the burden of disease representing a further $7.7 billion (Bromfield *et al.* 2010).

In the United Kingdom there are 60,000 'looked-after children' in the care of local authorities. Of these around 80 per cent are in care due to child abuse and neglect and related difficulties (Hannon, Wood and Bazalgette 2010). The annual cost of this is over £2 billion and this is just the cost for children actually taken into care. Hannon *et al.* also show how these costs continue into adulthood, especially for children whose care is badly planned. Interestingly, the cost is often greater for children who are taken into care at a later stage and with additional longer term costs. Through their research they show that early well planned intervention, with placement stability and well planned transitions for care leavers, though more costly in the short term, is actually less costly over the duration of time in care and into adulthood.

One of the particular concerns of the Lighthouse Foundation is how children are supported in making the transition from out of home care to interdependence. Research on children leaving out of home care also illustrates the high financial cost associated with inadequate support for children transitioning from care to interdependence (Raman, Inder and Forbes 2005). Children leaving care are often forgotten by the welfare system and society as a whole. As a result they fall into a gap, fending for themselves with limited support networks, internal resources and life skills, at a time when they are especially vulnerable and in need of support.

Though we have focused on the financial costs and costs to society, it is also important that we don't underestimate the cost of abuse at a more personal and humane level. As Perry states,

While not all children who suffer neglect or physical, sexual or psychological abuse become violent adults, the majority of these victims carry their scars with them in other ways, usually in a profound emptiness, or emotionally destructive relationships, moving through life disconnected from others and robbed of their humanity. (Perry 1997, p.113)

THE NEED FOR EARLY INTERVENTION, TREATMENT AND PREVENTION

William Castell, the former CEO of GE Healthcare, states that, 'The 20th century was about treating disease. The 21st century is about prevention' (Dowdy et al. 2010, p.2). However, at the turn of the century, Prilleltensky and Nelson (2000) point out that in the field of mental health we have a long way to go in terms of making this a reality: 'We all know the adage that prevention is better than cure, but departments and ministries of health in Canada and the United States devote less than 1% of their budgets to prevention of mental health problems'.

The population of children we work with have suffered serious levels of abuse and neglect, have often experienced up to twenty placements, have little or no contact with their families, become homeless, and have been excluded from school. They have been denied their birthright of being protected and nurtured. On the one hand, we have the challenge of responding to the present problem, but the only way to make progress in the long term is through preventative work. There is an urgent need for abused and traumatized children to be provided with the most effective treatment to enable recovery and to heal the damage that has been done. Even more importantly, we need early intervention programmes that support and educate parents, families and communities so that inroads can be made into this huge social problem and start a virtuous cycle where resilience and the capacity for appropriate parenting can grow.

We also need change on the macro socio-economic-political level to positively alter the conditions within which parenting takes place. Prilleltensky and Nelson describe the continuum of these interventions:

We can divide social and preventive interventions along a continuum of social change. Ameliorative interventions try to help victims of injustice, illness, or abuse without challenging the societal status quo. This type of help alleviates problems but does not strive to eliminate the social antecedents that contribute to the problem in the first place. Reformist initiatives adopt a more active role in perfecting existing institutions. Although a radical transformation of oppressive institutions and damaging norms is not called for, an effort is made to make them work better for people. Transformative agents are not content to tinker with existing sources of social ills, the goal is to envision more humane forms of co-operation and re-build public structures so that they will conform with the new ideal. (Prilleltensky and Nelson 2000)

Prevention and treatment must always work hand in hand. As long as there are children who are exposed to abuse and neglect, we have a duty to respond not just to the physical injury, but to the enormous and distorting emotional damage done to young minds. Genuine recovery for this group is also a preventative measure that will protect future generations, through enabling traumatized children to achieve in life and go on to parent successfully in their own right. It is one of the hopes of this book that a contribution can be made to understanding the type of approach that is needed.

CHAPTER 1

The Importance of a Theoretical Base

He who loves practice without theory is like the sailor who boards a ship without a rudder and compass and never knows where he may cast.

Leonardo Da Vinci

When we are faced with the challenging and complex task of facilitating recovery for traumatized children, it is essential to have a theoretical base to draw upon. There are a number of important reasons for this:

- Without a clear idea of theoretical approaches that work it is easy to do things that will make no difference and at worse even re-traumatize the children. Many well intentioned but ill-informed approaches do exactly this, which partly explains why so many traumatized children suffer many failures and breakdowns in the placements that are meant to help them.

- Working with traumatized children can be an extremely challenging and overwhelming experience. Having a body of theory to draw upon can help to make sense of things and to maintain the capacity to think, and find meaning in the most difficult situations.

- There is an increasing amount of research which provides evidence of how trauma impacts upon the development of the brain and what can aid recovery. Making use of findings from research can save precious time and help ensure efforts are focused appropriately.

- When traumatized children are being worked with by a team of people, a common theory can help ensure there is a consistent approach. Consistency, reliability and repetition are especially important for children who have experienced the lack of a safe and predictable environment, which is often associated with trauma and neglect.

- Whilst a theoretical base can provide consistency and guidance it also provides a benchmark by which new approaches can be tested and evaluated.

- Having a theory, which is well researched and evidence based can give the professionals involved a degree of confidence that can be supportive when faced with what can be felt to be an overwhelming task. The fact that others have been there before and used various approaches that have worked helps to give a sense of hope.

THE RELATIONSHIP BETWEEN THEORY AND PRACTICE

The relationship between theory and practice in the helping professions is complex and challenging. There are many reasons for this and they probably begin with the nature of the work itself. By their nature, the caring professions involve carrying out tasks in a professional manner that has many similarities to the most personal tasks in our lives. Such examples are bringing up children, supporting friends and family who are distressed, taking care of the ill and infirm, comforting the bereaved – as well as our own experiences of being parented, cared for and comforted. Normally we do these things with little formal guidance or teaching. We learn from experience, and wisdom is passed down through families and wider society. Even so, when we find ourselves suddenly faced with our first child or ill parent we might feel out of our depth and unprepared. Normally we muster the strength with the support of others to manage. However, things might not always work out so positively and there may be times when we need the help of a professional service.

What we have seen with many people who begin work with traumatized children is that they often believe qualities that have been successful in their lives with others, especially their own children, will also be effective in their work. To some extent this is true. However, the idea that there are theories about how to work with children clearly implies there are also things to learn. This may challenge our own beliefs and ways of doing things. One of the big differences about learning in this profession compared with others, such as manufacturing, is that the learning in our field is very close to our most personal experiences. For example, what kind of parent am I? Theories related to childhood might be felt to support or challenge one's view of oneself in a very personal way. Feelings of guilt and regret can easily surface. It can be threatening to accept that there are theories about child development and interpersonal relationships when these things seem so intuitive and part of who we are. People often use the phrase 'it's common sense'. This phrase immediately suggests that everyone regardless of their own experiences and cultural background would have the same view. Therefore it tends to be culturally engrained and to reflect the dominant culture. Closed forms of knowledge like 'common sense' are not easily open to critique and challenge in the same way that theory is. As Thompson (2000, p.28) points out, 'the use of theory implies a critique of common sense'. He argues that 'common sense' protects dominant ideological perspectives and can deter critical thinking which, he says, raises questions rather than provides answers. In eschewing common sense, he advises, a critical perspective is one which relies on thought rather than 'thoughtless assumption' (Thompson 2000, p.97).

At the other extreme, theory can be used in such a way that personal experience and judgement are diminished. We might feel as if we don't know what to do without referring to some kind of manual telling us what to do. This can happen particularly at times when we are unsure of ourselves and anxious about taking responsibility. If someone else or some theory can tell us what to do and it doesn't work it won't be our fault.

As Thompson (2010, p.11) suggested, referring to the philosopher Nietzsche, theory is not supposed to provide the Truth, with a capital 'T', to a problem. Nietzsche argued there is no absolute Truth, only smaller specific truths with a lower case 't'. In the same way a theory does not provide us with a Truth, but a framework within which we can also draw upon our experience and make choices about what to do. We then consider what happens next and test out whether our actions have been effective or not. We move on, testing outcomes against the theory, learning from experience and sometimes making discoveries that contribute to theoretical development. This process has been referred to as reflective practice and, as Ward (1998, p.218) states, the concept of reflection is 'a central theme in the relationship between theory and practice'. Theory in the humane professions is not static but something that is constantly evolving in the light of new experience.

Some people argue that theory is not necessary and that we only need action and positive outcomes. So if we do things and they appear to work we don't need a theory, we just need to know that such and such works. This argument has a number of flaws. Thompson (2010, p.7) argues how many actions which we take – whilst not consciously informed by theory – often have a long history of theoretical development that underpin the way we think and act. Theories are developed and influence our culture and the way we do things. For instance, it is clear how strongly different theories of child development, during the post Second World War period, had a huge impact on parenting even if the parents had no idea where the ideas they were implementing came from. So theory is influencing our actions, but if we have no awareness of it we can't easily challenge and test the theory. We might learn that something doesn't work but if we have no concept as to why, whatever we learn is limited.

THEORY IN THE CARING PROFESSIONS

Inevitably in the field of the caring professions many different theories have developed. In the field of psychotherapy, there are literally hundreds of different types of therapy. Admittedly many of them are variants on a particular approach. There has been much research attempting to look at the merits of the different approaches based on outcomes achieved (Loewenthal and Winter 2006). Interestingly, the conclusion has often been that it is not the particular theoretical approach that determines positive outcomes but the quality of the relationship between the therapist and client. It is as if there is something more fundamentally human involved that transcends a particular approach. Clearly, research can rule out approaches that don't work and identify approaches that appear to work better for certain problems. Similarly, in ordinary family life there are many differences within what might be considered appropriate styles of parenting. For example, some parents might be regarded as strict in their parenting whilst others are more permissive. Children from both types of family can grow up to be socially well-adjusted adults. Unless the parenting style is on the extremes, there is little evidence to suggest that different approaches can't at least be 'good enough'. What has been proven to be important to children is a reliable and consistent approach, without too much conflict between the parents on how things should be done.

Children need a secure environment, where they know what to expect and what is expected of them (Perry and Szalavitz 2006). In the same way, a theory can provide a consistent way of doing things which enables a team of people from different backgrounds and experiences to work together. In this sense the theory can provide a form of containment, which helps professionals to think about their work, especially when things become overwhelming and difficult to make sense of. Bloom pointed out the potential risks where there is not a clear and consistent theoretical approach, 'The staff often work at cross-purposes without even recognizing that their conflicts are due to conflicts in basic theoretical models and instead attribute the problems to the resistance of the children or personality conflicts among the staff.' Emphasizing the need for a trauma-informed approach she continues to advise that,

To avoid unfavorable outcomes, residential treatment programs need a coherent, integrated conceptual approach that does not reinvent the wheel but instead offers the flexibility to do whatever is in the best interests of the child. It must be a framework that can consistently guide treatment in the cottages where the children reside, in the schools that they attend, and in their formal therapy sessions. It must be a bio-psychosocial framework that is simple enough for everyone to understand, puts everyone on the same page, does not sacrifice complexity or diversity, is universally applicable, and provides an organizing framework for what everybody already does well. Such an organizing framework must also address what may turn out to be the most critical aspect of any approach that seeks to adequately treat children in residential settings: a 'trauma-informed approach'. An approach to childcare that takes into account the impact of overwhelming stress on child development is particularly important since it has been established that a large proportion of a residential treatment population have a history of exposure to violence, abuse and neglect. (Bloom 2005, p.56)

Less helpfully, theory can be used defensively to provide a sense of certainty, which can be a defence against feelings of doubt and not knowing what to do. When we are feeling overwhelmed, useless and not having a clue what is going on, rather than stick with these uncomfortable feelings until a meaningful understanding emerges, the temptation is to prematurely seek an explanation, however false, because it makes us feel better. So when we have theoretical knowledge, there is a constant tussle between using theory in a helpful way and at other times putting all theory aside so that we can concentrate fully on the unique situation we are in. If there is already an answer to a problem, based on previous experience, maybe we are overlooking something that is different. This can be one of the painful learning curves in work with traumatized children. If a worker too readily thinks he knows how to respond to a child based on previous experience, the child will most likely sense that the worker is thinking about the past and not him. Only when the child is satisfied that we are able to give up preconceived ideas, and approach him with a completely open mind, can real progress be made.

As suggested above, the relationship between theory and practice is complex, but it is also necessary. Workers with a theoretical understanding tend to become more confident in their work as their own actions, attitudes and thoughts are supported externally, and as they are also increasingly perceived by others to be professional (Thompson 2010).

PSYCHODYNAMIC THINKING

To begin understanding why a theoretical base is particularly important for organizations and individuals that work with traumatized children, it is necessary to understand something about the nature of the therapeutic task. It is essential in our work with traumatized children that we can attribute meaning to the situations we find ourselves in. The children have often been cared for by adults who are unable to think of them and their needs, and in the worst cases have only been able to think of them in terms of meeting the adult's needs.

The psychoanalyst and consultant child and adolescent psychotherapist, Waddell, states the following:

> Psychoanalytically based psychotherapy has, for many years, presented an unwavering and increasingly evidence-based picture of the degree to which the developmental capacities and lasting inner resources of infants and children are shaped, from the first, by the quality – that is the consistency and love – of the earliest relational environment. Initially that means the mother's or primary carer's mind. It is almost a truism that children learn to think by being thought about; that an infant's essential learning about him or herself takes place in the encounter of one mind with another from the very moment of birth. (Waddell 2004, p.22)

Theorists have also highlighted the importance of other adults in the relational environment of the child as being a vital element for their early development. As van Heeswyk (2004, p.11) has pointed out, 'It is not, as Franklin Giddins once observed, that two heads are better than one. Rather, it is that two (or more) heads are *needed* for one.'

Whether we are talking about difficulties with individual children, groups, ourselves or staff teams, it is essential that we 'think' about the whole situation and not just part of it. This includes looking at the individual, the environment, internal and external worlds as constantly interrelated parts of a whole. This work is not easy – the following extract from *Emotional Milestones from Birth to Adulthood* by Schmidt Neven illustrates our point:

> The psychodynamic approach puts forward the view that all behaviour has meaning, and that there is no such thing as communication and activity which has no specific communicable direction. In that sense, everything we do is part of a communication, and this of course is of vital importance in the communication between children and parents. For example, parents may be angry and irritated by what they perceive to be the destructive behaviour of their child. They may seek help and advice about specific ways of controlling this behaviour. A behavioural or cognitive approach to the problem would

probably refer to ways of helping the parents to evolve 'strategies', or ways of managing the problem of destructiveness. However, in using a psychodynamic approach, one would view the problem in a different way. First of all, one would postulate that the destructive behaviour is in itself *an important communication*. It might, in the context of the family, be the only way in which the child is able to communicate something about what he or she feels. So we would ask the question 'What lies behind the destructive behaviour?' The other question we would ask is 'Why does this behaviour emerge *at this particular point in time?*' So the questions '*What does it mean?*' and '*Why now?*' are all-important.

Fundamental to the idea that all behaviour has meaning is the belief that the recognition of meaning behind behaviour is actually very important to our emotional well being. If we are not able to attribute meaning to our personal experience and to our relationships with the important people in our lives, it is difficult for us to exist in even the most fundamental state of relatedness to others and to the broader community. (Schmidt Neven 1997, pp.4–5)

She continues to explain, as we have mentioned, why this type of thinking can be challenging for us:

The problem of denial – the importance of understanding that all behaviour has meaning is one that is slow to be recognised. Very often, in working with parents and families, one becomes aware of the cultivation of an attitude in which there is a denial of the links between life events, between the childhood experiences of parents and their own children and between making connections at all. The reasons for this are complex and may largely lie with the fear that we all have, at times, of becoming emotionally overwhelmed if we allow ourselves to recognise and make links between the different experiences in our lives. (p.8)

Maintaining the capacity to think and act constructively can be especially challenging in work with traumatized children (Tomlinson 2005). In particular, it has been argued that the residential treatment of 'emotionally disturbed' children is an extremely difficult task – if not verging on the impossible. Richard Balbernie (1971, p.14) drew attention to this in his paper actually titled 'The Impossible Task?' stating, 'Our task in both residential and field work is one of daily, increasing uncertainty, confusion, complexity, doubt and anxiety.'

PSYCHODYNAMIC CONCEPTS

There are a number of psychodynamic concepts that are specifically important in therapeutic work with traumatized children, particularly in therapeutic residential care settings. We will be referring to and elaborating on them throughout the book and shall briefly describe them here.

Transference and countertransference

Transference was first described by Freud (1912, 1914) who observed in his analytic work that patients transferred feelings that belonged to past relationships onto the analyst in the present. Most commonly, but not exclusively, it is feelings associated with the formative relationship with mother and father that tend to be transferred. Freud (1950, p.116) wrote that 'a whole series of psychological experiences are revived, not as belonging to the past but as applying to the physician at the present moment'. If these feelings are thought about, it is possible to gain an understanding into earlier conflicts and enable psychological changes to take place in the patient. Whilst this concept initially developed in the context of a psychoanalytic relationship between analyst and patient, the same dynamic is now understood to take place within a wide variety of different relational contexts. For instance, a child may transfer his experiences, both positive and negative, with parental figures onto other adults in the present who have a parental type of role, such as a therapist, teacher or caregiver. To some degree we all transfer some of our feelings associated with past experiences onto people in our present relational context. Therefore it is important in our work with traumatized children that we attempt to recognize these tendencies in ourselves, so that we can reduce the unhelpful aspects of this being acted out towards children and our colleagues.

One of the key ideas in psychodynamic thinking is that

> the patient and therapist have two separate subjectivities that interact in a meaningful way during the course of therapy. The psychotherapist is not a scientist looking through a microscope at a specimen. Rather, she is a fellow human being with conflicts and emotional struggles of her own. She unconsciously experiences the patient as someone from her past at the same time that the patient experiences her as someone from her past. (Gabbard 2010, p.15)

When we are on the receiving end of transference it is likely that we experience a feeling in reaction to this. So, if a child is treating us as if we are uncaring or even abusive, we may find ourselves feeling angry or punitive towards the child. This happens at an unconscious level and has been termed countertransference. If we are able to recognize and think about our countertransference feelings they become another avenue for understanding, which could further illuminate the nature of the child's and our own earlier experiences.

Gabbard (2010, p.15) referred to countertransference as a 'major therapeutic and diagnostic tool that tells the therapist a great deal about the patient's world'. Recognizing and thinking about our feelings in this way, they become a vehicle for therapeutic change rather than an unhelpful reaction. So, if we feel punitive towards a child we don't punish the child but try to understand why punitive feelings are being evoked in ourselves. It could be that the child is behaving in a similar way for which we were punished as a child, in which case our countertransference is more to do with our own past experiences. On the other hand, the child may be unconsciously provoking us to react in a punitive way, similar to how he may have been treated by his parents. The understanding we reach will then influence our response to the child. Winnicott emphasized how important it is that we are able to acknowledge the existence of our countertransference feelings, however uncomfortable we may be about them:

> However much (the psychiatrist) loves his patients he cannot avoid hating them and fearing them, and the better he knows this the less will hate and fear be the motives determining what he does to his patients... Above all he must not deny hate that really exists in himself. (Winnicott 1992, p.195)

If we are not in touch with these powerful feelings it is more likely that we act them out either directly or indirectly. Therefore it is necessary that we have the opportunity to openly and safely discuss these feelings in professional forums.

Projection and projective identification

Projection is a similar but in some ways more primitive process to transference, and is what psychodynamic theory refers to as a defence mechanism. Whereas transference takes place in the context of a relationship that may evoke aspects of previous relationships, projection is a way in which someone gets rid of overwhelming, distressing or persecutory feelings by projecting them into someone else. This begins in earliest infancy, where the infant who is becoming overwhelmed projects this feeling through his behaviour into a caregiver. The caregiver finds herself suddenly feeling anxious, for example, and tries to understand what this is to do with – that is, the infant may be hungry or feeling discomfort. It can be seen that the infant has not only got rid of some of his troubling feelings but has also communicated something to the caregiver. Stien and Kendall argue that,

> Getting someone else to feel the same emotion we are experiencing is one of the most basic techniques that human beings use to feel understood. Rather than becoming enmeshed in the negative emotions of the traumatized child, adults must try to empathize, and simultaneously maintain a 'meta-mood' of relative calmness. (Stien and Kendall 2004, p.148)

Where things go well the caregiver thinks about the infant's feelings and responds, often intuitively, by meeting his needs. This provides the infant with the experience that his overwhelming feelings can be thought about, understood and responded to positively. Gradually, through the emotional containment provided by the mother, the infant internalizes this experience and becomes increasingly able to think about his own feelings and communicate them more specifically.

The way in which the infant's projections are handled and responded to is crucial to the infant's development and lays the foundation for mental stability. However, as Trevithick described, this process is not straightforward,

> For instance, it is recognized that as the infant develops he may become envious of the mother's capacity for creativity, which includes thinking. This can result in envious attacks towards the mother by the infant, which can cause difficulties in her thinking. The realization that the mother has her own thoughts, which the infant is not in control of, is also the cause of anxiety for the infant, related to separation and fear of not being in control. If the mother is able to contain these anxieties, they can be a spur to the development of the infant's healthy curiosity and individuation. (Trevithick 1995, p.4)

Where the caregiver is not able to think about or respond to the infant's feelings, the infant will feel that these feelings continue to exist but are located outside himself, in a way that feels threatening to him. For example, feelings of intense hunger that belonged with the infant are now felt by the infant to be located in the caregiver. In a primitive sense the caregiver then becomes someone who may literally devour him. As adults we may be able to recognize a similar process where, for instance, we deny our own anger and project it into another who we then feel afraid of. To take this a step further and confirm our fears, we then provoke the other person into becoming angry with us. The other person can find himself becoming angry and expressing these feelings in a manner whereby he feels he is acting out of character, as the feelings did not originate in himself. Talking about the therapeutic context Gabbard (2010, p.13) explains, 'Thus the patient may behave in an irritating way until the therapist becomes irritated and unconsciously conforms to an angry object from the patient's past.'

To describe this process and developing Freud's concepts of transference and countertransference, Melanie Klein (1946) first used the term projective identification from her observations of relationships between babies and their mothers and infants. Gabbard (2010, p.13) explains how the process manifests itself in therapeutic work: 'In projective identification, the patient unconsciously projects a self or object representation into the therapist and then, by exerting interpersonal pressure, "nudges" the therapist into taking on characteristics similar to the representation that has been projected.' The major difference between projection and projective identification is that in projective identification the person who is targeted with the projection begins to behave, think, and feel in a way that is consistent with what is being projected into him.

Splitting

The process of splitting is also connected to projection as specific feelings are split off and disowned. Splitting is normally used to describe the way in which polarized feelings such as 'good' and 'bad' feelings are separated and split off. Initially both good and bad feelings are projected into the mother whom the infant does not yet perceive as a whole person. So there is the 'good' mother and the 'bad' mother. As the infant develops and begins to realize that the good and bad mother is the same person this creates a conflict for the infant. The good mother whom the infant projects positive feelings into is also the bad mother whom he projects negative and hostile feelings into. Therefore, the infant becomes concerned about hurting the good mother. The infant may respond to this in a number of ways. With the mother's support he may begin to recognize that the mother is neither all good nor all bad. He may develop reparative behaviour towards the mother to compensate for his attacks on her. This is what one would hope for in healthy development. Alternatively, in conjunction with the mother's lack of capacity to contain these splits, he may find this too difficult to resolve and continue to keep the mother as a split rather than whole person. This will hinder his development and result in a relationship that swings from being all good to all bad. If he perceives the mother to be vulnerable or reactive to his negative projections, he may either find another person to project these feelings into or repress these feelings, possibly by turning them inwards. This response can be seen in children who project all bad feelings into one adult whilst preserving all good feelings for another adult, or who turn their difficult feelings, such as anger, on themselves.

It is clear from this brief description to see how the handling of projection and splitting processes is central to a child's development. Where there are difficulties in this, the child's development will be hindered and potentially distorted. When this happens, as it invariably does with children who are severely traumatized, we can expect projection and splitting to become major areas of work until the child's developmental difficulties are resolved.

Emphasizing the importance of these concepts to the work we are writing about in this book, Stokoe states that,

I believe that projective identification is the main language of the therapeutic community. The young people are continually filling staff and other young people with those parts of themselves that they are unable to handle. A classic example is bullying: the bully is unable to handle fear, so he uses projective identification to make someone else experience fear. In this way the bully has the pleasurable experience of seeing fear outside himself and, therefore, controllable. (Stokoe 2003, p.86)

THE RELATIONSHIP BETWEEN THE ORGANIZATION AND THERAPEUTIC TASK

Menzies Lyth (1979, p.234) also drew our attention to the difficulty of management in those institutions that care for people and possibly aim to help them change – collectively known as the 'humane institutions'. She claims that the management of these institutions, 'calls for an unusual degree of management skill from people who do not easily see themselves as managers'. Menzies Lyth and Balbernie (1971) both give similar reasons why this task is so difficult.

- Working with clients who are 'in care', vulnerable and dependent, evokes high levels of anxiety in those that work with them. Menzies Lyth (1959, 1961, 1970), in her papers on the task of hospital nursing, gave a detailed account of this process. In turn, the propensity for the worker to develop a defensive, unhelpful and 'anti-task' response to protect themselves against the anxieties involved is also high.

- There is often a high level of ambivalence connected to being 'in care'. Ambivalence will be evoked in the child, the worker, the organization and society as a whole. This often revolves around conflict connected with such issues as being cared for/rejected; getting better/worse; being dependent/independent and being helped/deprived.

Given the challenging nature of the work it is essential that organizations who work with traumatized children are clear about their primary task. The primary task is the task the organization must perform over and above everything else – the reason for its existence. Take for example an organization like the Lighthouse Foundation, which works with homeless children – is the primary task to keep a roof over children's heads or to enable the children to recover from their experiences? Clarity on this makes a significant difference to all matters of the organization's activity. The precise definition of the 'primary task' is essential and constant vigilance is needed to stay 'on task', faced with the ever-present pull of anti-task tendencies.

As well as having a clearly defined task, the approach to the task or methods and tools used also need clarifying. Menzies Lyth states that,

> The performance of the primary task of an enterprise requires an appropriate organisation. Such an organisation has two aspects: (i) The choice and application of an appropriate technology and (ii) the choice and application of an appropriate social system – what Trist and others (1963) have called a socio-technical system. (Menzies Lyth 1959, 1961, 1970, p.227)

This means that the treatment approach in all of its details, the resources used and how they are applied and organized, should give the best possible fit with the primary task. Both the 'clinical' approaches (technology) used in work with children and the way the whole organization (social system) works are relevant to the task. The organizational culture needs to support and facilitate the work with the children in a complementary way. If the primary task and socio-technical system are to be defined in a residential treatment setting, a theoretical understanding of what is being 'treated' – and with what 'aim' – is necessary, so that theory can be applied to practice.

THE TREATMENT APPROACH

Fahlberg emphasized the importance of a theoretical base to residential treatment:

> The most important task of treatment must be clearly and succinctly stated. Specific problems and dynamics vary from child to child, but a philosophy of treatment must clearly identify the category of problems that are most essential for the programme to confront if successful treatment is to occur. (Fahlberg 1990, p.51)

Without a theoretical base, it is difficult for staff to be trained to a level that enables them to provide consistent, coherent and appropriate care. In her paper 'The Importance of Child Care Training', Barbara Kahan argues that we would expect lawyers, dentists, doctors and teachers to be trained, qualified and up to date with recent knowledge,

> so why are we prepared to tolerate a situation in which, by definition, some of the most needy and traumatized children in our community are cared for by people who, however well-intentioned, are neither trained, qualified nor, in many instances, knowledgeable about their needs and how best to deal with them? (Kahan 1995, p.1)

If we are to understand how to treat children whose development has been disturbed, then first of all we need to have an understanding of what constitutes ordinary development. As Phillips (1988, p.96) points out, 'In order to recognise a developmental distortion, one must have a confident sense of what 'true' development consists of.' These children are specifically ones whose emotional development has been severely impaired, due to 'environmental failure' such as abuse, neglect and trauma within the first year or so of life. The factors central to the child's predicament are environmental rather than biological, constitutional or medical. We use the term 'environment' to mean the immediate environment of the infant and specifically the individuals most closely involved with the infant. So this means that where the infant does not receive adequate 'maternal' provision, this may be related to the mother, her partner, the extended family and the societal context. Shapiro and Carr (1991, p.36) also pointed out that the use of the word environment directs us to think of the family as an open system, an organization interacting with the external world, rather than merely a collection of individuals. From this point of view, 'environmental failure' may be the result of difficulties between people within the infant's environment, including the infant, and/or between those people and the external world.

ATTACHMENT AND TRAUMA-INFORMED THEORIES

Trauma and attachment theories, together, can provide a useful interpretive frame for carers, support staff and others to understand better the needs and challenges of traumatized children. They can provide a sound platform for guiding responses to children both in care and in other environments in which they find themselves. Such theories offer a more comprehensive and holistic means by which the emotional, psychological and behavioural functioning of abused and neglected children can be deconstructed and understood.

There have been significant developments in theory related to child development over the last fifty years or so. However, the fundamental view of John Bowlby (1969) that the attachment of the infant to a caregiver is of central importance in the infant's development remains true. As Cameron and Maginn (2009, p.28) argue, 'Bowlby's theory has stood the test of time remarkably well and current neurological studies are able to confirm both the positive impact on childcare (extensive development of neural pathways and brain growth) and the negative (lack of brain growth and development).' The need for attachment and parental acceptance is universal, regardless of culture, age, gender or ethnicity. In the 1980s and 90s there was much research that looked at the interactions between mother and baby (Stern 1985). Video technology was used to analyze this in greater detail than had previously been possible.

This led to some revisions of theory, such as the infant's awareness of itself as separate from the mother – happening earlier than previously recognized.

This research led to a greater understanding of the importance of maternal attunement (McCluskey and Duerden 1993). Contemporary research on the brain has made major leaps through the capacity we now have to actually see what is happening in the brain (Perry and Szalavitz 2006). To a large extent this scientific research is compatible with psychoanalytic theories of child development. As Panksapp (1999) argues, 'affective and cognitive neuroscientists are now in a position to link concrete neural entities to various abstract psychological and psychoanalytic concepts' (cited in Green 2003, p.2). While our understanding of the process of brain development has advanced significantly, the fact that early childhood attachment is the central influence is supported. The detail of exactly how the attachment works and how it impacts on the brain's development has been debated. For instance, how important is it for the mother to be the primary attachment figure? The research on brain development has indisputably shown that the first years of life have a major impact on the infant's development and that trauma during this period can cause major developmental difficulties (Perry and Szalavitz 2006).

During the last seventy years or more, there have been many pioneers establishing children's homes and schools, specializing in the treatment of emotionally disturbed children. Bridgeland (1971), in his book *Pioneer Work with Maladjusted Children*, provides an overview of the history of these developments. These pioneers often drew their ideas from a theoretical understanding of child development. Emphasizing the important influence of psychoanalysis in particular, he states that, 'The most extensive single body of theory related to the needs of therapeutic education is that of psychoanalysis' (p.269). He goes on to argue that pioneers in residential treatment – Lane, Neil and Shaw – applied the theories of psychoanalysts such as Freud, Jung, Anna Freud, Reich and Klein, showing that psychoanalysis 'was not done but lived'. More recently, Ward (1996, p.22) claimed that, 'The characteristic which emerges as probably most distinctive of the current British therapeutic communities for children is their commitment to the psychoanalytic theory-base.' This approach is also consistent with the work within our own organization.

THE INFLUENCE OF WINNICOTT ON THERAPEUTIC RESIDENTIAL CARE

In post-war years, the work of Winnicott (1947, 1955, 1956b) in particular has been applied to this field of work. Winnicott has been especially influential on those working in residential settings with children. This is partly because of his view that early infant development problems caused by 'environmental failure' needed to be treated in a planned twenty-four hour a day therapeutic environment. This co-relates with his concept of the 'holding environment'. As a result, any 'localized' form of treatment, such as psychotherapy, will only work if the child feels all aspects of the environment are responding to his needs. Winnicott (1955, 1956b) directly applied some of his theories to residential treatment settings. In discussing the 'overall influence' of Winnicott's work, Jacobs (1995, p.122) claims that, 'Winnicott is perhaps most influential as an inspiration to other pioneers, especially those working with children.'

Winnicott's theory of the mother–infant relationship also referred to the wider setting of the relationship, and the importance of this in providing a supportive context for the mother and infant. Menzies Lyth (1990, p.xii) points out that Winnicott emphasized the importance of a well-managed setting, if the mother–infant relationship is going to be facilitated: 'Such management ensures that the environment runs smoothly enough, that boundaries are held, disturbing intrusions are prevented or the effects mitigated – and that the mother is free and protected in her maternal pre-occupation.' The management of the whole organization in which the children are being cared for and treated is essential in enabling treatment and care to happen. It is also actually beneficial to the treatment task in itself. The children internalize a sense of an ordered, reliable environment, rather than a chaotic, unreliable environment. This highlights the importance of implementing clear boundaries, definition of roles and appropriate sharing and delegation of responsibility.

In a similar vein, Stapley (1996, p.211) argues that Winnicott's theory of the mother–infant relationship has great relevance for all organizations, 'what Winnicott refers to as "A Facilitating Environment", one which encourages (or facilitates) the development of the child – seems to be the sort of organisation holding environment that is required in today's organisation'. The psychoanalytic influence can also be seen in the approaches of pioneering 'therapeutic' organizations in other countries, such as Browndale in Canada, the Orthogenic School in the USA and the Lighthouse Foundation in Australia.

INDIVIDUAL, FAMILY, COMMUNITY AND SOCIETAL WELLNESS THEORY

Whilst we draw from the field of psychodynamic, psychotherapeutic and analytic approaches, like Winnicott, we do this within the context of recognizing the wider influences of community and society in influencing and shaping children's development. There is a danger when our primary task is to provide treatment for individuals that we ignore the wider context. Hence we reinforce the cultural norm of individualism, which can be argued to be one of the causes of ill-health. We find that theories of psychological wellness are very helpful in this respect and Prilleltensky and Nelson (2000) eloquently summarize this point:

> Despite what we know about the impact of various systems and levels on families, most preventive and reactive interventions in child welfare and mental health deal with individuals or dyads, such as parent–child or marital relationships. Our actions seriously lag behind our understanding of wellness. An enormous corpus of evidence points to the powerful impact of socioeconomic, cultural, and contextual factors in shaping the lives of children and families … yet in apparent disregard for this knowledge, workers continue to focus on counselling, therapy, or person-centered prevention as the main vehicles for the promotion of wellness (Albee 1996; Cowen 1985). The causes for maintaining an individualistic and intrapsychic orientation in child welfare and mental health are many and have been reviewed elsewhere (Fox and Prilleltensky 1997; Prilleltensky 1989, 1994, 1997; Wharf 1993). A culture that promotes selfishness and blames victims for their misfortune is bound to want to fix people and not structures. So ingrained in our society is the individualistic mentality that professionals rarely question the narrow focus of social interventions. In a sense, changing individuals in light of ominous social forces is like searching for the penny where there is more light, never mind the penny got dropped in the dark. We offer counselling because it is what we are accustomed to, not necessarily because it is the best means of helping. Never mind societal structures and economic policies need a serious overhaul to lift people out of poverty, we sit down with our clients and teach them how to budget their ever shrinking dollars, sermonize them not to get too upset with their children even if there is not enough to eat, and urge them not to expose their kids to lead when all they can afford is deplorable housing with lead paint and lead pipes (McKnight 1995). (Prilleltensky and Nelson 2000)

Where we talk of inadequate parenting we need to remember that all parenting takes place in a context, within wider family, community and society dynamics. For instance, it is clear that poverty and a lack of resources impact on the challenges of parenting, increasing stress levels, contributing to psychological problems such as excessive aggression and making child maltreatment all the more likely (Trickett et al. 1998). Therefore, our theoretical approach needs to incorporate an understanding of wellness in the widest sense. This will have a number of benefits: the approach is more compassionate and less judgemental towards individuals, which is also likely to be more helpful in enabling children to develop empathy; a recognition of the importance that community and society plays in our lives is likely to help us ensure that the children we work with are enabled to take their place positively within these settings; working with communities will also be educational and supportive to those communities in understanding the needs of children, the problem of trauma and what can be done to change things. There is a strong argument that also claims the necessity of tackling things on the macro political level. This is often dismissed as being unrealistic given the challenges of our day-to-day work. However, wherever it is possible it is a worthy aim to have some influence.

CONCLUSION

Because of the link between the infant, trauma and the environment it is clear that the treatment of traumatized children cannot take place entirely on a one-to-one basis. Both the individual relationships with the child as well as the environmental context are crucial in the therapeutic and recovery process. As Winnicott has shown, theories of object relations, attachment and child development whilst focusing mainly on the mother–infant relationship also paid attention to the wider environment. Others such as Menzies Lyth, who adopt a psychodynamic and systems perspective on understanding organizations, have developed theories that are particularly compatible. It is crucial in the residential treatment of traumatized children that the whole organization and every activity within it are aligned to this work. For this to happen there has to be a theory – as Phillips (1988) put it – of 'true' child development, of trauma and its impact on true development and of organizational systems and dynamics. In addition, these theories need to be compatible so that they complement each other, and the nature of the organization enhances and supports the individual work and attachments that take place within it. Confirming the importance of this, Canham (1998, p.69) argues that, 'the whole way the organization functions is the basis for the possibility of an introjective identification'. The children will internalize not only the relationships they are most directly involved with but also the way the organization as a whole functions. Similarly, the children will internalize the nature of the organization's relationship with the wider community and society. This will be especially important to them when they make their transition as young adults into the wider the community.

CHAPTER 2

Trauma-Informed Practice

Traumatized children cannot heal within traumatizing – or traumatized – organizations, and instead such organizations can make children's problems worse.

Bloom 2005, p.63

Psychological trauma involves an experience of such intensity that it damages underlying assumptions and expectations about the world or the self, and can be understood to mean a profound emotional shock (Oxford Pocket Dictionary 1992). A 'traumatic event' has been defined by the American Psychiatric Association's (2000) Diagnostic and Statistical Manual (DSM-IV)

> as one in which a person experiences, witnesses, or is confronted with actual or threatened death or serious injury, or threat to the physical integrity of oneself or others. A person's response to trauma often includes intense fear, helplessness, or sheer horror. Trauma can result from experiences that are "private" (e.g. sexual assault, domestic violence, child abuse/neglect, witnessing interpersonal violence) or more "public" (e.g. war, terrorism, natural disasters). (Witness Justice 2011)

Trauma can have a particularly profound effect when it is experienced during the formative years. Gordon (2010, p.6) argues that, 'when traumatic experiences occur in early childhood they undermine the development of the very sense of self and the basis for future developmental stages.'

If out of home care systems are to become more attuned and responsive to the needs of children in care, concepts of wellbeing must be contextualized within a trauma-informed framework of understanding.

History has shown that if children are provided with positive parenting experiences they can recover, or at least significantly improve, from even the most severe trauma caused by abuse and neglect (Perry and Szalavitz 2010). Cameron and Maginn (2009, p.28) stated that, 'The more secure children feel, the more time, energy and inclination they have to seek and make sense. Whereas fear constricts, safety expands the range of exploration.'

HOW TRAUMATIZATION DEVELOPS IN CHILDHOOD

Though many children experience trauma this does not mean that the child always becomes traumatized. Whenever a child or adult experiences a traumatic event, the natural responses of the body and mind to protect the person are likely to keep aspects of the experience out of consciousness. The mind takes in what is happening and responds before all of the details are consciously registered. This is a normal survival response and serves to prevent the person from being overwhelmed so that he or she can take protective action. Therefore, the aspects of the experience that are kept out of consciousness are experienced as feelings, such as anxiety rather than as thoughts.

The potential difficulty is that these feelings can be triggered in the future by scenarios that are reminiscent of the traumatic event. This happens at an unconscious level and the person is left with unpleasant feelings that are difficult to understand. For example, a person may suddenly feel anxious or panicky, or they may experience visual images such as flashbacks or nightmares, or find themselves having obsessive ruminations (Janet 1904). The feelings associated with the traumatic event will need to be understood and related back to the trauma so that they can be integrated as part of the experience. This then helps the person to differentiate between a feeling that belongs to the present and one that is related to the past event. Gradually the person is then able to regulate their emotions and the intensity of feelings related to the past reduces. So for instance, a person who has been in a car crash may initially feel very anxious when getting into a car again. But over time, as she recognizes what feelings belong to the past and what belong with the present situation she returns to her normal state of mind, albeit with maybe a little more caution. To achieve this return to a state of equilibrium a person needs a number of capacities and resources. They need the emotional and cognitive capacity to process the event and ideally support to help them work through their experience and feelings. Often a partner, a family member or friend can provide the necessary support and sometimes a professional such as a counsellor may provide the needed help. If the event was an isolated occurrence most people recover from trauma in time.

Alternatively, as van der Kolk and Newman (2007, p.7) explain, 'The posttraumatic syndrome is the result of a failure of time to heal all wounds. The memory of the trauma is not integrated and accepted as a part of one's personal past; instead, it comes to exist independently of previous schemata (i.e. it is dissociated).' Dockar-Drysdale (1990a, p.122) explains one of the effects of repeated trauma:

> I found myself considering the problems of a small boy assaulted by a violent adult. Of course after the first occasion such a child would feel acute anxiety and dread that the experience might be repeated. However, when such a trauma occurred constantly, this anxiety would change into severe panic states, such as we have seen in our experiences.

Another key factor in determining the impact of trauma is a person's unique disposition. What may be traumatizing to one person, whether they are an infant or adult, is not always predictable, regardless of similarities in circumstances. Some children manage to survive extremely difficult experiences more positively than others. Something that might be a small difficulty to one infant could be quite traumatic to another who is more sensitive: 'So although the reality of extraordinary events is at the core of PTSD, the meaning that victims attach to these events is as fundamental as the trauma itself' (van der Kolk and Newman 2007, p.6).

Trauma causes an excess of emotion and the ability to regulate emotions is something that develops throughout childhood and to some extent adulthood. The traumatized children we work with have often experienced repeated trauma at an early age, when they were most vulnerable in terms of emotional resilience. In many cases the environments of neglect and deprivation they were living in meant that they were underdeveloped compared to a 'normal' child of their age, which will have increased their vulnerability. Often the people responsible for their trauma were their closest carers and therefore there may have been no one to turn to for support. In some cases, maybe someone in the extended family provided an element of support and care. This may have made a significant difference.

Once the cycle of trauma begins the effects begin to spiral. Rather than the trauma being a one-off event it becomes an expected occurrence. The child becomes highly anxious and is unable to switch off from this state. This then interferes with all aspects of her daily life and makes it difficult to do any of the ordinary things, like playing, relaxation and the enjoyment of any nurture that might be available. The child therefore becomes increasingly deprived of the experiences that are necessary for growth and to redress the imbalance. The child learns to turn away from relationships and not to seek comfort. This leaves the child in a situation where she is unable to integrate her experiences, is preoccupied with danger and where the 'split off' feelings related to trauma are being continually triggered and re-experienced. In the most severe cases, the child may completely shut down in a disassociated state. This occurs at an instinctive level to at least make the child less visible.

Children who are withdrawn in this way may seem as if they are not too much trouble, but they are barely living in any way that could be described as meaningful or real. It is literally like curling up into a ball and waiting for the inevitable attack to pass. Traumatized children who are not so withdrawn and who are still hyperactive, waiting for the sign to take cover and run, are likely to be highly emotional. Their experiences and inability to integrate them, cause fearful and defensive reactions to anything that triggers their anxiety. Often this means that they create tension and if they are still in the abusive environment, further abuse and punishment is a likely consequence.

Bloom explains how traumatization in childhood can develop into adult pathology:

> Recent research on childhood trauma is helping to understand how children's exposure to overwhelming stress is traumatized over time into adult psychopathology. As evidence accumulates it becomes clear that the brain organizes itself in response to environmental pressure that may be far more potent than even genetic influences because the central nervous system is so vulnerable to stress (Garbarino 1999). For these children, what begins as an adaptive response to threat – a fear state – becomes instead a fear trait that they carry into adulthood (Perry *et al.* 2005). Children who are exposed to violence show disturbing changes in basic neurobiological and physiological processes and it is postulated that these disturbances have profound developmental consequences. Bruce Perry and his colleagues have observed persistent hyperarousal and hyperactivity, changes in muscle tone, temperature regulation, startle response, and cardiovascular regulation as well as profound sleep disturbances, affect dysregulation, specific and generalized anxiety, and behavioral impulsivity in children who have been traumatized. Over time, these growing children proceed down a number of different pathways in order to help themselves adapt to disordered physiological stability and emotional dysregulation. Some will become addicted to drugs and/or alcohol. Others will develop an eating disorder. For others, anxiety and depression will be the predominant presenting problem. Still others will have recurrent difficulties with relationships that will dominate the clinical picture, while others manifest their underlying unresolved conflicts via bodily illness and dysfunction that can affect virtually any organ system. As a result, by adulthood, the presenting picture can look amazingly diverse and, consequently, the common traumatic

origins of the pathological processes of development can easily be overlooked or ignored (Trickett and Putnam 1993). (Bloom 2005, p.57)

It is relatively easy to see from the way trauma develops in an abusive environment that the outcome is likely to reach a point of total breakdown. The carer's inadequacy leads to abuse and neglect, the child becomes increasingly traumatized, which impacts further on the carer's resources, and so on. Clearly, if the situation is not too endemic and there is the possibility of support from extended family or professional services, it may be that some stability can be achieved and a recovery process can begin. For the child to have any possibility of recovery within the environment the carers will have to begin their own recovery first.

Where the child is removed from the 'trauma' environment, she will continue to be in a traumatized state until any treatment process has a positive impact. The child will be in a new and unfamiliar situation, which may be equally as frightening from her perspective. Adults can't be trusted and all manner of things are likely to trigger the child's heightened state of arousal and anxiety. As van der Kolk and Newman (2007, p.9) state, 'Because of this timeless and unintegrated nature of traumatic memories, victims remain embedded in the trauma as a contemporary experience, instead of being able to accept it as something belonging to the past.'

One of the key tasks in work with traumatized children is to reach a point where the trauma can be named, accepted and integrated as part of the child's past. 'In important ways, an experience does not really exist until it can be named and placed into larger categories' (van der Kolk and Newman 2007, p.4).

The children we work with have suffered the double impact of trauma within a context of general neglect and both will need addressing if the child is to recover. Stien and Kendall (2004, p.138) argue that, 'Research shows that new experiences are the most effective way to change the pattern of connections between nerve cells, networks, and systems.' In practice, this means that the first task is to provide a safe, calm and reliable environment. Once the child feels safe and contained, which may take a long time, it may then be possible to provide her with the kind of nurturing experiences she needs to fill the gaps in her development.

TRAUMA CAUSES HYPERAROUSAL AND FEAR IN CHILDREN

Experiences of trauma create states of hyperarousal and fear in children that cause the brain to produce adrenalin, which stimulates the mind and body to be prepared to fight or take flight. This can be seen as a normal healthy response to danger that improves the likelihood for survival. We take flight from the danger rather than stay in its proximity. However, when a child is continually in a state of danger, the brain is in a constant state of arousal and the excess of adrenalin that is produced actually damages the brain's development. Additionally, the part of the brain that reads danger signals becomes hypervigilant and begins to exaggerate warning signals. Danger is increasingly read into situations that are not actually dangerous. Hence, the child becomes highly anxious and hyperaroused by ordinary everyday experiences. For instance, touching a sexually abused child in an ordinary way may be perceived by the child as a precursor to abuse, leading the child to become aroused. Something that the child might not even be conscious of, such as a certain tone of voice or smell, can trigger the child from being in a calm state into a sudden state of hyperarousal, anxiety or panic.

This can be one of the most difficult and bewildering things to deal with in work with severely traumatized children. The behaviour of the child is often as chaotically unpredictable as their own experiences. As Whitwell describes,

> A typical 'frozen' child in a therapeutic milieu presents a curiously contradictory picture. He has charm, he is apparently extremely friendly and seems to make good contacts very quickly... In contrast he may become suddenly savagely hostile, especially towards a grown-up with whom he has been friendly. He will fly into sudden panic rages for no apparent reason. (Whitwell 1998a)

Traumatized children benefit from caring environments that are attuned to their emotional states, where the carers can adjust the environment to support emotional regulation, and can provide predictable responses and routines that assist in reducing hyperarousal (Tucci *et al.* 2010). By attunement we mean the capacity to be so in tune with a child that you can anticipate without being told what the child's needs might be and how they are feeling. This is just as a mother might anticipate the needs of her infant and understand how they are feeling (SACCS 2010). For the reasons we have described, this is particularly challenging when working with traumatized children whose moods can change so rapidly.

Cameron and Maginn emphasize the central importance of attunement to the child's development and sense of security:

Underpinning secure attachment appears to be the key child-rearing process of 'attunement'. This occurs when a care-giver is not only aware of his or her own emotions, but can also recognize how his or her child is feeling and can convey this awareness to the child. An attuned relationship is a prerequisite to the development of both security and empathy in the young child. (Cameron and Maginn 2008, p.1158)

Hannon *et al.* refer to recent research explaining the importance of 'sensitive parenting' in enabling traumatized children to achieve positive outcomes:

Schofield and Beek (2005) studied a cohort of children placed in foster care, who were a 'high risk' group according to the age at which they were placed and the abuse and neglect they had been exposed to. They found that the degree of 'sensitive parenting' demonstrated by one or both carers was associated with whether children settled stably in their placement and made good progress. 'Sensitive parenting' was defined as: The carer's capacity to put themselves 'in the shoes of the child', to reflect on the child's thoughts, feelings and behaviour and their own thoughts, feelings and parenting style – all features of reflective function that link to resilience in the carers themselves as well as to resilience-promoting parenting. (Hannon *et al.* 2010, p.85)

CHILDHOOD TRAUMA REDUCES THE BRAIN'S CAPACITY TO THINK AND REGULATE EMOTIONS

Traumatized children are likely to find it difficult to utilize reasoning and logic to modify their behaviour or reactions. These children are also unlikely to learn from consequences, in particular when they are in heightened arousal states. During early infant development the brain develops in a sequential and hierarchical way which begins in the lower part of the brain. The first stage of development is the brainstem and this actually begins in the womb. This is the part of the brain that controls basic bodily regulation functions such as heartbeat, blood pressure and body temperature – the regulation of arousal, sleep and fear states. Perry (2006) provides a comprehensive account of how the brain's development moves on from the brainstem during the first nine months to the diencephalon, to the limbic and finally the prefrontal cortex parts of the brain.

The diencephalon integrates multiple sensory and fine motor control. The limbic system regulates emotional states and the capacity to read emotions in others. 'Brain growth and development is profoundly "front loaded" such that by age four, a child's brain is 90% adult size' (Perry 2005, p.1). The majority of this development and growth of the brain takes place during the first three years of life. Without the satisfactory completion of one stage of development the brain cannot move on to the next. The needs of the infant during the different developmental stages are also different. For example, brainstem development requires rhythmic and patterned sensory input and attuned, responsive caregiving. The diencephalon development requires the introduction of simple narrative as well as emotional and physical warmth.

This understanding of how the brain develops has significant implications for us in our work with traumatized children. It is natural that we first of all relate to children in a chronological way. We see a sixteen-year-old and we have normal expectations of a sixteen-year-old. However, if a child has been traumatized in early childhood her brain may not have developed at a pace with her chronological age. If a child has been so traumatized that the limbic and cortex parts of the brain are largely undeveloped, a sixteen-year-old may be functioning in many respects as an infant. Even where a traumatized child does have some capacity to think, often she actively avoids thinking as her inner world is dominated by thoughts related to her traumatic experiences. Therefore, it is essential that we have a clear understanding of how the child's traumatic experiences have impacted on her development. As van der Kolk and Newman (2007, p.7) state, 'Thus, in dealing with traumatized people, it is critical to examine where they have become 'stuck' and around which specific traumatic event(s) they have built their secondary psychic elaborations.'

We then need to respond to the child in a way that is relevant to their actual development rather than chronological age. For instance, to use reasoning and logic which requires cortex functioning, with a child whose development is stuck in the lower part of the brain, would be no more use than trying to reason with a baby. This is one of the most common mistakes made in work with traumatized children. Approaches such as talking therapies are sometimes used with children who are not able to relate in a meaningful way to this approach. More appropriate approaches might be related to physical and sensory experiences, which stimulate the lower parts of the brain. It is understandable how challenging this can be in practice, especially when we are concerned about the child's inappropriate behaviour, and we feel the need to explain this to them. Similarly, a traumatized child who is feeling 'bad' or unhappy may benefit far more by doing something physical, such as dancing, or playing a game to gain a sense of physical mastery, rather than trying to talk about their experiences. As Smith (2009, p.ix) has argued, 'It is an interesting reflection on how residential child care is perceived that recruitment processes often target individuals who want to counsel children around their difficulties, rather than run around a park with them.' Seligman (2002, p.11) advises to, 'Augment positive emotions in your children to start an upward spiral of more positive emotions.' This approach makes perfect sense to us in normal child development, but seems counter-intuitive when working with children whose development has been disrupted and held back. So, if a two-year-old was unhappy we would not spend too long in dealing with the detail of her feelings. We would quickly establish what the problem was and then move on to a positive and enjoyable experience, most likely of a physical nature.

CASE EXAMPLE: LEE

Susan shared her experience of tucking her young daughter in bed at night. She would wrap the duvet around her daughter as if in a womb and read her a favourite fairytale. This is an ordinary childhood experience that many parents provide intuitively for their children.

A sixteen-year-old male, Lee, who Susan cared for, began acting out one day by running out into the backyard of the home, yelling profanities and saying he wanted to die and that the pain was too hard to bear. Susan could not work out why he reacted, and thought something terrible must have happened that she hadn't seen. In unpacking the chain of events with Lee, it became clear that he had never been tucked in by his mother and had never been read a bedtime story. Susan was able to respond in a natural way and asked him if he would like to be tucked in and for her to read him a fairytale. He agreed that he would love this. Susan tucked him in the same way she had with her daughter and read him the same fairytale, which calmed him down.

This experience, repeated over time, had a huge impact on Lee's development, as he was provided with a need that was not met in his early childhood. Lee had experienced being abandoned by his family who he never saw again. He spent his childhood in institutional settings where his need for nurturing experiences remained unmet. Lee had missed out on some of the basic primary experiences (Dockar-Drysdale 1990a) that a child needs as part of early development. To enable recovery, it is vital to focus on providing children with the opportunities to experience what they may have been deprived of in their early years. What is also important to note about this example is the focus on developmental needs, rather than chronological expectations. A child at sixteen years of age who has experienced early trauma and neglect will at times need to be treated as if he or she were younger. The recovery process in a sense requires returning to provide what has not been provided in infancy.

It is interesting that Lee who had literally been abandoned, which can feel like being totally emotionally dropped, sought a kind of provision that feels exactly like being held, both physically and emotionally. Waddell describes the significance of this to the child's treatment:

Repeatedly demonstrated is the endless enactment by such children of the feeling of being dropped, of being got rid of (often painfully reproduced by the 'caring' agencies themselves). The task is not to offer substitute care and parenting in order to rectify past deficiencies; rather, it is to enable the individual to respond to what may now be on offer. The significance of the awareness of a space in someone's mind cannot be minimized; this kind of receptive attention may be a unique experience for such a child. As one therapist puts it: 'the legacy of the abandoned child is usually not only the burden of being abandoned but of being left with extremely inadequate mental resources to cope with a degree of pain which would overwhelm the most favourably brought-up child' (Boston and Szur 1983, p. 76). (Waddell 1989)

TRAUMA DISCONNECTS CHILDREN FROM RELATIONAL RESOURCES

One of the consequences of trauma is that it disconnects children from relational resources that can alleviate its effects. Stien and Kendall explain that,

> for maltreated children, abuse has shattered their ability to trust. These children must go against the grain of their prior experience to seek and expect nurturance. Usually, distraught people seek connection with others. This impulse is innate. Young children are naturally drawn to adults for protection and comfort when they feel frightened. Normally, a nurturing parent comforts a child by establishing eye contact, using soothing touch, and a calm, reassuring voice. For maltreated children, however, their cries for help were usually met with indifference or perhaps further abuse. Adults were the source of pain, not comfort. Abuse 'teaches' children that dependency is dangerous. To defend themselves against further hurt, they ward off their feelings of vulnerability and act as if they have no need for affection. (Stien and Kendall 2008, p.149)

According to Tucci *et al.* (2010, p.5), children who have experienced trauma require 'opportunities to experience attachment relationships which offer consistency, nurture and predictability'. Carers can be trained to understand the significance of daily interactions in providing the basis for children to modify their internal working model (Levy and Orlans 1998) and previous attachment patterns. For example, a child who experiences their carer being trustworthy and reliable over a long period of time will begin to believe that adults can be reliable and trustworthy. The carer's sensitivity to providing attuned responses to children with traumatic backgrounds is a core competency in caring for them.

TRAUMA RESTRICTS THE ATTENTION CAPACITY OF CHILDREN

As we have discussed, traumatized children are likely to be in a state of hypervigilance. They are constantly scanning their environment for the slightest sign of danger. Inevitably this means that they are unable to concentrate on other things and can appear to be very easily distracted. It is likely that some children who are diagnosed with attention deficit disorder may have been traumatized. In addition, if the child's developmental stage is not understood they may be expected to join in with an activity which is beyond their capacity. This can lead to frustration and lack of interest, which may give the impression of not being able to pay attention. These children will benefit from environments that enable them to engage in experiences, which redirect their attention away from past trauma-oriented activation to the here and now. The environment will need to be as calm and predictable as possible so that the child's state of fear is reduced.

Stien and Kendall explain that,

> Typically, treatment begins with techniques that are aimed at reducing stress and helping children find new ways to regulate their emotions and calm themselves. This step, in turn, enables children to develop their cognitive resources. Strengthening cognition further enhances the ability to regulate emotions. (Stien and Kendall 2004, p.137)

The Australian Childhood Foundation's 'Response to the National Standards for Out of Home Care' informs that carers should be supported to offer children opportunities to act and react in playful ways, which are likely to provide more intensely positive experiences. 'These opportunities also relieve the burden of unrealistic expectations on traumatized children. They also powerfully connect children and carers in shared activities that promote trust and belonging' (Tucci *et al.* 2010, p.6).

TRAUMA-BASED BEHAVIOUR HAS A FUNCTIONAL PURPOSE

We can understand the purpose and meaning of trauma-based behaviour in children, shifting our interpretations away from judgemental blame to greater acknowledgement of the ongoing impact of children's traumatic experiences. Traumatized children develop responses to trauma that are in essence survival responses. The responses are a solution to the problem the child is faced with. The more traumatized the child becomes, the more likely it is that the child's responses will become patterned in response to any situation the child perceives to be threatening, whether it actually is or not. Therefore, over time the response that originally might have been an appropriate response and solution becomes increasingly dysfunctional. This understanding enables carers to develop the confidence to plan helpful and empathic responses to children. The aim is to help the child to feel safe enough to recognize that whilst their responses may once have been a solution to a problem, they are no longer functional in the present. This approach can also be translated into other settings such as school, where similar behaviours can intrude on children's everyday experiences.

TRAUMA RESTRICTS CHILDREN'S ABILITY TO DEAL WITH CHANGE

Traumatized children tend to organize their experience in such a way that makes their reading and responses to various situations simple and quick. If a child experiences regular threats to her physical and emotional safety, quick mental processing is necessary to recognize potential threats and to respond so that the child's survival is protected. Therefore, the child will tend to perceive numerous variants on a specific situation as a threat and will have a similar response, such as to take flight. The child might respond to any situation that suggests intimacy as a threat of sexual abuse and respond by attacking and/or taking flight. The child will need considerable support from the adults in their care environment to reshape their responses. This will take time. Carers and other significant individuals will need to focus on introducing change in small increments, preparing and supporting children to become accustomed to one change before initiating another. In this context, carers and others need to understand the benefits of predictability and routine for traumatized children. Perry and Szalavitz's (2006) extensive work with traumatized children, with a focus on trauma and its impact on the brain, highlights the importance of predictability and consistency of care in supporting the development of traumatized children.

TRAUMA UNDERMINES IDENTITY FORMATION IN CHILDREN

The impact of ongoing trauma on children prevents them from developing a coherent sense of self. As discussed, the traumatic experiences, especially in early infancy, disrupt and distort the child's development. Children become preoccupied with protecting themselves and have little concern with anything other than survival. In this state, it is not possible for children to develop interests and discover what they enjoy and what they like. They are mainly concerned with the avoidance of pain. Additionally, the lives of traumatized children are often chaotic with frequent breakdowns and changes in their circumstances. Some traumatized children may have had multiple placement breakdowns, perhaps living in ten or twenty different homes by the age of ten. All of these factors result in children often having little sense of who they are, the people involved in their lives or where they have come from (Rose and Philpot 2005).

Object relations theorists refer to this as identity diffusion. The work with these children may initially be providing experiences that enable them to develop a positive sense of what they like, enjoy and dislike. It also enables them to begin to assert their sense of identity. This might be by providing many nurturing experiences and opportunities for the child to begin to enjoy things and to play. Many traumatized children are unable to play. Being able to play simple games can help a child begin to establish her identity. Once a child has a foundation of knowing what she likes and dislikes, what she feels, that she is safe and loved for being who she is, she can then begin to consider the bigger questions of where she has come from and her life journey. This work could take a number of years and be part of a programme of life story work (Rose and Philpot 2005).

The aim of the work is not just to establish the child's history. It is also to work through the meaning the child attaches to different aspects of her life and to correct distortions in her perception. For example, traumatized children often feel responsible for the things that have happened to them, including abuse. Whilst this might seem quite dysfunctional, by assuming responsibility the child is able to replace feelings of vulnerability and helplessness with an illusion of having some control. Additionally, the child may need to preserve a positive image of the parent or caregiver responsible for the abuse. This protects the child from potentially overwhelming feelings of loss, rage and fear (van der Kolk and Newman 2007). Therefore, an important task in work with such a child is to help the child see where the responsibility really lies, shifting the child's inappropriate sense of responsibility. To do this work it is necessary to explore not only the child's memories and thoughts about her experiences, but also her emotions in relation to different people and events in her life. This work can be particularly difficult and painful. Not only are distressing memories being worked on, but also the child's feelings about those memories. A child might feel shame and guilt about some of her feelings. Only when these feelings are named and explored can the child be helped to put them into perspective and let go of some of the most negative self-persecutory aspects.

Some of the child's negative views about herself may be gradually replaced with other feelings such as sadness. If the feeling of responsibility is let go of, the child may then be in touch with exactly how helpless she was, and how awful it was to be treated like that. This then requires a modification of how the child may view the abuser, which is again very challenging, especially if it was someone who was supposed to love and protect the child. From this brief example, it is clear how complex and necessary the work is for the child to develop a more coherent and positive sense of identity, which now includes being cared for and understood by those working with her.

TRAUMA AFFECTS SOCIAL SKILLS DEVELOPMENT AND IMPACTS ON PEER RELATIONSHIPS

Children with trauma backgrounds are likely to have difficulties in all social situations including those with other children. They will have difficulty in forming appropriate attachments, reading social cues and situations, managing disagreements, and knowing how to respond appropriately. Their state of hyperarousal and fear is likely to cause them to behave in inappropriate ways. They may be overly aggressive, controlling or withdrawn in situations that would be considered non-threatening to other children. Some children due to their specific experiences may also be highly sexualized in their behaviour. Carers and other adults have a very important role in helping traumatized children to manage their relationships and interactions appropriately. It is essential that carers also role model respectful and appropriate interactions with others. This will gradually enable traumatized children to build a network of relationships which promote connection and provide opportunities to reconstruct their attachment styles.

THE IMPACT OF TRAUMA ON THE CHILD'S INTERNAL WORKING MODEL

Traumatized and homeless children predominantly have histories which include childhood trauma, abuse and neglect, in many cases dating back to their infancy. Early difficulties and breakdowns in their family environments have often been compounded by further negative experiences, for example, breakdowns in foster placements and exclusion from school. Inevitably these experiences will have had a damaging impact on the child's development and internal working model. These children develop a view of the world that is unsafe, of caregivers who are hurtful, unresponsive and untrustworthy and of themselves as bad and undeserving (Levy and Orlans 1998). The defence mechanisms that have formed to survive and cope with this fearful and negative expectation are often entrenched and deeply rooted. In some cases, however traumatic and negative their circumstances may seem, they are at least familiar to the child. It can seem safer to the child to hang on to this familiarity rather than take the risk of letting someone offer help only to be let down again. The problems that the children present, which can be anything along the continuum of emotional disorders to mental illnesses, are therefore additionally difficult to treat.

The following two brief vignettes by young people talking about their initial experiences of moving into Lighthouse, vividly show how unusual and potentially frightening it is to be in a new environment. They also highlight how being shown care and concern can feel so unfamiliar and anxiety provoking. It is completely at odds with their internal working model.

CAROL'S STORY: MY FIRST DAY

I still remember the first day I moved into Lighthouse, I was a young girl, scared, nervous and also insecure because my life was being upheaved again. I remember my carer Vicki. As I was heading to bed for the first time in my new environment and saying goodnight, Vicki asked me would I like a goodnight hug. This was such a foreign concept to me, so many thoughts and emotions ran through my head.

ANNIE'S STORY: LOTS OF QUESTIONS

I was still painfully shy and quiet. I kept to myself a lot. It took so much energy to come out of my room and interact with others; however, slowly I did. I had no idea how to interpret Sue's immediate kindness towards me. Why was I rushed into admittance to Lighthouse before others? Why did she offer me new, really nice clothes? Why was she giving me hugs? Why was she spending one-to-one time with me? Why was she organizing people to do things for me? Why the kind compliments when no one really knew me? Why would these people want to do things for me? Why was I being given movie tickets, free fun nights out and Christmas presents? I don't deserve this. Why were the other children even being nice to me? Why did people want to hear me talk at these family meetings? Why didn't they get rid of me when they saw my cuts? When they knew I hadn't stopped doing it? When I had to be readmitted to hospital over and over? Why did Sue like me? This all scared the utter hell out of me but I also liked it. So I still kept quiet in case it all stopped.

RELATIONSHIP AND ATTACHMENT DIFFICULTIES

For children who have been abused and neglected, attachment difficulties are often central to this experience. In particular, children who have become homeless could be considered to be in a situation where they are completely detached from pro-social relationships with others. They are learning to live in a situation where they are reliant on no one besides themselves. The child's homelessness can be seen to be the end of a continuum of failed attachment, leaving the child feeling completely abandoned, alone and isolated. The child's internal working model of attachment is likely to be mistrustful and negative. It is one where other people let you down, hurt you or are only interested in you for their own gratification. In some cases, there will have been some positive experiences of attachment in the child's history, albeit too brief and disrupted. Helping the child connect or reconnect with the possibility of a supportive and meaningful attachment is possibly the biggest challenge involved in the work.

Hannon *et al.* argue that,

Child development literature tells us that if children are to develop in a psychologically healthy way and develop the important character traits and skills they need to succeed in life (such as application, self-regulation, empathy and resilience), they need to experience:

- a secure attachment

- 'authoritative' parenting that provides a combination of 'responsiveness' and 'demandingness' (or warmth and consistent boundaries)

- stability. (Hannon *et al.* 2010, p.12)

PHYSICAL WELLBEING

Traumatized and homeless children often suffer a number of difficulties in relation to their physical wellbeing. It is now well known that emotional trauma has a general impact on a child's ability to thrive in all senses. Perry and Szalavitz (2006) have shown how the brains of traumatized children can literally fail to grow; other aspects of their physical development can also be affected. Perry and Szalavitz explain:

However, a groundbreaking study of more than seventeen thousand Californians enrolled in the Kaiser Permanente health plan has shown that childhood trauma is a critically overlooked factor in the obesity epidemic – and in virtually every other major cause of death studied. The risks for heart disease, stroke, depression, diabetes, asthma, and even many cancers are all affected by trauma-related changes in the stress response system. Empathy and connection affect physical – not just mental – wellness and health. (Perry and Szalavitz 2010, p.162)

In addition to this, traumatized children often have no appropriate model of being cared for. Being emotionally immature, with a lack of concern for themselves and others, traumatized children are likely to do things that are neglectful and harmful to themselves. This might include self-harming behaviour, lack of concern for their own safety, putting themselves in dangerous positions, unhealthy diet, lack of personal hygiene, use of drugs, and so on.

THE BASICS OF TRAUMA TREATMENT

We have explained how childhood trauma, especially when it is reoccurring and within a general context of neglect, has an impact on the child. It affects all aspects of development in a profoundly damaging way. We shall summarize some of the basic aspects of treatment that we have referred to.

First of all a child needs to be safe and protected from the risk of further trauma. The environment the child is in needs to be calming, predictable and reliable so that the child can actually begin to feel safe. Those working with the child need to have an understanding of trauma and its impact. They need to be capable of responding to the child in an attuned and sensitive way. 'To calm a frightened child first you must calm yourself' (Perry and Szalavitz 2006, p.67). At the same time, the child needs to experience adults using their authority appropriately to set clear limits and to manage the child's behaviour when necessary. The child's destructive and violent behaviour, whether towards others or the self will need to be stopped in a firm but empathetic way, as this behaviour may be normal to the child. This work in establishing safety will help to reduce the child's stress responses, gradually allowing the child to use parts of the brain that are more to do with relating and thinking. Once the child is settled, depending on their stage of development and needs, different elements of the work can take place. Stien and Kendall (2004, p.135) refer to the ISSD Guidelines for Treatment (2000) and mention the following helpful points:

- Help the child learn how to regulate her emotions.

- Promote acceptance of painful feelings.

- Promote the direct expression of feelings in healthy attachments and relationships.

- Help the child to reduce symptomatic behaviour, e.g. withdrawing or acting out.

- Desensitize traumatic memories and correct the faulty beliefs about life caused by traumatic events.

- Promote a unified identity by helping the child achieve a sense of cohesiveness about her own thoughts, feelings and behaviour.

- Enhance motivation for growth and future success.

For children who have been severely deprived and abused from infancy onwards, attachment work and the provision of experiences that will fill developmental gaps is especially important. Emphasizing the importance of this in work with deprived and traumatized children, Winnicott (1986, p.112) claimed that 'cure at its roots means care'. Working on issues related to trust and safety within relationships will be necessary before a child feels attached to anyone, in such a way that they will allow themselves to be looked after and cared for. Therefore, patience is required to avoid the temptation to rush any kind of work before the child is emotionally ready. Important attachment relationships can be considered on the individual, group and community level. Severely traumatized children have often experienced inadequate and damaging relationships in all these areas, with negative experiences of the parent–child relationship, the extended family and wider community. This is not to say that there weren't also some positive experiences for the child in these areas. One of the aims of treatment is to enable the child to relate on all levels, one-to-one, in a group, and the wider community. The way in which the child learns to relate should become something that they feel comfortable with. This enables them to achieve their personal aims and wishes, in their own way. For instance, some children may prefer individual relationships and others may relate better to a group.

The development of self-mastery and an appropriate sense of control are particularly important for the recovery of traumatized children. Working with children in an environmental setting like a residential or foster care home provides a wide range of opportunities to achieve this. Children can be supported and encouraged to develop their skills and interests. This can give a feeling of physical and psychological competence. Children can be fully involved in having a say in how things should be done for them and generally in the home, and what their role will be. There are unlimited opportunities for working on relationships, with carers, other adults and children. Cowen, talking from a 'wellness' perspective, outlines the following elements of a healthy environment for development:

> Key pathways to wellness, for all of us, start with the crucial needs to form wholesome attachments and acquire age-appropriate competencies in early

childhood. Those steps, vital in their own right, also lay down a base for the good, or not so good, outcomes that follow. Other cornerstones of a wellness approach include engineering settings and environments that facilitate adaptation, fostering autonomy, support and empowerment, and promoting skills needed to cope effectively with stress. (Cowen 1996, p.246)

Finally, another core aspect of treatment is helping the child to live more in the present than the past. To be more engaged with others, and her own interests. To achieve this, the child may need to work through her past experiences of trauma and loss so that they become integrated as experiences that can be moved on from. As the child becomes more engaged, there are opportunities to name and acknowledge experiences, feelings and emotions. This enables the child to develop a repertoire for understanding herself, relating to others and also for exploring her traumatic experiences. As Stien and Kendall (2004, p.150) state, 'Learning to tolerate emotion depends on gaining emotional awareness. Many maltreated children need to go back to square one, that is, to learn to identify and label the emotion(s) they are experiencing.'

CAROL'S STORY: DISSOCIATION

Carol was at Lighthouse during her late teenage years and is now twenty-eight. She describes her experience of reoccurrences of her traumatic experiences and how she survived by dissociating.

While living at Lighthouse I had to deal with the reoccurrence of past traumas. These occurred in the form of flashbacks and dissociation. If it wasn't for the patience and care I received during these times, I know for a fact that I would not be alive today to tell this story. Dissociation is the brain's way of saying I've had enough. My brain could not deal with or comprehend what was happening to me as a child so it switched itself off. Quite often a flashback experience would lead to dissociation.

After one incident of dissociation I had two quite deep 10 cm cuts under each breast. I was bleeding and in shock. I felt such shame and fear from this incident that I did not tell anyone. I took myself to the doctor; I knew I needed stitches. I waited for hours at the doctor's, just sitting, alone and afraid that I couldn't even remember doing this to myself. I was numb to the core of my body. I couldn't say anything to the doctor. I just stood there and slowly lifted up my top, showing him the wounds on my breasts. He gave me a letter and sent me to emergency across the road. I walked to the hospital in a daze. Still numb, I gave the lady at the counter the letter and they put me on a bed and stitched me up. I remember Violet, my carer, coming into the room; she hugged me, kissed my head and told me it was going to be OK. I was safe and it was OK for me to feel the pain.

There were many times after this incident that I lost my memory; they were painful episodes and often brought back feelings and emotions from the abuse in my past. I have scars on my body that will never go away. I was hurt so much inside; the pain from cutting took it away. For that split second when the knife pierced the skin, all I could feel was that sensation, not the pain in my heart.

We have briefly explored some of the issues related to trauma, its impact on development and some of the aims of treatment. The remainder of this book will explore how some of these issues can be worked with in a residential treatment setting, and how this can be particularly complex and challenging work.

CHAPTER 3

Therapeutic Relationships

Therapeutic relationships take place in a facilitating environment, which allows relationships to form and develop in an emerging way. 'Reportedly, Michelangelo described his work as a sculptor as a process of removing the excess marble concealing the beauty of the figure within. His job, he was reported to have said, was a process of uncovering rather than creating. Working with people is often like this' (Fuller 1998, p.177).

BEGINNINGS

The saying that 'in every ending there is a beginning' seems appropriate. Likewise, in every beginning there is an ending. So, the arrival of a new baby, as well as bringing joy and hope, also brings the end, and loss of how things were before. New beginnings bring hopes and expectations, as well as fears and anxieties about the future. A new beginning, however positive we feel about it, is a change. It will evoke feelings of loss of what went before and comparisons between new and old.

The beginning of a new placement for a child is an emotionally charged occasion for everyone – the child, the carers, the children already in the home and the organization. As Salzberger-Wittenberg (1988) describes, it is a time of hopeful and fearful expectations, which may be unconscious as well as conscious. She refers to the following hopes for the worker – to be a helpful parent, to be tolerant and to be understanding; and for the child – to rid himself of pain, to find someone to help carry the burden and to be loved. Among the fears she mentions, for the worker – probing and digging into the past, and doing harm. For the child – to be blamed, to be punished and to be abandoned.

The other children will also have hopes and fears about the new child. How will they get on and how will the new arrival alter their own position in the group? The organization will be hopeful of a positive placement and fearful of things not working out positively. Where the child's family are involved there will also be hopes and fears.

The arrival of a new child is a hugely significant event and none more so than for the child, who has probably experienced numerous placements. He has had many experiences where any hope has quickly been replaced by disappointment and fear. We can expect that the child will be predominantly in a fearful and anxious state. Therefore the way the whole induction process is managed is extremely important in building a bridge into the new home.

The first step is the referral process, where the child's worker identifies the potentially suitable placement. For this stage to be effective there needs to be clarity about the nature of the child's needs and the therapeutic service being offered. Any confusion at this point can cause great difficulties once the placement has started. For example, if the service is to provide treatment, then this is quite different to purely providing a safe place for the child; though safety may be an essential part of the treatment. If the social worker is particularly anxious about the child's immediate safety the more complex matters to do with treatment may be overlooked. This could cause difficulties later on in the placement. If the organization has concerns that the child isn't responding to treatment the worker may have difficulty appreciating the concern as long as the child is safe. All parties, including the child, need to have an understanding of the reasons for placement and a commitment to it. Normally it is not helpful to involve the child until the professionals involved have reached clarity on this.

The traumatized children we work have suffered major levels of abuse and neglect, such that their development has been seriously hampered, delayed and distorted. The experience of multiple and prolonged experiences of trauma has been referred to as complex trauma (Cook *et al.* 2003). The following are some of the difficulties the children often have:

- difficulties building and maintaining any healthy relationships
- limited education and possible learning difficulties
- poor body image
- mental health problems and disorders
- physical health problems
- substance abuse

- suicide risk

- self-harming

- lacking basic life skills such as personal hygiene

- limited social skills

- antisocial or oppositional behaviour.

Many of the children have experienced so much trauma, neglect, disruption and placement breakdown in their lives that their basic sense of identity is often highly confused and fragmented. So, to begin with we need a clear history of the child's life and experiences. This will help to shed light on the nature of the child's needs and where the various difficulties stem from. As Perry and Hambrick (2008, p.40) state, 'In order to understand an individual one needs to know his or her history.' It is not unusual to find the child has been given many diagnostic labels such as attention deficit disorder or oppositional defiant disorder, yet the underlying history may not have been fully connected to the child's symptoms. Read *et al.* explain how the underlying causes are often overlooked:

> We leave the last words to a group of service users who, during the planning of the Auckland training program, were asked what they thought about asking all patients about child abuse. 'There were so many doctors and registrars and nurses and social workers in your life asking you about the same thing, mental, mental, mental, but not asking you why. I think there was an assumption that I had a mental illness and you know because I wasn't saying anything about the abuse I'd suffered no one knew. I just wish they would have said, "What happened to you? What happened?" But they didn't.' (Read *et al.* 2008, p.249)

We know that trauma, particularly in early childhood can have an impact on all aspects of a child's development, including physical growth and development. van der Kolk, McFarlane and van der Hart state the importance of gathering a thorough history and what should be included. Where they refer to a patient, the same applies to the children we work with.

> Prior to the start of treatment, a thorough history needs to be taken. This should include the nature of the traumatic stressor; the patient's role in the traumatic experience; the patient's thoughts and feelings about actions taken and not taken; the effect of the trauma on the patient's life and perception of self and others; exposure to prior traumatic experiences; habitual coping styles; level of cognitive functioning; particular personal strengths and capacities; prior psychiatric history; medical, social, family and occupational history; and cultural and religious explanatory beliefs. (van der Kolk *et al.* 2007, p.420)

In the case of work with traumatized children it is particularly important to have an understanding of their relationship with 'parents' and other caregivers during the first years of life.

> A crucial element in figuring out any brain-related clinical problems, therefore, is getting an accurate picture of the patient's experiences. Since much of the brain develops early in life, the way they are parented has a dramatic influence on brain development. And so, since we tend to care for our children the way we were cared for ourselves during our own childhoods, a good 'brain' history of a child begins with a history of the caregiver's childhood and early experiences. (Perry and Szalavitz 2006, p.83)

Annie's and Carol's stories clearly describe what it is like to live a life of abuse and neglect. The experience might feel normal to the child but can have such a profound and distorting effect on their development.

ANNIE'S STORY: ABUSE AND NEGLECT

I was a painfully shy and inhibited child and teenager. I lived in constant fear of physical and emotional punishment of which I believed I was always deserving. All I cared about was pleasing others as perfectly as possible so as to avoid further punishment. I had no idea that this was not normal. My childhood did not foster a healthy development of my own personality, nor my own sense of personal worth. I left my father's home in 1994. I was fourteen years old. In retrospect, I am sure that I was severely depressed at the time. Before this, life consisted of being locked in my room for weeks on end where I did not dare to open the curtains or turn the light on. I lost track of day and night. During these times my father would randomly enter yelling and throwing things at me. He would also throw and slap me around – this was a lot easier to take than when he wanted to speak to me. My father would use me as some type of sound board, where he would wake me in the night to talk of all his problems, berate me and others, and ask my advice. I learnt very well how to act as if I was listening, as these talks would always go for at least five to seven hours at a time. During these periods of seclusion I was also irregularly rationed bread. I would sneak out to feed and water my dog which was always chained to the side of the house – she lived her whole life in her own faeces. I hate that I never saved her. She suffered more than me. When those weeks were over I had to lie to my school about my non-attendance. At school I had to exceed, I had no option but to be the best. I still don't know why. But when it seemed that I had achieved this I was again ignored and physically isolated for weeks on end.

Outside of these times I slept in my father's bed every night. I was his 'special one'. I was proud to be this. The family said that I was the 'strong one' and that I had to support him. I was seven when this expectation began. I prided myself on this praise. In short, I became my father's little wife. I was watched when I bathed, watched when I dressed and watched when I slept. The pain, the paralytic fear, the isolation, the malnutrition, the bruises and scars, the extreme pain from sexual abuse, the self-loathing, the coaching on what to say to doctors, teachers and the department of child services, the learned hatred towards women (especially female doctors), the obsession for Catholic doctrine and Mass services, the utter adoration and loyalty towards my father, the need for complete personal perfection…this world of secrecy was my unquestioned 'normal'.

I think I stopped my father from killing us once. My mother got custody of my sister; she never asked for me. Now I see that my father became manic and irrational as he had lost to my mother. After a long all-night drive where again I had to do nothing but listen to his continuous rants in silence, he had driven us both to the edge of some beach cliff. The engine roared the more upset he got. I think he asked me to save him. He even started to cry as we got to the edge. He said he did not want me to leave him and that he loved his special girl. As he accelerated forward I promised I never would. The front right tyre went over the edge. I was completely calm and talked him through reversing. I put him to bed.

The weeks after are another gap in my memory. I just know that I ended up at my cousin's house and kept moving on until two years later I was admitted to Monash Medical Adolescent Psychiatric Ward. Five months later they referred me to the Lighthouse Foundation. I don't know why but Lighthouse took me in immediately.

CAROL'S STORY: MOVING INTO CARE

I was brought up in quite a strict religious environment and as part of this a lot of my independent thoughts and beliefs were crushed. My emotional development was stunted. The religious group had told me what to do, how to do it in my day-to-day life. They also had my life planned out for the future. At a young age I had a husband picked out for me, I was to leave school at the age of fifteen, become a housewife and child bearer. Throughout my childhood I was also physically and sexually assaulted. My parents being the main perpetrators, but the elders of the church also played a role in this abuse; the abuse went on for over ten years.

My memory of moving into care is a nightmare. I was being removed from everything I'd known and my whole life was turned upside down. I was moved into a strange house, with none of my belongings except for the clothes I was wearing. It was a weekend and I didn't even have school to look forward to the next day – at least that would have been familiar. I was safe from abuse, but not happy. It was dark already and late, I hadn't eaten since breakfast, even if they had offered me food, I would have refused it – too stressed to keep it down. I was taken to an old lady's house, it smelled funny and I had to borrow some of her clothes to sleep in. She took me to a small room at the front of the house and wished me goodnight, then left. I was scared, cold, uncomfortable in a stranger's clothes and house. I cried myself into a restless sleep.

My time in care was brief but substantial enough to leave an impression. Yes I was safe now from physical, sexual and emotional abuse, but I was constantly moved from house to house. This in itself is a form of emotional abuse. Foster care to residential care, to hospital, to secure welfare, I even stayed with some of my extended family for a stint, but this just led to more abuse. One time, I had to wait at the police station till 9 pm because DHS had nowhere to place me. They said I was going to have to sleep in a hotel room for a night with a worker. On many occasions I sat waiting in the DHS office in my school uniform wondering when and who I would be staying with that night, and if they would be nice to me. At last count, I had moved fifteen times in two years while in government care. Unfortunately for some children in government care this is a small number of moves and it has a massive impact on their lives. After some time, I was coming to the age where DHS couldn't look after me anymore. I was going to be old enough in state terms to look after myself. This really wasn't the case. I was old enough in legal terms to look after myself but not emotionally, socially or financially. I was still completing high school. At this point in my life I was introduced to Lighthouse.

INFORMATION GATHERING AND ASSESSMENT

As we can see from the stories above, all children come into care with a unique story. It is therefore vital that we gather as much information as possible about the child to ensure that the placement is in their best interests and that we can provide the best level of care. At intake our Community Care Team gather summary information about the child. This is for basic demographic, holistic and clinical purposes and to provide a framework for the placement of the child. We acquire relevant documentation on the child from other services, departments and where possible significant people in the child's life. This is a vital and comprehensive stage of intake, and entry cannot occur until the documentation has been received and reviewed. The data provided by past agencies and relevant connections to the child assists us in predicting risk, protective and resilience factors in the home.

At the completion of the initial contact, and if it is agreed that the placement is potentially suitable for the child, an intake interview date is set. The interview is an opportunity for everyone involved to explore the nature of the child's difficulties and needs, and how the placement will work. We explore what it is like to live in one of the homes and what kinds of things will happen. Following this, we carry out a comprehensive psychosocial screen. During this we assess the child for clinical and non-clinical risk factors, resilience capacities, historical data and specific support needs. The screening is a holistic psycho-social assessment. It looks at mental health history, cognitive functioning, general health, mental health issues, substance use history, family history and attachment styles, strengths and coping skills, family and community networks and readiness for treatment. Screens are carried out by either our psychologists or clinically trained professionals under supervision and take approximately ninety minutes. All children are entitled to have a support person present at the screen and should have as much information as possible to ensure they are aware of what the process entails. It is also important that the child has the opportunity ask questions and to provide feedback.

Naturally, much can be observed at this stage. Part of the assessment will be based on how the child responds, and what potential for engagement was shown. During the interactions the child will also be making his own observations, consciously and unconsciously of the messages given verbally and non-verbally. For instance, if the people meeting the child are preoccupied with other things, perhaps difficulties within the organization, or if there is any ambivalence about taking another child, this will be picked up by the child and will give some indication of the environment he is entering into.

THE INTAKE PROCESS

The initial contact with the organization is the first opportunity to begin the therapeutic process with the child. To ensure that the first contact is a positive one the whole organization understands the significance of the beginning. The face of the organization (reception and intake workers) approaches the child in a way that is consistent with our therapeutic approach. It is also important that the reception understands the therapeutic task and has the appropriate level of training to be able to have an appropriate relationship with the child. At Lighthouse, our receptionists are employed with a youth work background, as the reception plays a dual role – as an administrator and a resource to the children.

The intake process needs to be carried out in a way that reflects how the organization will work with the child once the placement begins. Therefore, an organization like Lighthouse tries to demonstrate a thoughtful and nurturing approach. This will give the child a sense of what to expect in the future. The intake workers are the first point of contact for the child, and as such they need to ensure that the child is provided with all the signs that the organization is a welcoming place, and that the child is always at the centre. All our intake workers have had experience as carers. They have an in-depth understanding of the key tenets of the programme such as trauma-informed practice, attachment and object relations, child development and strength-based approaches. This provides them with the knowledge and the skills to offer the child a nurturing entry into the organization.

The process of entry to the programme is based on suitability, which includes: age and gender; risk and protective factors; sexuality; proximity factors and supports in place; employment (for older young people); education; and the child's presenting psychosocial challenges. The aim of the process is to ensure the child's suitability and that a child entering the home does not threaten the safety or therapeutic process of any of the current children. Once the placement has been agreed it can be supportive to ease the child into the transition, through visits, telephone contact and outreach support. We welcome every child with great enthusiasm, whilst being sensitive to their anxieties. We ensure they have time to digest things at their own pace. The purpose of this stage is to assist the child to feel welcome and that someone cares, thus building a bridge into our community.

As with all change, and especially for traumatized children, time to digest what is happening and work through some of the initial anxieties is necessary. A period of time for the child, the carers and other children to think about and process some of their feelings can prevent a sudden reaction when the child arrives. Making practical arrangements, such as getting the child's room ready can make the change feel concrete for everyone involved – in much the same way that parents prepare for the arrival of a new baby.

Once all documentation on the child has been acquired and assessed and it is deemed that the programme is in the best interest of the child, he is now ready to move in. The process from initial intake to admission varies between a few weeks and a few months, depending on various factors. These may include access to relevant material, assessments, initiative and specific needs of the child, cooperation of other services and dynamics in the home. The focus is on integrating a new child at the earliest possible time.

ATTACHMENT

A therapeutic relationship with a traumatized child is one that heals and enables the child to recover. The child will have a primary relationship with a carer and also other carers in other homes as part of a therapeutic community. From this secure base, there is the opportunity of relationships with many others in the wider community of the organization. It has been shown that traumatized children are more likely to recover if they form a primary attachment to a caregiver, and also have a wide network of positive relationships. With each relationship the child has there is a therapeutic window of opportunity. As Perry and Szalavitz argue,

> What maltreated and traumatized children most need is a healthy community to buffer the pain, distress and loss caused by their earlier trauma. What works to heal them is anything that increases the number and quality of a child's

relationships. What helps is consistent, patient, repetitive loving care. (Perry and Szalayitz 2006, p.231)

A child develops from birth onwards through relationships, beginning with a primary attachment relationship. A baby is totally dependent on his carer, normally his mother. Providing things go well a strong attachment develops. Ideally, the mother's partner is also closely involved and the parental couple have the extended support of family and friends. Many parents struggle with the demands of meeting a baby's needs without the support of a wider network. The attachments of the parents to each other, their own families and friends can provide a strong network of attachments, which provides a secure base for the baby.

As discussed earlier, traumatized children often come from chaotic family environments, where many of their relationships have been broken. Often the parents will have been unable to meet their needs and a supportive environment will have been lacking. Many of the children fear relationships and have developed a lack of trust in relationships. It is vital that we role model to children that relationships can be healthy and supportive. One of the ways we do this is through the way we interact with each other as team members. As an example, the 'I feel like saying' process, which we describe in Chapter 8, provides an opportunity to build strong relationships. It is also an opportunity to resolve any difficulties in relationships, so that children are not adversely affected. An organization can also be viewed like a family system, and it is vital that the culture of the organization supports the therapeutic work with the children. The work environment needs to be centred on respectful and trusting relationships. This enables individuals to feel comfortable to debrief and share the impact that the work is having on them, without fear of judgement or criticism. Furthermore, the effective resolution of conflict also role models to children that disagreements don't need to result in loss or abandonment; and that there are healthy ways for differences to be resolved that result in stronger relationships.

Central to the Therapeutic Family Model of Care (see Appendix 2) is the role of live-in carers. The carers live in the home with the children, taking on a parental role as 'therapeutic parents' (Pughe and Philpot 2007), guiding, protecting and nurturing the children in their care. The carers are generally recruited as individuals rather than as a couple. Whilst the model provides a lot of similarities to a family, it is not foster care. The aim is to provide a high level of continuity, primarily from the two carers. The carers are supported by respite carers that are attached to particular homes, which also helps provide continuity and familiarity. Hannon *et al.*, drawing on their research, state the importance of providing a reliable level of care, where children have the opportunity to form close relationships with a small number of carers, rather than experience the kind of indiscriminate multiple caretaking that Bowlby found so damaging:

> Several of the young people we spoke to who had experienced placements in residential care explained that they found the changes in staff destabilising and that it was more difficult to form attachments than in foster families. The young people who described positive experiences of residential care attributed this to the close relationships they had been able to form with staff: 'some of them treated me like their own', or with other children: 'My children's home was good to me and the kids there got really attached together and none of us wanted to separate anymore because we were all we knew and that's what we thought was family.' (Hannon *et al.* 2010, p.86)

There are up to four children living in any home. At times, though, we may have members of the extended Lighthouse family live in for a period of time, such as outreach children and children from other homes. Through experience, we have made a decision that any more than four children would not be appropriate. The children in the home require intensive support and we try to ensure that they have emotional and physical access to their carers, which would be very stretched with more children in the home. In Australia there has been a move towards having a smaller number of children in residential care homes. Some programmes have a capacity of two children to ensure that the complex needs of the children are supported, so the children have access to staff that assists in promoting a sense of safety and stability. In other residential care centres in Australia four children in a unit appears to be standard (Burt and Halfpenny 2008). Similar trends can also be observed in the UK.

Carers enter into therapeutic relationships with our children, aiming to offer unconditional love and support, and role modelling effective relationship development and management. However, as van der Kolk, McFarlane and van der Hart explain, this is a hugely challenging task:

> The therapeutic relationship with PTSD patients tends to be extraordinarily complex, particularly since the interpersonal aspects of the trauma, such as mistrust, betrayal, dependency, love and hate, tend to be replayed within the therapeutic dyad... The devastating effects of trauma on affect modulation, attention, perception, and the giving and taking of pleasure bring both patients and therapists face to face with the full range of human emotions – from the desire to love and feel safe, to the wish to dominate, use and hurt others. (van der Kolk *et al.* 2007, p.420)

A central aim of the therapeutic relationship is to provide a safe relationship in which the child can then work through and integrate unresolved aspects of his traumatic experiences. As we shall see in the next chapter, the way the carer manages this work and the support she receives is the critical factor in any progress the child makes.

From the position of being engaged in a positive attachment relationship and through observing other healthy relationships, the child can then acquire experience and skills to develop and manage other relationships in his life. This includes relationships with carers, other children they live with, friends, future employers, community committees, social and professional supports, or partners. A child's ability to develop and maintain positive relationships with important individuals in his life ensures that he always feels part of a community. This notion of being connected is the fundamental rationale of the Therapeutic Family Model of Care and the carer–child relationship is central to its delivery.

JACINTA'S STORY: ATTACHMENT

The second time I moved in it took me a while to relax before I genuinely started focusing on learning about myself. In time I learned to avail myself of all the opportunities and support that this environment offered. It is like Lighthouse is its own habitat. It does not encourage being away from the world – but it is more like the attachment theory – you learn to attach and when you are attached you are much more resilient to interact with the world and know that you have a safe place to return to – but mostly I learned to be with myself, to self-sooth, – if you can't do that you can't even identify your own goals or move forward.

I continued therapy and I am still doing it. I followed my interest in study and knew I wanted to do something that was in the same field as the role models I experienced at Lighthouse. Where I could return the opportunities availed to me through this programme, and be part of the circle of giving and receiving and supporting other children in the same predicament. For them to witness that you can get to the other side of your pain and sadness and use that to move forward – in a caring environment. It is not about getting rid of the pain but saying what can I do with the pain – and be positive.

So that is why I have my body art – not to forget but to add positively to my experience. And use it as strength to move forward and be a companion to others who have had similar experiences. In the beginning I got a job through Julie in a café that was known locally to Lighthouse – she was kind and understanding and gave me a chance. The next step was that I got a job on my own in a fairy shop using my creativity…by telling stories to children at birthday parties. The owner of the café never doubted I was honest and wanted to move forward, but she understood I needed to move slowly due to the medication I was on. But I knew she trusted me and that meant a lot. It gave me time to sort myself out slowly. So the encouragement she gave me helped me feel safe and gain confidence. The knowledge that I was trusted gave the confidence to continue to move forward. So really what I want to say, is that all along it is about relationships and trust and other people identifying the positive in you before you are ready to see it yourself. If no one reflects that back to you – you will never see that yourself and develop the impetus to move forward. It is the mirror thing. It opens that little window in your mind, and your spirit to grab hold of your self-worth through others reflecting back to you – you are worthy, you are contributing, and that I am worth spending time with.

SECURE BASE

According to Joseph Chilton Pearce,

> children's emotional experience, how they feel about themselves and the world around them, has a tremendous impact on their growth and development. It's the foundation on which all learning, memory, health and well-being are based. When that emotional structure is not stable and positive for a child, no other developmental process within them will function fully. Further development will only be compensatory to any deficiencies. (Mercogliano and Debus 1999, p.1)

In addition to providing children with positive relationship experiences, the carer–child relationship provides a foundation where children may experience safety and security. Through the carer's attunement to a child a close emotional relationship and intimacy develops between them. The nature of this bond allows trust to evolve at a very deep level, facilitating the sense of safety and security. It is this secure base that enables children to grow, to try new things and to address their difficulties. All the while knowing that whatever challenges life may bring, they can always seek security, respite and comfort in the relationship with their carers. As Bowlby wrote,

> evidence is accumulating that human beings of all ages are happiest and able to deploy their talents to best advantage when they are confident that, standing behind them, there are one or more trusted persons who will come to their aid should difficulties arise. The person trusted, also known as an attachment figure, can be considered as providing his or her companion with a secure base from which to operate. (Bowlby 1979, p.103)

More recently Hannon *et al.* stated that,

> Research on attachment has also shown how important it is for young children's development that they experience a warm bond with their primary caregiver. The caregiver's show of affection and responsiveness towards the child gives the child the sense of security they need to develop an attachment with their carer. Through this process of *attunement* with their caregiver, children are able to develop empathy, which provides the basis for other social skills and the ability to form relationships. (Hannon *et al.* 2010, p.74)

Cameron and Maginn claim that,

> Increasingly, too, it is the development of empathy which is now being viewed as the antidote to both childhood and adult violence – an argument which is well evidenced in the 'Worldwide Alternatives to Violence' report (2005). Children who do not experience attunement with a caregiver may fail to develop empathy altogether. Secure attachment is therefore fundamental to children's socialisation and wellbeing. (Cameron and Maginn 2008, p.1158)

CAROL'S STORY: RETURNING TO A SECURE BASE

The second time I moved into Lighthouse was life changing. The first time I did not know what Lighthouse could do for me. I just moved in and went on with my own little patterns. I continued with self-harm and addiction, and denial of my past. If I did not come the first time, I would not have realized what a special place it was and had the trust and confidence to come the second time. But the trust was there and I knew that – that was what got me back the second time – the trust in people there, the relationships I had and that I knew people really cared about me, loved me and valued me. And I knew that this was the place to be if I wanted my life to move forward. I had learnt to communicate differently.

I worked with Julie and Kate, my psychologist and next carer. They had enormous influence on me through their care, education and role modelling. This time, gradually I started becoming aware of my own patterns and the way I connected with people and about positive relationships versus negative ones. I could talk to them about the negative behaviours without being judged and as I did this, they helped me to learn different ways of dealing with my pain. Over time I learnt about engaging and expressing myself in more positive ways. Using my strengths rather than harming myself. That was really crucial in changing the way I dealt with my experiences and feelings. So even though it is still habitual in me to want to self-harm, I now have inner strength to make more positive choices and to express and experience my feelings positively and without harming myself. Not just in a physical sense but not doing drugs, not harming myself and not choosing bad relationships. Learning to value myself, knowing I am worthwhile and that people want to spend time with me and I don't need to create drama for them to be with me – they do it because I am me. That I know I have things to offer. I don't know if this makes sense but I know what I mean.

Talking to Kate regularly and seeing Julie a lot more than weekly was the catalyst. It took me a long time though. They hung in with me. They cared. I believe they knew that I was more than my behaviours, but it took a long time to find the strength to see that in myself. To understand and realize that I had a mentality of harming myself, creating drama and being moved on again. Gaining insight into that pattern – and to then turn it around by finding more positive ways of expressing and experiencing my world. It is about feeling the feelings, but now I can externalize those feelings, memories and flashbacks – and know I can get through these moments by using my skills of singing, theatre, creative arts and creating writing. To realize that these crisis times of most intensity are transient and I can get through them – I have the skills and I have the strength to reach out if I need to.

COMMITMENT

The commitment of a Lighthouse carer is significant and continuous. Whether they are actively engaging with the children or spending time carrying out daily household tasks, their role as caregivers to the children is ongoing. This continuity of care is central in emulating the family experience that is at the core of the Therapeutic Family Model of Care. Carers make a commitment to stay for at least a period of two years, due to the attachment focus of the programme. The carers generally adhere to this, as they really become committed to the attachment approach. They see the benefits not only to the children, but also to their own development.

To support the carers in this work we offer the following:

- Clinical supervision – carers receive at least fortnightly clinical supervision from one of our psychologists. It is psychodynamic focused, and aimed at understanding the transference that occurs in the relationship with children. It is about looking inward, to understand the carer's role in the therapeutic process for the child, and to develop the internal resources to work in a challenging environment.

- Operational supervision – carers receive fortnightly operational supervision, which is focused on the task of caring for children.

- Extra annual leave and flexibility of hours to ensure they are also taking care of themselves.

- Access to various leisure and recreational facilities. For example, all carers receive free access to full gym membership.

- Carers meeting – all carers attend fortnightly peer supervision sessions facilitated by a psychologist.

- Fortnightly training – carers attend in-house training that supports their personal and professional development. Some of the areas covered include attachment, psychosocial development, grief and loss, language and communication and preventing vicarious trauma training.

As Whitwell (2010) has said, in talking about a similar task in the UK,

> Love by itself is not enough. Many carers will intuitively do the right thing without knowing why. Unless carers receive training to help make sense of

behaviours which are symptoms of the underlying emotional disturbance (panic rages, disruption, no guilt, splitting), they will burn out.

The live-in component of the programme is an essential element in providing a sense of family for the child. These children have missed out on many of the basic experiences of childhood that we take for granted, like being put to bed and woken up by the same person. When the child comes home at the end of the day, he knows who is going to greet him. There is consistency and predictability for the child. The commitment of living in with children requires significant sacrifice on behalf of the carer. The home is as much the child's as it is the carer's. Often, a carer's personal space, privacy and other boundaries may be compromised and in some circumstances relinquished altogether. Sharing a home with children means sharing personal space, personal belongings and giving up many of the social liberties that living independently entails. Clare Winnicott, in her paper 'The Stress of Residential Living', emphasizes the potential difficulty involved in this:

> There is no doubt that the life of the group in the residential living invades the central core of the personality of each individual, and constitutes a threat to personal living. Children and adults alike are affected by the situation, and each one is permanently engaged in the struggle to maintain personal existence and to create a space in which to be themselves and to act independently. (Winnicott 1968, p.2)

CONTINUITY OF CARE

The continuity of care provides carers with an opportunity to continuously role model and engage in positive therapeutic relationships with children. It also provides an opportunity for repetition of response and interactions, which as we have described is vital in the recovery process. When conflict presents, children and carers are required to take a relationship-focused approach to managing the conflict. The skilled carer needs to have the capacity to work from a non-judgemental paradigm. This is more focused on working with pro-social behaviour modification, rather than blaming the person. We call this 'challenging the behaviour not the person'. It is more effective to give the message that it is the behaviour that we find unacceptable rather than the person. The carer also needs to be consistent with her own boundaries and responses to challenging behaviour, as well as being open to innovative solutions that the child may feel works for him. By living in with the child, over time, the carer gains insight into the triggers for the child, as well as effective strategies. There is no quick fix, it takes time. The carer learns what works for the child, and through this continuity and repetition the child also learns what behaviour is appropriate. He also learns that he is loved and that he is accepted.

There is little room for avoiding conflict while living with a child, as most parents will know. However, how the conflict is responded to is the key issue. It might be responded to in a way that is helpful or unhelpful and it is not always easy to know what kind of response is best. The nature of conflict is likely to mean that we experience some degree of anxiety and our response can easily become reactive. The relationship-focused approach to managing conflict provides opportunity for children to learn how to manage conflict. Waddell (1989) argues how this supports the child's development by requiring the child to face rather than avoid painful issues. It is actually the adult's capacity and willingness to do this that comes first and provides a model for the child: 'The inability to establish boundaries, to assert limits – though usually easier as the line of least resistance – may often engender a difficulty in tolerating *any* pain or frustration, and thereby actually hinder development'.

Children also learn that relationships can continue to strengthen, as they develop a sense of trust in relationships, despite the challenges involved. For many children, this is a new experience. Often conflict has resulted in relationship breakdown. However, living with their carers, children learn that it is possible and beneficial to openly address conflict and move forwards rather than remain stuck with painful and unresolved feelings.

The commitment of a carer is long term, often lasting over years and in some circumstances a lifetime. The carers living in with the children, much like a parent, have an unflinching commitment to keep children safe. It is a significant role that is seen as the most important role within the organization. It is a role that one cannot clock off from. Even when on leave, carers are still thinking about the child that is going for an operation, or the child that is starting school or a young person's new job. Although not physically there, the carer is emotionally and psychologically there. For a child, knowing that their carers are going to be in it for the 'long haul' greatly facilitates the development of trust. This trust enables children to open up to their carers, knowing that they are more than just another worker that comes in and out of their lives. Ultimately, the carer's commitment is not just to the children, the role also requires that they continually develop and improve. The commitment is also to oneself. Thus, being a carer is not about 'having a job' or going to 'work', rather it is a vocation. This point is illustrated by Carol.

CAROL'S STORY: DEALING WITH THE PAST

Over my five years of living with Lighthouse, I not only had the time and space to grow up, but I also had the love and support I needed to deal with my past experiences. It is amazing what comes up when you are finally in a safe environment. It's like your body is in survival mode and then as soon as you relax and feel safe, a memory, a flashback, a horrible feeling emerges and you are a mess once again. On many occasions at the beginning I just sat with disbelief; these people actually cared about me. They showed interest in my schooling, asked what I would like for dinner, wanted to take me to appointments and help me with homework. I would have a bad day at school and they would try to cheer me up. I would have a flashback and they would sit with me for hours. They wanted to spend time with us. Yes, they had a wage, but trust me, it wasn't what they came or stayed for. I would cry with pain and they would sit with me, hug me, and sometimes even cry with me until I fell asleep.

At times, carers may take a period of time away and work in other organizations or sectors, but will remain connected with the Lighthouse community. They often return refreshed to work as carers, or take on other roles in the care team. The relationships with children do not end when the carers move on to other forms of work, they take a different form. With the support of the organization and with appropriate boundaries, the carers are encouraged to maintain relationships with the children if it is of therapeutic benefit for the child. This role models to children that relationships can change over time, but continue to be important.

WORKING WITH LOSS

Inevitably, work with traumatized children involves huge amounts of loss and grief. In itself, the experience of any trauma involves the loss of how things were before the trauma. The traumatized person's sense of continuity and predictability in their life is disrupted. The traumatic experience now needs to become integrated as part of the person's identity. When trauma is repeated and happens within the context of neglect and abuse the losses are continually compounded. For children who are traumatized in early life, there is not always a great sense of loss as trauma and neglect may be the norm. Whereas deprivation is associated with loss of something good, privation is a more accurate term to describe a situation where the child never experienced something that could be called 'good enough'. These children may seem to be 'unfeeling' and cold in relation to their experiences. Similarly, children who have experienced overwhelming losses have often developed powerful defence mechanisms to help them survive and block out painful feelings.

As Tomlinson (2005, p.46) states,

> The traumatized children we work with will have suffered many losses. We use the word suffered rather than experienced, as in many cases they will have not had the necessary support to make sense of their losses and to integrate the experience. Eva Holmes (1983, p.75) summed this up with a comment made to her by a child, which became the title of a paper about children and loss – 'I'm Bad, No Good, Can't Think'. She talks of the child's struggle to come to terms with pain and loss, and says, 'Central to this struggle seems to be the transformation of pain from something which has the character of an overwhelming physical attack into something which can be carried in the mind as experience'.

Bloom (2005, p.68) states that working with loss is one of the four core components in the treatment of traumatized children, alongside safety, emotional management and work on the future. As we begin to establish attachments with traumatized children, their fears and anxieties related to loss are likely to surface in a powerful way. The children often become highly anxious, in that just as they are beginning to experience something positive and nurturing this will be followed by further losses. As a result, the child is likely to become testing and defended to either bring about the loss they fear or to create an emotional distance. Containing and working through feelings related to loss will be a central part of day-to-day work. However, it is also important to focus on providing new enriching experiences and to do this in a balanced way that is not about avoiding the child's pain. As Whitwell states,

> *Depression can be a good thing.* We are working with children who live in a permanent state of excitement, fending off painful, difficult thoughts. It is going to be helpful for them to begin to feel sad and depressed. That was new to me, and I think it is common currency in our society that if anybody is depressed they've got to be jollied out of it. (Whitwell 1998b)

> During a child's time with us in a residential setting, there will be further losses. However, we have the opportunity to help the child experience these further losses in a meaningful way. At the same time, we can potentially work through unresolved matters related to earlier losses. Because of our awareness of a child's history, we may become worried and feel guilty about any further losses imposed upon the child by ourselves. For example, by our decision to leave for another job. Similar feelings of guilt can apply to other instances of our absence. Such as, when we have leave or time away for training and illness. Unfortunately, if we do not understand and process our feelings of guilt,

negativity is likely to dominate absence and loss, in a way that undermines the opportunity for therapeutic gain. (Tomlinson 2005, p.46)

Experiences of loss in the day-to-day work are an opportunity to provide a more positive model of how loss can be managed. As mentioned above, often traumatized children had no emotional support in containing, processing and integrating their experiences. When a child we are working with becomes anxious about separation and potential loss, we can support him to manage and think about these feelings. For example, if a child is missing or even feels abandoned by a carer who is on leave, we can help him to contain these feelings and think about how they may be related to past experiences, gradually distinguishing between the past and present.

> If we can maintain the capacity to think about loss, as with change there is the opportunity for growth and development. In his account of child development, Bion (1962) emphasized how the infant's experience of the absent mother or breast, can be a key point of growth in the child's development. By helping him to manage separation and deal with feelings of loss. Bion argued that the infant's first thoughts would happen in response to the gap created by absence, i.e. by thinking about the mother who is not there. (Tomlinson 2005, p.46)

Working with traumatized children will also evoke feelings of loss for those working with them. This may be related to the worker's relationship with a child and feelings of loss connected directly to this, such as when a worker is away from the child. As Lanyado argues,

> Whilst we are usually aware of the significance of loss or separation from a loved adult, for a child, we do not often consider its counterpart. What does it mean to the adult to give up caring for a loved child? When a child has got under an adult's skin, even in a highly ambivalent manner, it is not easy to hand them over to another member of staff's care. (Lanyado 1989, p.139)

The work may also surface aspects of our own experiences, especially during childhood. When these experiences involve losses, which have not been fully integrated into our consciousness, this can be painful. Where this happens the worker may become emotionally defended and unable to work with the child's feelings. Support and supervision is very important in enabling the worker to acknowledge and process her own feelings. As with the child, in the same way this then becomes an opportunity for the worker to develop and integrate her own experiences.

ROLE MODELLING

Living in a home with children means that all facets of carers' lives are essentially on display. The children experience the carers as human beings with strengths and weaknesses, through the way they deal with conflict and the way they face challenges. They become role models for what healthy relationships should look like. Carers are required to continually be mindful of the way they present to children; they should continually reflect on all their interactions, their thoughts, emotions and experiences. Essentially, carers are required to be 'switched on' when in the presence of children. In a role where the majority of their time is spent in the presence of children, this level of active awareness is very demanding.

PERSONAL GROWTH

The benefits that carers experience, however, are significant. Observing children's journeys, their achievements, celebrating milestones and bonding with children on a deeply emotional level, can be extremely rewarding for a carer. Additionally, the commitment of being continually 'switched on' provides carers with the opportunity to develop themselves. They are continually self evaluating, learning about their own patterns of behaviour and proactively ensuring that they are always working to the best of their ability. We provide many opportunities for carers to challenge themselves and grow as individuals. Our psychodynamic approach to clinical supervision and peer processes ensure that carers are continuously reflecting on who they are, their practice and their place in the world. Carers learn much about themselves. Those of us who work with traumatized children also know that the children will bring much of our unresolved issues to the surface. Our psychodynamic processes provide an opportunity to make sense of this, which is potentially empowering.

CREATING CAPACITY FOR RELATIONSHIP BUILDING: ONE-TO-ONE TIME WITH CHILDREN

The primary focus of the Therapeutic Family Model of Care is developing positive and supportive relationships with children. Central to our philosophy is the notion that 'it is the relationship that is the foundation for success'. Primary carers' one-to-one time with children is vital for the development of the primary attachment, and for fostering a supportive and reciprocal relationship. As part of their role, in addition to living with the children, primary carers have weekly one-to-one time with the child they care for.

Secondary carers also engage in one-to-one time with children when time permits. The major focus of these times is on relationship building with the child. During one-to-one time children also have the opportunity to raise any issues that may be impacting on their care. This provides an opportunity for the carer to provide the appropriate support. Information can also be relayed to the senior care team to develop systems to provide the best possible support to the children.

Challenging behaviours demonstrated by children are ideally managed through the relationship with their carers. Open discussion about how certain behaviours impact on the relationship is a core strategy in managing behaviours. One-to-one time is the ideal forum for these conversations. It provides carers and children with an opportunity to spend quality time together, and to build a strong relationship that will provide a secure base from which behavioural issues can be addressed. Individual time with children, where the carer can build rapport and develop a sense of safety, is essential. For a child who may have never formed a secure attachment in his life, who has experienced relationship breakdown, and had carers who were not emotionally available or consistent, the time provides the space for the carer to be totally concentrated and attuned to the needs of the child. This is an essential element in the formation of a healthy attachment and helps the child develop a sense that people can be trusted. However, becoming emotionally involved with a traumatized child is not an easy task. Lanyado, referring to Winnicott, elaborated on what is meant by emotional involvement:

> In a paper on 'Residential Management of Difficult Children' that Winnicott wrote in 1947,
>
>> 'It might be asked why...get emotionally involved? The answer is that these children...do not get anywhere unless someone does, in fact, get emotionally involved with them. *To get under someone's skin*' (my emphasis), 'is the first thing these children do when they get to begin to hope.'
>
> I am not advocating a kind of wholesale, no holds-barred type of emotional involvement – as I am sure Winnicott was not. I am trying to describe a considered and thoughtful awareness of how one feels, professionally, about the relationship with a particular child. This requires careful honest sifting of what belongs to one's own personal propensities when forming relationships – such as being touchy over certain matters, or insensitive over others – from what is evoked by that particular child. (Lanyado 1989, p.138)

The getting under the skin that Lanyado refers to can take different forms, such as the child rejecting the one-to-one time; behaving difficultly during the time; trying to spoil the time; or, as Clare Winnicott states,

> At some time or other some of the children will be unable to make use of what the staff member himself could offer by way of positive experiences in the present, because they are needing to live through the past and the adult can feel wasted and exploited. (Winnicott 1968, p.6)

It is important that the times are regularly and consistently scheduled on a weekly basis. Ideally it will be at the same time on the same day each week, for at least one hour. If a time is missed, it is rescheduled for another time as soon as possible. A consistent one-to-one time helps to contain the children's anxieties and concerns and provides them with an opportunity to regulate their emotions. It is common for the children to exhibit symptoms of poor impulse control. When confronted with an emotionally laden experience like conflict, children will often 'react' to the emotions with a specific behaviour. Often this behaviour is directed towards gaining the carer's attention. Knowing that a one-to-one time is only a short while away, where they will receive the carer's full attention, may reduce the frequency of object-seeking behaviour (behaviours to seek the proximity or response of the carer).

Ideally, children will learn to respond to emotional content in a way that best serves them. Part of the process of cultivating this skill is for children to learn to 'sit with' their emotions until the intensity has worn off and then decide upon an appropriate response. For children to learn to do this they need to experience adults, sitting with and being able to think about their own feelings. The kind of thinking we refer to involves becoming more conscious of our own feelings and this can be painful, hard work. It is emotional rather than intellectual thinking. Waddell explains,

> Thinking and feeling constitute hard, emotional work – active processes, at the heart of this model of parenting: the taking in of the infant's or child's painful experience, the containing of it, the relieving of the most distressed aspects, and the handing of it back in a more tolerable form. (Waddell 1989)

In the same way that children may avoid sitting with their feelings, we might also find ourselves escaping our difficult feelings by becoming busy and doing something to avoid our feelings. Waddell (1989) compared the difference between thinking and doing, with different modes of parenting, 'The difference between the two modes might be made by the mother who *serves*, by being available by "thinking" emotionally, as opposed to the mother who *services* by doing instead of thinking.' In terms of helping the child to sit with, tolerate and think about difficult feelings, it can clearly be seen how too much doing or 'servicing' as Waddell says, can be anti-developmental for ourselves and the child.

In aiming towards considering strategies for regulating emotional experiences, carers ask the child whether a particular issue can wait until one-to-one time to be addressed. This type of enquiry requires the child to reflectively assess the issue he is facing and make a decision about the enormity or intensity of the issue. If the child does wait, the carer can explore with him what strategies he used to manage himself until their time. Approaching issues in this manner facilities children's' awareness of the strategies they employ to manage their emotional states.

Carers normally have one-to-one time outside the home. This enables children to view their carers in different environments and perspectives. It enables them to see their carers as individuals and not just carers. Many of the children struggle to acknowledge that it is possible to perceive someone as 'good', but at other times as 'bad'. Often they will see an individual as either a 'good' or 'bad' object depending on their experience of them. This is a process known in psychodynamic terms as 'splitting'. This conception can also change from day to day, creating a very emotionally unstable relationship between the child and carer, and also between carers. As Clare Winnicott states,

> Another feature of the transference of past experiences into the present living situation is the need that many disturbed children have to split their positive and negative feelings, and to project positive feelings onto one member of staff and reserve their negative feelings for another. This must be particularly difficult in a residential setting and obviously staff could get a view of each other, which might cause unnecessary strain among themselves if they were unaware of what is going on. (Winnicott 1968, p.6)

To help prevent these patterns from becoming fixed it is important that children observe carers in different contexts. For example, from giving a child a consequence to having fun rollerblading. In this way children learn to develop a relationship with different 'parts' of their carer. They are able to have fun and enjoyment with one part of the carer (fun carer) while experiencing firm boundaries with another part of the carer (consequence-giving carer). This continued dichotomizing experience will support the children in seeing the carer as a 'whole' individual with both good and bad aspects existing simultaneously. This is an essential part of 'normal' psychosocial development.

However, before a child can reach this point, which is a healthy level of development, we may need to tolerate long periods where the child splits their feelings. Our task is to hold the splits emotionally, rather than react to them. If two staff members who are holding polarized negative and positive feelings can discuss and think about these different aspects of the child, they are beginning the process of holding the fragmented pieces of the whole child together. Holding the negative aspect of the split is generally the more demanding part of the work. When a child begins to transfer negative feelings onto a carer, it can be an indication that the child feels that person is safe and reliable enough to contain their most difficult feelings. Whitwell (1998a) explains the importance of this role, which Dockar-Drysdale terms as a 'reliable hate object':

> I had come from a hostel where, in the staff group, if anybody was working a shift and had had a bad time from the clients, the other staff would say, 'I do not know what he's doing wrong, it is all right when we work.' Or 'I do not have a problem with this child, I can manage him perfectly, he smiles OK for me. What's your problem, you cannot handle him?' The staff team needs to understand that children will relate to staff members differently, and that coping with the hatred that a child invests in you at a particular time is important. In a sense the team ought to celebrate that you are doing it on their behalf, and support you, rather than being in any way critical, implying that you may not know what you are doing, and that is why you are getting a bad time. (Dockar-Drysdale 1990a, p.14)

On the other side of the split, being treated by a child as completely good, whilst possibly engendering positive feelings in the recipient, will also need thinking about and responding to in a way that doesn't reinforce the child's unrealistic idealization.

UNIQUE NEEDS

It is important that one-to-one time is unique for that individual. For instance, playing a game of pool with every child in their time may devalue the importance of this time. Ideally, each child's time will involve an activity that uniquely represents their relationship with the carer. This may be going bowling, or visiting the same coffee shop. Where feasible, carers allow the children to choose the location and to set the agenda for these times. We have noticed that a unique and 'special' format to each individual child's one-to-one time can have a profound positive impact on the relationship. For example, one child's time may predominantly occur at the beach, while another's predominantly occurs at a park. In this way, each child can feel that their time is special to them.

Generally speaking the time will last at least one hour. This allows for the likelihood that deeper issues will be brought to the surface. A good period of time enables the child to become more comfortable with the carer and to potentially be more open. A reliable, significant time also facilitates relationship development, which ultimately will support carers in managing behaviours through the relationship when required.

THE IMPORTANCE OF THE RELATIONSHIP WHEN CHALLENGING BEHAVIOUR

The effectiveness of addressing challenging behaviours in the one-to-one relationship will depend on the stage of the relationship. The progression of the relationship will determine the strategies utilized in managing behaviour. The more secure the attachment and the more skilled the carer is, the more able she will be in managing the behaviour. As the child develops a sense of safety and belonging, he becomes more capable of receiving feedback and taking consequences on, with trust in the carer. As the strength of the relationship is developed, the carer is more able to explore the underlying needs of the child and to see the behaviour as a manifestation of underlying needs, rather than taking it personally. When a child behaves in a challenging manner, our initial impulse can be to punish and deprive the child, rather than realizing that these behaviours are due to unmet needs, and unexplored potential.

The carer's ability to be attuned to the underlying needs of the child can only occur through the building of a relationship. Having this attunement and insight can assist the carer in developing less reactive ways to dealing with the child's behaviour. Perry and Szalavitz (2006) highlight that although we need to set boundaries, if a child is to behave well, he needs to be treated well. Children who are treated with love and concern are more likely to develop a sense of concern towards others. They are more likely to comply and cooperate with others, not out of a fear of punishment, but because they recognize that their efforts are appreciated by those who also care for them.

CHALLENGING BEHAVIOUR AS A SIGN OF HOPE

Inevitably the work with children will at times be very challenging. The children's challenging behaviour should be thought about carefully rather than reacted to. This can be demanding as the carers may feel the difficult behaviour is a sign that things are going wrong and they aren't doing a good job. Clearly, boundaries need to be set around behaviour that is unacceptable, especially when this is to do with the safety of the child and others. However, this can be done firmly in a way that is non-punitive. It is quite possible that the child actually hopes that his behaviour will evoke the kind of response from those around him that he needs. He needs boundaries and limits to his behaviour. At the same time he needs to be understood and accepted, even though his behaviour may not be.

As Perry and Szalavitz explain,

Traumatized children tend to have overactive responses and, as we've seen, these can make them aggressive, impulsive, and needy. These children are difficult, they are easy to upset and hard to calm, they may overreact to the slightest novelty or change and they often don't know how to think before they act. Before they can make any kind of lasting change at all in their behavior, they need to feel safe and loved. Unfortunately, however, many of the treatment programs and other interventions aimed at them get it backwards: they take a punitive approach and hope to lure children into good behavior by restoring love and safety only if the children first start acting 'better.' While such approaches may temporarily threaten children into doing what adults want, they can't provide the long-term, internal motivation that will ultimately help them control themselves better and become more loving towards others. (Perry and Szalavitz 2006, p.244)

Rather than viewing antisocial and challenging behaviour in a negative light, Winnicott (1956b) saw it as a sign of hope. There are a number of potential reasons for this. Traumatized children who have become withdrawn and passive as a way of protecting themselves, as they begin to feel safe, may begin to express themselves in an assertive way. Whilst this might feel challenging it might be a sign that the child is coming alive emotionally. As Winnicott (1964) states in *The Child, the Family and the Outside World*, 'A baby in a rage is very much a person'. For some of our children, one of the few times they feel like a person with real feelings may be when they experience a feeling like rage.

Children who have been so badly let down and mistreated by those they depend on most cannot be expected to trust another person until they have tested that person's commitment and capacity to stick with them through difficult times. They will have been told over and over that the new situation they are in is going to be permanent, only to be rejected and moved on again when they show challenging behaviour.

JAMIE'S STORY: MOVED AROUND

It's hard when you start to build a relationship and then you're thrown out into the streets. Before arriving you have nothing and start to build your life and then you get moved around. This is hard when you are traumatized. You are putting them back in the same situation.

The child fears this is going to happen every time, so rather than wait, full of anxiety for the inevitable, they create the scenario they expect to get it over with. If they don't get the rejecting and reactive response they expect, it can be anticipated that they will push the boundaries further. This was a consistent

93

pattern of behaviour during Jamie's placement at Lighthouse. He was defiant, and constantly pushed the boundaries with the carers. Surviving this stage is crucial and one of the most important things in the child's treatment. This work isn't easy and sometimes the most important thing is to just survive and be there the next day. Winnicott explains the therapeutic value of this:

> It may be a kind of loving but often it has to look like a kind of hating, and the key word is not treatment or cure but rather it is survival. If you survive then the child has a chance to grow and become something like the person he or she would have been if the untoward environmental breakdown had not brought disaster. (Winnicott 1970, p.288)

It can seem understandable that children might react to us in an angry and challenging way if we are setting boundaries and limits. It can be more challenging to understand a child who attacks our attempts to be more generally thoughtful about him and his needs. Tomlinson argues that,

> The children we work with will also attack our attempts to think about and understand them. This is linked to their overwhelming sense of mistrust. While adults who are feeling retaliatory and punitive may show this in their response, children are also likely to attack the benign response. Children may react in a paranoid way to benign interpretations that adults make, as if they are being persecuted. Feelings like persecution, hopelessness and despair may be projected or displaced onto the adults. There could be a tendency for the adults to take flight from these feelings rather than recognize them and continue working with them. (Tomlinson 2005, p.47)

We often consider this with our carers, when explaining the process of projection and how to manage the uncomfortable feelings. In some instances it might be helpful to imagine a person over their shoulders that the child is angry with, and that the child is not actually angry with them. This cognitive process can sometimes help the carer to experience things less personally and to understand that the child is projecting feelings associated with his trauma. However, a cognitive approach is particularly difficult when the child's trauma happened in early infancy, before the child was able to integrate his experience in any way. The 'transference' from such a child can be so powerful that it feels almost 'delusional' in quality. It can feel as if we really are the child's parent and there is no 'as if' in the feeling. It is extremely difficult to withstand the powerful nature of this. As Clare Winnicott explains,

> Everyone who works with children (or adults) who are disturbed, is familiar with the phenomenon of the transference. Some of the attitudes and behaviour which we see are only explicable in transference terms, because the present situation does not warrant the reactions produced. However, there are children

who will unconsciously so manipulate the present, that their own reactions are justified. Staff members can find themselves fitting into the child's pattern and unless they are aware of the drive within the child to reproduce the past, they can find themselves acting out of character and at sea in the situation. (Winnicott 1968, p.5)

A child who has been severely deprived, as Winnicott states, may become most challenging just at the point where they begin to feel hopeful. Winnicott argues that when the deprived child experiences a sense of hope in the environment's capacity to recognize and meet his needs, he may well develop antisocial behaviour, such as stealing or destructiveness that has a high 'nuisance value'. The child is not interested, at this stage, in stealing things for their own sake, but stealing 'in symbolic form only what once belonged to him by right' (Phillips 1988, p.17) and which has been lost. He is also 'alerting the environment to this fact' (p.17) and testing the environment's tolerance towards the nuisance value of such behaviour. The nuisance caused by the child also contains hope, which provides an opportunity for us to respond and nourish. Alternatively, reacting only to the symptom and missing the need will diminish the child's hope. If treatment is to be successful, the people that make up the child's environment will need to notice his antisocial behaviour as a sign of hope and an attempt by the child to: 'return to the point at which the environment failed the child. He returns to find where what he hasn't got came from, to the gaps in himself' (Phillips 1988, p.17).

Whilst the child's antisocial behaviour may be a sign of hope, it can be very difficult for us to feel hopeful. As well as being faced with very challenging behaviour, it is also likely that a traumatized child may need us to feel and contain some of his own feelings of hopelessness. It is possible that just when our hopes are raised the child will violently dash them to let us experience what has happened to him. We reach a state of hopelessness similar to that he may have felt. If we can experience this, survive it and somehow muster up a belief that things can get better, maybe the child can begin to feel a 'better time' is possible. Describing therapy work with sexually abused children, Trowell (1994, cited in Tomlinson 2008) concluded that, 'The importance of sustaining hope in the child, the family and the therapist should not be underestimated.'

CASE EXAMPLE

Robert's first two years of life were characterized by an absent father and traumatic separations from his mother, in a generally chaotic and unreliable environment. His development from then on had been fraught with difficulty. At the time of referral,

Robert was described as uncontrollable and unable to take responsibility for his actions. His antisocial behaviour included stealing, destructiveness (vandalism), stealing cars and running off. A few months into his placement, we noticed a number of yoghurts hidden in his room and empty cartons lying on the ground outside his bedroom window. He was evidently taking yoghurts from the fridge in the night, eating them and then throwing the cartons out of his window. As Robert was normally very adept at stealing and hiding things, it seemed odd at first that he was making little attempt to conceal these cartons. Having discussed this with Robert's carer, Terry, we decided that this might be a 'sign of hope', that Robert was looking for us to provide him with an experience, symbolically representing the provision he lost in early infancy, and to help fill some of the gaps left by that. Dockar-Drysdale (1961, 1963), describes the significance of this provision and how it may be provided, throughout her writing, and terms the provision 'adaptation to individual need'. She compares this to the way a mother responds to her infant's 'spontaneous gestures', as described by Winnicott.

Rather than confront him, Terry simply asked Robert if he liked yoghurts, to which Robert smiled, looking rather embarrassed, and said yes. Terry asked him if he would like to be provided with yoghurt as a special thing (adaptation) at bedtime, just before settling down. Robert replied with enthusiasm that he would. This then became a reliable provision from Terry for Robert, on the same evenings every week for over a year. Robert kept the empty cartons and eventually had a stack several feet high. McMahon (1995), referring to the same case, pointed out that the yoghurt cartons may have symbolically represented the emotional experience which Robert now had stored up inside him. Certainly, at those times that Robert received his yoghurts from Terry, he seemed to feel very much like a small child enjoying a very meaningful feeding experience. As this provision was important to Robert, representing early 'primary experience' of which he was then deprived, it was essential the provision was reliable. Terry would never be asked to do anything else at those times and his time with Robert would be protected, ensuring the provision would not be disrupted.

From this example, it can be seen that there are key elements that make the treatment possible.

1. There is an understanding, shared by the care team, of the kind of emotional experience a child needs to facilitate his emotional growth and development.

2. There is also a shared understanding of how deprivation of those experiences may manifest itself and how it may be responded to in terms of treatment.

    This understanding is conceptualized explicitly, so that all of those working with Robert are approaching the situation from the same angle. For instance, the nuisance value of Robert's behaviour was first of all tolerated, then thought about and understood in terms of his needs. If, instead of this, Robert had been confronted about his behaviour, it may not have been possible for Terry to make the provision and an opportunity would have been missed. As Winnicott states,

> The antisocial tendency implies hope. Lack of hope is the basic feature of the deprived child who, of course, is not all the time being antisocial. In the period of hope, the child manifests an antisocial tendency. The understanding that the antisocial tendency is an expression of hope is vital in the treatment of children who show the antisocial tendency. Over and over again one sees the moment wasted, or withered, because of mismanagement or intolerance. This is another way of saying that the treatment of the antisocial tendency is not psychoanalysis but management, a going to meet and match the moment of hope. (Winnicott 1956b, p.309)

3. Without a shared understanding of why the provision was important, Terry would not have been protected and supported in meeting the provision over such a long period of time. Indeed, without such an understanding, the provision may have been seen as an unnecessary indulgence or spoiling, or just 'silly'. This would have undermined the provision, making it difficult to sustain. Dockar-Drysdale (1963) describes the vulnerability of a worker making such a provision and some of the primitive feelings, such as envy, that may be evoked in all those involved.

Sometimes challenging and antisocial behaviour may be a way a child takes flight from painful feelings. If a child is feeling anxious or worried about something, those feelings may be hard to acknowledge and stick with. So becoming challenging might feel like a distraction or can take the focus away from those uncomfortable emotions. Whitwell describes the pattern of behaviour of such a child:

> We know that he cannot risk being left short of satisfaction for a moment because when the level of his pleasure drops, pain will flow in. Having withdrawn from frustration he must use any means in his power to maintain the pleasure level and this tends to be delinquent. (Whitwell 1998a)

This might be especially true for children who are, maybe for the first time, getting in touch with some painful feelings to do with their past. As the work progresses and reaches this positive point, there can be a reaction from the child, which might lead us to think progress isn't being made.

When behaviour is particularly challenging another possibility is that carers collude with the child, through the fear of provoking even more challenging behaviour. Collusive anxiety is where an adult may turn a 'blind eye' rather than confront the reality, due to a fear of possible reaction (Dockar-Drysdale, 1990c). So to work with challenging behaviour, understanding and thoughtfulness is essential. This can only be maintained under such difficult circumstances by effective communication and support within the therapeutic team.

PSYCHOLOGIST'S CASE DIARY: THE SYMBOLIC MEANING OF TRAIN TRACKS

Sharon was eighteen years of age and came from a background of long-term neglect and physical and sexual abuse, and had been with us for two years. Much of her trauma occurred in the pre-verbal stages of development. The trauma was further compounded by a number of sexually abusive relationships with young men throughout her adolescence, and at least two sexual assaults in her adolescent years. Sharon had a history of hospital admissions for self-mutilation and attempted suicides. As I began working as a psychologist with the organization I heard much about her risk-taking behaviour, defiance and at times aggressive behaviour towards carers.

I began working with Sharon more closely, following a number of incidents of threatening to take her own life and concerns about an abusive relationship that she was involved in. Some boundaries had been put in place by the carers around her abusive boyfriend visiting the home, as it was placing the carer and other children at risk. Sharon reacted to this through a number of incidents of parasuicidal behaviour, self-mutilation, abuse of prescription medication, which resulted in an overdose, deep visible cuts on her arms, an attempted self-asphyxiation, sexualized behaviours, and further threats of suicide. The major focus of my work and that of the team, at this stage, was on keeping Sharon alive, so we placed her under twenty-four hour supervision.

My analysis was that, through her behaviour, Sharon was asking to be contained. She was unable to regulate her own emotions, and to act in a way that would keep her safe. As a clinical team, we believed that her behaviours were what we refer to as object-seeking behaviour. She was acting in a way to bring on a caring response from a parental object. Sometimes this type of behaviour is mistakenly labelled as attention seeking rather than object-seeking behaviour. The team worked around the clock to provide a sense of containment through the carer providing proximity maintenance for Sharon. This was very challenging, given that with every attempt to put in a boundary, and to provide love and safety, this triggered acting out which was extremely difficult to manage.

One of the keys in supporting Sharon to work through the current issues was to understand the meaning of her behaviour. A common thread was that she often gravitated towards the local train track, where she could be found sitting on the edge of the track. In my experience as a psychologist, I have seen this similar scenario being acted out many times, particularly working with young people that have borderline presentations or histories of pre-verbal trauma. It was common with Sharon and with other young people with a similar presentation, to threaten to jump in front of a train or to regularly find themselves on train tracks quite impulsively. There have been a number of occasions where we have had to contact the train operators to close down the tracks, as we attempted to remove children from them. It was when working with Sharon, that I really started to explore the meaning of the train tracks, and why this was such a common response of the children in dealing with the emotional turmoil of their lives.

Our interpretation of what the train tracks symbolically represented was as follows. Train tracks and trains are symbolic to all of us and may have a special meaning to children who sit on the margins of society. The term 'off the rails' has been used as a metaphor in Western societies throughout the last century to describe those who are considered the 'other', those who sit on the margins of society such as homeless people. The messages given to the children we work with throughout their lives has been that they are 'off track', 'off the rails' or 'need to get on the right track'.

Traumatized children often have not developed the capacity to self-soothe due to their developmental trauma and interrupted attachments. They have not had the role modelling of parental figures to direct them on the 'right track'. They often develop relationships in a maladaptive way and constantly become the victims of abuse. For such a child, it is very difficult to know what the 'right track' is. What the child does know, and has been made very clear by society, is that she is not on that track and she does not fit. In essence, what the railway track could be seen to represent is the right track, and the train represents the people the child should be like, the people that are on that right track. The train has a direction, it is going somewhere. In essence the child's life involves observing the train passing by, but never really understanding how to get on that train.

By going on the track, the child is symbolically on the right track. It could be seen as a physical acting out of a positive desire, though with little recognition for the consequences of the impulsive behaviour. The child is trying to do something positive, she wants to be on the right track, but it is being done in a maladaptive way.

We viewed Sharon's acting out as an attempt to get on track. Understanding the possible symbolic nature of the behaviour helps us to see the behaviour differently. This provided an avenue to explore her behaviour with her. Sharon responded well towards this approach and began to feel more emotionally contained. We could have judged Sharon's behaviour as being only destructive, which may have resulted in a punitive response. In contrast, seeing the behaviour as an attempt to act out a positive desire, which is to get on the 'right track', led to a more empathetic response. Through her behaviour, Sharon had introduced the symbol of the train tracks. Travel metaphors such as trains and train tracks are full of symbolic possibilities – excitement, envy for those on the train, danger, change, escape, being on the move, a new life. It is important that the interpretation takes into account the personal story for that particular child. Our attempt was to find the meaning behind Sharon's behaviour and in particular a positive meaning to her behaviour, a sign of hope, and discuss this with her. This symbolic interpretation began the process of working through with Sharon, and exploring the meaning of her behaviour became a major step towards her recovery.

THE ROLE OF TOUCH IN THE HEALING PROCESS

As we have been talking about the development of attachment relationships with children we need to consider the role of touch in these relationships. This is especially so, as the children we work with have experienced major deprivation in their early years, where touch is such a central part of the attachment relationship. The issue of touch in relationships between adults and children has become particularly complex in recent years. We are all aware of the moral panic, which has had some impact within families and a huge one within settings that work with children. There has been a proliferation of guidelines produced by schools and all organizations that work with children, advising professionals on appropriate behaviour and how to protect the safety of children and themselves from false allegations of abuse. Piper and Smith (2003, p.880) refer to numerous studies on this subject and highlight the nature of confusion and anxiety that has developed:

> The literature relating to 'touch' is extensive but most is concerned with promoting a particular viewpoint. For some, touch is good, for others it is a danger or therapeutic, but relatively few are concerned with the confusions and contradictions identified in this article.

Perry and Szalavitz (2006) advocated the positive benefits of touch and argued that it is critical to human development. They claimed that sensory pathways related to touch are the first to develop and are more elaborated at birth compared to sight, smell, taste and hearing. They claim research has shown that premature babies who experience soothing skin contact mature and develop more quickly. In older children, massage has also been found to help reduce stress hormones, blood pressure and depression.

We work from an attachment perspective with children who have experienced long-term abuse and neglect. Our approach is aimed at redeveloping the capacity for secure attachment in the children. As part of this the use of appropriate physical contact is encouraged. This is made additionally difficult as the children have often experienced not only a lack of healthy and nurturing touch, but also inappropriate touch involved in sexual and physical abuse. Therefore, we have to be especially careful as children are likely to have previous memories triggered and react anxiously to touch. On the other hand, they may become overly sexualized, believing our intentions to be sexually motivated. Many children who have been abused believe that adults are only interested in them for sexual reasons. They may encourage this as a way of keeping the adult happy, and preventing other repercussions such as violence or punishment. van der Kolk *et al.* argue that,

> In patients with histories of sexual abuse and other violations of personal boundaries, the meaning of touching needs to be clearly spelled out, understood and agreed to before it is introduced in the treatment. Interventions that involve touching need to be properly timed, after a secure relationship in which a patient can confidently register reactions has been established. (van der Kolk *et al.* 2007, p.321)

However, the answer to this is not to do as some organizations have done, which is to ban all physical contact. Not only does this potentially doubly deprive the children, it also reinforces the message that adults cannot be trusted. There are many benefits of appropriate physical contact, such as non-sexualized hugs, holding hands and pats on the back. Appropriate touch helps create the capacity for attachment, which is partly learnt through touch and proximity maintenance. Other benefits of physical contact are listed below:

- It teaches appropriate forms of touch that are non-sexual and non-predatory. This is vital for children who haven't experienced appropriate touch and who lack boundaries due to sexual abuse.

- It allows for dyadic emotional regulation, which assists in the development of emotional regulation skills in children with attachment difficulties.

- It provides a sense of 'normal' caring and family for the child. Some children, due to attachment-related trauma may be operating at a pre-verbal stage of development. They may require physical approaches as part of their developmental process.

- It can assist in the relief of stress in children who have difficulties with emotional regulation.

- It can help promote positive body image, through the link between positive emotions and the body.

- It role models appropriate forms of affection.

We understand that children who have experienced abuse may have difficulty and discomfort with physical contact. Any form of physical contact should be consensual, and the child should always be asked if he is comfortable with it. This is especially important at the beginning of the relationship where the child may be wary and likely to misinterpret things. We can gauge a child's comfort by observing his reactions to touch. There is a balance to be struck between being thoughtful and respectful towards the child and not losing all spontaneity, so that touch becomes an orchestrated clinical event! Physical contact with children is appropriate if it has a therapeutic purpose and is acceptable to both the carer and child. Examples of appropriate physical contact include: when it is part of comfort or emotional support; a hug to settle a child who is distressed; or as a greeting when meeting a child. It is vital in assessing the appropriateness of the physical contact that the following be considered:

- the therapeutic benefit for the child
- the intent behind the physical contact of the carer and child
- the length of relationship with the child
- the closeness of the relationship with the child
- the level of trust the child has towards the carer.

If touch is to feel natural and meaningful in a positive way to a child, we need to feel confident rather than anxious about our position. If we are perceived by the child to be acting anxiously around touch, this is likely to arouse his own anxieties. It might suggest that there is something wrong with physical contact between children and adults. Within an organizational setting it will help workers to know exactly what the organization's policy is, so that they can feel their practice is openly supported and not something worked out by individuals on their own.

CONSEQUENCES VS PUNISHMENT

Within the context of rights and responsibilities, the way we work with challenging behaviours, consequences and punishments are particularly important. It is also a very complex area of work. Many children we work with are used to being punished, often unfairly and for reasons they can't understand. Many times they will have been punished and treated harshly by their parents, in an arbitrary fashion based on the parent's mood and needs rather than on the child's behaviour. For children who have been abused, traumatized and who have hyperaroused stress response systems, punishments are often likely to make matters worse, because they increase stress levels and reinforce a negative view of the world as a hostile and unforgiving place. It is generally far more effective to have clear expectations about what is acceptable and what isn't. When a child crosses the line, help them think about it and find ways in which things could be put right. Making reparation for something hurtful or damaging that they have done provides them with the experience of contributing to making it right. Many traumatized children believe that the mistakes they make or their negative behaviour has catastrophic and long-lasting damaging consequences. They have learnt this through experience, where a small misdemeanour may have resulted in a severely violent response from a parent, or where challenging behaviour led to another placement breakdown. The capacity to make reparation also requires a person to have empathy with another and to feel some concern.

For children who are so emotionally underdeveloped, it may take time before they can be expected to feel any genuine concern towards others. Normally, this capacity develops in infancy in response to feeling concern from others, and through the role modelling of caregivers. Reparation begins with an infant's wish to 'repair' his caregiver, whom he fears he has hurt through his aggressive impulses. In healthy development the infant's concern and wish to make his caregivers happy is based on the love they give him and not out of fear created by punishment. For a child to love and care for others he needs to feel loved and cared for. We can also encourage the development of empathy by discussing with the child his behaviour and how it might make others feel. Perry and Szalavitz (2010) suggest that, 'To encourage empathy, discipline by reasoning, perspective taking, consistency of appropriate consequences, and above all, love' (p.313). And 'If you teach children to behave by using reason, they are likelier to be reasonable' (p.314).

Some of the complexity involved in this area of work is to do with our own feelings and the children's perceptions. For instance, we may need to manage the child's behaviour because we feel it is unsafe. If the child is in a volatile mood and the group is about to go on a trip together and we decide the child can't go, he might perceive this as a punishment rather than an appropriate consequence. At the same time, the child's behaviour may easily evoke a punitive feeling in ourselves and we might feel like punishing him. We might explain things to the child in terms of safety and so on, but if we feel punitive and aren't acknowledging this to ourselves we might act punitively, even if we say that we aren't. To check that we aren't becoming punitive in our response, it can help to think about the behaviour we are unhappy with and talk about this with the child, rather than being very judgemental – as we discussed earlier, focusing on the behaviour rather than the person. We can give messages such as, we don't like that behaviour or that behaviour makes me feel angry, which is a less threatening message than I don't like you and you make me very angry. This can be difficult when the child's behaviour towards us may feel very personal. One may feel like retaliating in a way that might be humiliating, shaming and crushing for the child.

Dockar-Drysdale argues that a punitive approach may actually damage the child's potential to develop a capacity of concern towards others:

> I suggest that punishment not only anticipates but hampers and probably blocks the natural process of restitution, thereby preventing the further process by which the child may direct into constructive channels the hostile feelings which have led to guilt and the need for making restitution. (Dockar-Drysdale 1953, p.7)

Traumatized children are very familiar with being punished, humiliated and hurt. Punishing such a child is likely to trigger his memory of these experiences, causing him to feel angry and resentful towards whoever is punishing him.

However, children should be helped to understand that there is a consequence for their behaviour, both positive and negative. We need to help them understand the positive consequences of their behaviour, as much if not more than the negative consequences. This is because these children know only too well that they can do hurtful and destructive things, but they often have no idea that they do things which can give pleasure and make others feel good. They often feel that they are insignificant to others and the only way they can have an impact and feel of any significance is by being challenging.

When we do need to help a child understand something about the negative consequences of their behaviour and to do something if possible to put it right, the more relevant or 'logical' the consequence is to the behaviour, the more likely it is to make sense to the child. For example, if the child has damaged something in the home, helping to fix it is more relevant than having to go to bed early. For children who are just beginning to develop feelings of concern towards others it can also be important to give them the space to find their own way of making reparation. For instance, the child may suggest that he does something for someone he has upset. As Bridgeland (1971) states, 'damage, theft, aggression will be followed by feelings of guilt which will be relieved, not by punishment or enforced restitution, but in a way appropriate to the child's inner need'.

It has often been quite common in children's homes that arbitrary punishment and reward systems have been introduced. The child may be fined a certain amount of money, lose a privilege or have to carry out a chore for everything he does wrong. This approach is simplistic. It doesn't help the child to learn about the real consequences of his actions. Rather than encourage the development of concern towards others, it actually reinforces a concern for oneself and how to avoid punishment. The child who is emotionally underdeveloped sees difficult behaviour in terms of how it affects and makes him feel rather than how others feel. We are also trying to prepare the child, particularly adolescents, to develop the skills to be parents one day themselves. To break the cycle of abuse, neglect and homelessness, we must prepare children to develop the qualities and skills to manage relationships – something that their own caregivers were unable to role model:

> Punishment can't create or model those qualities. Although we do need to set limits, if we want our children to behave well, we have to treat them well. A child raised with love wants to make those around him happy because he sees his happiness makes them happy too; he doesn't simply comply to avoid punishment. (Perry and Szalavitz 2006, p.243)

PROMOTING RESPONSIBLE CHILDREN: EMPOWERMENT PROCESSES

What can be most distressing about trauma and makes it most difficult to recover from is the experience of being out of control and being unable to do anything. As Mollon (1996, p.5) states, 'Children who are abused often develop dissociative mechanisms that are specifically aimed at escaping from the body that is being violated or tortured.' A normal response to a threatening situation is that the person becomes hyperaroused in preparation to take flight and escape the situation. Where this is impossible, as is often the case for small children, they are trapped in a frightening situation and powerless. This is where the child may disassociate to block out feelings of terror and the body literally closes down to improve the chances of survival. Perry and Szalavitz explain:

> Dissociation is a very primitive reaction: the earliest forms of life (and the youngest members of the highest species) can rarely escape dire situations under their own steam. Their only possible response to being attacked or hurt, then, is essentially to curl up, to make themselves as small as possible, to cry for help and hope for a miracle. This response appears to be driven by the most primitive brain systems, located in the brain-stem and immediately surrounding it. For infants and young children, incapable of or ineffective at fighting or fleeing, a dissociative response to extreme stressors is common. It is also more common in females than males and, if prolonged, dissociation is connected with increased odds for post-traumatic stress symptoms. (Perry and Szalavitz 2006, p.49)

Therefore, a sense of having some control over their circumstances is especially important to traumatized children. Our approach to service provision is based on the voluntary participation of children. It is underpinned by a commitment to supporting the rights of children and advocating on their behalf to the broader community. In particular, we support the rights of children for self-determination, to have their confidentiality and privacy maintained and to make informed choices about how they will address their future growth and development. We encourage all children to learn about their rights and to develop further their understanding of their rights and responsibilities within our programme. We work with children from an empowerment model, where children are encouraged to provide feedback to improve the quality of the service, and to ensure that the needs of all children are met accordingly. Children are encouraged to be leaders in their own recovery journey. We believe that with support children are often able to arrive at what is best for them. Our approach ensures that children's voices are heard, and that the organization's strategic directions are informed by their opinions, experience and knowledge. Hannon *et al.* state the importance of listening to and involving children in the decision-making process:

> If we are to prioritise looked-after children's and young people's emotional wellbeing, it is essential that they are able to influence decisions that affect them. All of the young people we spoke to mentioned the importance of feeling that their views and feelings were being listened to and acted on. (Hannon *et al.* 2010, p.97)

Referring to Judy Cashmore, they identify key reasons why it is essential to involve looked-after children and young people in making decisions that affect them:

- Compared with children who live with their family and normally have two parents making decisions for them, looked-after children often have a wide range of adults, sometimes unknown to them, making decisions about them.

- It helps the self-esteem and confidence of children who have suffered abuse or neglect to have their opinions respected, to feel like 'active agents' rather than 'powerless victims of the whims of adults'.

- Placement stability is improved by children having a choice about their placement. Decisions that take the child's views into account are more likely to be appropriate and acceptable to the child.

- Being involved in the decision-making process helps to build children's resilience and sense of agency, which is important in preparation for taking charge of their lives in the future.

We believe strongly that the rights of children must be at the forefront of what we do as an organization. All organizational policies and processes need to be aligned with the rights of children. The following rights based on the charter for children in out of home care are at the core of all decisions made in the organization:

- to live in a safe and caring home, where I can learn and grow
- to have a say and participate in my own care by being an active participant in creating my own Individual Development Plan
- to express any concerns, for my physical and emotional safety, to my carer and/or the care team
- to be allowed to be a child and be treated with respect
- to be provided with information
- to know that information about me will only be shared in order to help care for me
- to have a carer and a care team who is there for me
- to have fun and do activities that I enjoy
- to have my cultural beliefs respected.

We encourage children to be drivers in their journey. To speak out when they believe that their rights are been oppressed, or if they believe that service delivery is not in line with their best interests. At the same time, if a child is to accept rights in a meaningful way, they also need to learn that with rights come responsibilities. So, if a child has a right to be listened to he also has a responsibility to listen to others. If it is a right to not be physically hurt, he also has a responsibility not to hurt others. This does not mean that a child's rights can be taken away because of some misdemeanour. It docs mean that we have to continually work on supporting the children to understand that all children have rights and what applies to one also applies to others.

PARTICIPATION OF CHILDREN AND YOUNG PEOPLE IN THE ORGANIZATION

The involvement of children and young people in having a say in how services are provided is now a commonplace concept. It is clearly linked to what we have been discussing about promoting responsibility in children. However, how far this actually goes in reality is more varied and less clear. Hart (1992) provides the following hierarchical ladder to describe the different levels of young people's participation.

Rung 8: Young people and adults share decision-making

Rung 7: Young people lead and initiate action

Rung 6: Adult-initiated, shared decisions with young people

Rung 5: Young people consulted and informed

Rung 4: Young people assigned and informed

Non-participation

Rung 3: Young people tokenized

Rung 2: Young people are decoration

Rung 1: Young people are manipulated

It is likely that few organizations working with children and young people go beyond level five. The project is designed and run by adults, but young people understand the process and their opinions are treated seriously (Hart 1992). This level may be typified by young people sitting on advisory councils. Levels six to eight are considered to move beyond participation and are more challenging to achieve. One of the dilemmas in moving towards rung eight, which is where young people initiate, lead and make decisions, is whether a young person is emotionally and cognitively developed to a point where this would be appropriate. Fletcher (2008) describes level eight as 'when projects or programs are initiated by young people and decision making is shared between young people and adults. These projects empower young people while at the same time enabling them to access and learn from the life experience and expertise of adults'. This level is typified by youth/adult partnerships. It could be argued that it is not so much a question as to whether children and young people are capable of being involved at this level, but matching the scale of a project with their level of development. So for some young people, who may be eighteen years or older and whose development is in line with their chronological age, it may be appropriate to be in partnership with adults on large-scale projects.

It is possible for young people at this stage of development to have a role in the running of an organization. However, younger or less mature children, whilst not being ready to participate at this level, can be involved in initiating, leading and making decisions (with support) on small projects, for example, projects in a home to improve the quality of play materials; initiating a project, taking responsibility for making decisions and purchasing within a budget.

The skills learnt in this type of process can be built on as the child develops. The child is learning that they are expected and encouraged to be involved and this becomes the norm. In this small example, it is not difficult to see how a child's perspective can offer insights and knowledge that may be especially relevant. This knowledge has been referred to as 'experiential expertise' and is increasingly drawn upon, in all aspects of industry, through concepts such as consumer representation.

The aspiration should be to involve children and young people at the highest level they are capable of. This can be a challenge to adults and organizations that may have a paternalistic and hierarchical attitude towards authority. As Fletcher (2008) argues, 'This is somewhat controversial an issue for many people working with and around young people. Essentially, the debate is which of these levels of participation is actually the most meaningful?' The difficulty may be manifest at an unconscious level and need considerable working through. Without working through underlying resistances the organization's approach is likely to be tokenistic.

One of the objections often stated is that this type of thinking is giving children inappropriate responsibility and will lead to poor standards, blurred boundaries and even chaos. What we are suggesting isn't that children and young people's responsibility should be elevated in a carte blanche manner, but in a manner subject to an appropriate matching with their maturity, abilities and skills. It can be seen in recent years that when given appropriate opportunities, the capacity for children and young people's participation in organizations has successfully achieved levels that may not have been thought possible previously. Youth Coalition of the Australian Capital Territory in Australia outlines the potential benefits:

> Participation gives young people a say about what is important to them, allows them to 'own' decisions made about their lives, increases self confidence and skills, and empowers them. Young people's participation in decisions that affect them and the life of their community is valuable and has a range of positive outcomes for young people and those who engage with them (2008, p.222).

For this to be carried out in a genuine way that moves beyond tokenism, it is essential that the organization is fully committed and backs this up by ensuring the necessary level of resources are provided. It should be recognized that the concept of youth participation is not only about providing developmental opportunities for young people, but is also about improving the effectiveness of organizations, so that there is a mutual benefit. For instance, Boese, in a paper titled 'From Participation to Leadership', referring to an Australian project designed to support youth participation in a community programme, states that,

> The evaluation reveals that the program led to positive outcomes for most students and also for the participant program sites, the schools and the community sector organisations. The interviewed student participants and teachers, as well as the stakeholders from the community sector, agreed that the program generated valuable outcomes. (Boese 2010, p.ix)

Similarly in the USA, Youth on Board (2000, p.4) in 'Why and How to Involve Young People in Organizational Decision Making', state that,

> Inviting young people to serve your nonprofit is a concrete way to help your organization, your community and ultimately society as a whole. As anyone who works with young people knows, adults gain as much from bringing young people into the fold as young people do by being there.

They continue: 'Youth involvement leads to innovative solutions, stronger communities, and increased self-worth, among young people who feel supported by adults, rather than feeling ruled by them.' Youth on Board cite numerous benefits of involving young people up to the level of board membership.

As the central theme of this book is about working with severely traumatized children, we do not have the space to do full justice to this subject. However, the reason we raise it is because it is very relevant to all organizations that work with traumatized children, however young they are. There are very important reasons for this. The aspirations for the children we work with, as in an ordinary family, will influence the way we think about and respond to them, whatever their age and stage of development. If we have unnecessarily low expectations, from an early age these will be conveyed to the children. For children in care and who already have low self-esteem, this negative expectation can be particularly damaging to their long-term outcomes. For all organizations, the aim should be to achieve the highest possible rung on the ladder that Hart refers to. For organizations working with very young children, rung four or five may be the appropriate level. For an organization such as Lighthouse that works with older children and young people, some of whom have come back to work at the organization as well as sat on the board of directors, the highest rung of the ladder may be realistic.

CHAPTER 4

Demands and Rewards of the Work

Staff Support

Be kind, for everyone you meet is fighting a hard battle.

Plato

Working with traumatized children can be highly rewarding and also very demanding. Whether the demands involved lead to rewarding benefits for the children and those that work with them will largely depend upon how the demands are managed, thought about and responded to. The demands stem from the children's experiences, as well as our own values, beliefs, experiences and needs. If we are able to be reflective in our practice we are more likely to respond in a way that is therapeutic for the children and ourselves. When we are faced with particularly challenging work, there can be a dilemma in how we think about it. Is this what the work is all about? Is this what we are here for? Am I getting anywhere, am I on track? Am I able to do this, do I need to learn more, do I have the skill? Am I wasting my time? Do I need to shift my world view? Do I need support, will people think I'm not coping? These can be some of the questions that carers might ask themselves and the anxieties involved will need to be contained for the therapeutic work to continue.

CARER'S REFLECTIVE CASE DIARY

The last few weeks have been very tiring and demanding. As carers in the home we really set ourselves up for this by letting our communication slip to a low; we had allowed our daily routine to become quite mundane and we also let boundaries around daily routines slip. One of the children I provide care for was continually testing and rejecting towards me. I found myself drawn into this rejection and struggled not to react to it. One of the carers being away ill for a while highlighted the pressure we were experiencing. Everyone seemed quite shaken up by this, and it was difficult for me to accept that more needed to be done when I was already feeling drained. Up until that point I felt as if I, and things around me, were going backwards. The idea that sometimes 'the most important thing that you can do is to be there the next morning' helped a great deal, as it was about all that I felt I was able to manage. The eventual reaction to this was that a lot of individual effort was put in and we made some positive progress in stabilizing things.

Similar situations may arise in a family during times of illness, bereavement, absence, the arrival of a new baby or just a difficult to understand phase where everything seems to be hard work. It is during these periods that the support of the wider care team is needed to help make sense of the experience and to provide emotional containment. All carers, like parents, can experience ups and downs, and periods of questioning their skills and abilities, and the relationships in their lives. Much like an extended network of family and friends that are available to support a parent, the extended team of carers, case managers and psychologists in the Lighthouse model, provide the much needed support and sounding board. As well as this, it is important to identify what the skills and competency issues may be, and ensure that the management team is attuned to the needs of the carers, to provide the training and support that is required.

WORKING WITH CHALLENGING AND AGGRESSIVE BEHAVIOUR

Bridgeland, referring to the work of Dockar-Drysdale at the Mulberry Bush School, explained how aggressive and destructive behaviour needs to be understood within the context of a therapeutic approach:

> Society, both inside the school and in contact with it from outside, must understand the essentially therapeutic approach to destruction and aggression. Damage to property for instance, at times very apparent at the Mulberry Bush, is seen as an essential working out of the child's aggression. The transfer of this aggression to people will eventually be welcomed since it will then be more accessible to therapy. (Bridgeland 1971)

As well as dealing with the child's aggressive responses to everyday experiences such as frustration, anxiety and boundary setting, it is also likely as an attachment develops that feelings of anger and aggression related to previous carers will be transferred onto the new attachment figure. So whilst we can expect this, it is particularly challenging to manage and work with effectively. Some children who are not physically aggressive might create a threatening atmosphere by being verbally aggressive and defiant. This can create an anxiety that if one challenges the child, she might become physically aggressive.

Traumatized children, as we have discussed, are often hyperaroused and in a state of fear. They have little capacity to regulate their emotions and are easily overwhelmed. Day-to-day frustrations and anxieties can easily build up and become unmanageable for them. They are also likely to misread situations and perceive a threat where there isn't one. The typical responses to this for a traumatized person are flight, fight or withdrawal. To work with traumatized children, anticipation is essential. The carers need to be deeply attuned to the children, so that they know the things that might trigger anxiety and fear. Picking up on the children's anxieties, they need to take steps to support children in a way that calms them. For one child, this might be the opportunity to talk about a problem before it becomes overwhelming, while for another it might be to do something they enjoy and which will be relaxing. As Perry explains,

> One of the greatest lessons I've learned in my work is the importance of taking the time, before doing anything else, to pay attention and listen. Because of the mirroring of neurobiology of our brains, one of the best ways to help someone else become calm and centered is to calm and center ourselves first – and then just pay attention. When you approach a child from this perspective, the response you get is far different from when you simply assume you know what is going on and how to fix it. (Perry 2006, p.244)

Dockar-Drysdale (1990b, p.127) believed that with this level of attunement and intervention most violent incidents are potentially avoidable: 'One could start by saying that the management of violence is its prevention. By this statement, I mean that, since all acting out is a breakdown in communication, it is our responsibility to keep in communication with the children in our care.' Or as Farragher and Yanosy (2005, p.101) said, 'Our job is to help put feelings into words rather than act them out.' The quality of emotional holding will have a direct impact on the feelings of safety for children. As a child begins to feel safe and develop emotionally she will become more able to manage her own feelings.

CARER'S REFLECTIVE CASE DIARY

During the last few weeks I was involved in a number of violent or aggressive situations with Greg. Many of these were around sports games. Greg sometimes flies into a temper if he is frustrated with the game, or if he thinks another boy is getting at him. During these tempers he stomps around shouting, building up for a charge of aggression, such as kicking the football very hard at someone. The times when I have asked him to stop he has often responded with verbal aggression, physical intimidation and has run off. In one game he was accidentally kicked by Daniel. He reacted very aggressively by pushing Daniel. I had to step between them. Greg said that I was blaming him and became physically aggressive towards me. At this stage, I asked him to go for a short walk, and come back when he calmed down and could talk.

Another time during a game, I accidentally bumped Greg. He turned round angrily, stopped for a few moments and then walked away. He had time then to realize what he was doing. First of all he walked away and then came back, saying that we should phone his social worker to get him out. Later on Greg told me that he understood it was an accident and that he got angry because he was angry with himself. He has also reacted aggressively a number of times when he thinks he is being blamed for something.

Different children were concerning in different ways recently, with a number of them exhibiting very disturbed and disturbing behaviour. The questions I am left with are: were they safely contained and what is the connection between the behaviour and treatment for each child? By the very nature of our work with children, there will be challenges and difficulties involved. Obviously there is a limit to what we can contain, though the container should not be seen as some fixed vessel that has no room for growth. The difficulties in our work challenge us to understand the children and ourselves better.

Greg is an example of a boy that was extremely difficult, very controlling, disruptive, omnipotent, panicky, aggressive and regressed (including bed wetting) for about a six-month period. He was also, throughout his time here, a leader, helpful, creative, humorous and likeable. It was essential that Greg could be all of those things here. The progress he made has probably enabled him the chance of a satisfying life rather than a life spent living institutionalized.

CARER'S REFLECTIVE CASE DIARY – PROTECTING CHILDREN: RESPONDING TO ALLEGATIONS

The child protection work around the allegations made by one of our children about one of our carers, as well as a complaint by another child, was demanding and testing work. These types of issues are very complex and the procedures involved are rigorous. The impact on the community, carers, children and other key members is huge. These situations are difficult to manage in the best interests of the children. It is a challenge to balance the needs of the child, as well as the needs of staff members involved. For instance, how helpful is it for a carer to be away from work while a complaint is investigated? If the allegations are untrue, what is the impact on the child and the carer? Will there be an emotional backlash against the child if the allegations are unsubstantiated? The child may have made the allegations to test if they will be heard and this can be difficult to empathize with if it was untrue and you are on the receiving end. What if the allegations are true, what does that mean for the organization?

These are all tough and anxiety-provoking questions that we have to ask during these challenging situations. Emotionally unintegrated children often have major anxieties about their omnipotence and their destructiveness. It is common for these children to project their past experiences onto others, particularly parental figures. These projections can be positive and negative, seeing the carer as good or bad. It can often be difficult to differentiate between reality and fantasy for the child, which can be very hard when investigating allegations of abuse. One of the challenges for us in these situations is the containment of our own feelings, and to remind ourselves of the primary task, which is the care of the child. Due to the experience of abuse, powerful feelings are also aroused around the triangular dynamic of victim/rescuer/persecutor. Different staff members may take on, or are perceived by others to take on these roles. Then the danger is we start acting them out.

At times, serious allegations such as those of abuse can make it challenging to utilize our regular conflict resolution processes. For instance, it is not appropriate to place an alleged victim with an alleged perpetrator into a mediation process, which is our regular approach to managing conflict. We have to be realistic about the task at hand, and when entering the work be really aware of the inherent risks involved, as it can be common for workers to have allegations made against them. Some allegations are true, and others can be a result of fantasy, misinterpretation of a situation and, on occasions, false in a more deliberate way. The organization needs to be very clear about their processes for dealing with allegations. It also needs to ensure that systems and ways of working through these very complex situations are in place to protect children and carers, and that they are trauma informed and child centred.

PHYSICAL AND EMOTIONAL WELLBEING

As the research on trauma shows, we recognize that our physical and emotional states are entirely interconnected, in other words as Schmidt Neven (1997, p.259) explains, 'Psychosomatic – a recognition of the essential connection between mind and body which hopefully avoids a split between these two.

In this book the essential psychosomatic relationship between the infant and mother is presented as a cornerstone of development.'

In the care sector, it is common for workers to experience stress-related health concerns. We know that there are high rates of leave due to illness, there can be high rates of vicarious trauma, and there is often a high turnover of staff. We are also aware that in a programme which focuses on long-term care, the emotional and physical wellbeing of care staff is vital for a therapeutic care programme to be effective.

The occurrence of staff being signed off work with ailments described as stress related can be concerning and difficult to work with. When this happens does it mean that we are not understanding and managing stress effectively? For instance, what is it that causes pressure to lead to stress and illness rather than job satisfaction? What is the impact on those who are not ill, when other team members are ill, and what judgements are made about the person who is ill or struggling? Is there a lack of resources? Are we fully addressing the emotional impact of the work? Are we experiencing difficulties within our management structures, which are affecting containment? Is there a lack of effective leadership, ineffective delegation and role confusion? The original meaning of stress is – a system of pressures acting on a body which will either compel or constrain it in some way. The stress is the cause of an effect rather than an effect in itself. Menzies Lyth (1998) points out in her foreword to *Stress in Social Work* that an increase in emotional involvement, which may feel stressful at times, may also be desirable in terms of task performance and job satisfaction. Consulting to the role of hospital nurses she recommended that nurses became more involved with their patients, therefore at times making themselves more vulnerable to feelings such as loss and anxiety. The successful management of this then led to greater job satisfaction with diminished staff illness and turnover. She also refers to an observation made by Bion, who worked in a therapeutic community for soldiers experiencing difficulty in resettlement on returning from war: 'Bion made a similar point when he held that whether or not troops in battle developed panic depended on circumstances, whether the battle was properly managed' (Menzies Lyth 1998, p.7).

Whenever someone is ill, it can raise critical feelings, as well as ones of concern. At times, adults' feelings, as well as children's can be fairly primitive. It might be implied that the person who is off ill, isn't really ill or doesn't care. For some children it can be translated into 'I am too difficult' or 'not worth being loved'. When under this sort of stress, we need to think about how our emotional and physical state is affecting our ability to work with the children's emotions. Maintaining the space to keep ourselves thinking therapeutically is especially important and sometimes most difficult to find when the work is most stressful. On the positive side, it seems that when one person is ill or away for some reason it often provides opportunities that turn out to be productive for others. Whitwell reminds us of the importance of considering the group dynamic and how this may be impacting on a worker who has become ill:

> What is going on for that individual, and what are we as a staff group projecting into that person? Is that person carrying for us the feelings of hopelessness and helplessness arising from the work? The discipline of asking ourselves about the dynamic is a crucial part of therapeutic community work. (Whitwell 1998b)

The role of our senior care team in these circumstances is very similar to the role of a carer in caring for children. The senior care team in some ways is the carer of the carers, or the container of the containers; they must be attuned to the needs of the carers. The success of the care programme relies on the psychological wellness (Prilleltensky and Nelson 2000) of the carers. The team regularly monitors all aspects of carers' wellbeing. This is done through supervision and weekly meetings that discuss the wellbeing of carers and children. Attunement to the needs of the carers allows for early intervention; for example: providing a space to think about the work and the impact it is having on them; where necessary, supporting carers to take some leave; linking them into counselling and mentoring; and whatever else may be required for the specific needs of the carer. Emphasizing the importance of providing support for carers, referring to McMahon (2003), Sharpe states,

> that therapeutic work with young people puts extraordinary demands on the 'self of the worker' whose personal engagement with a young person can arouse powerful feelings which need to be thought about rather than 'defended against' by avoiding, projecting and splitting.

She also points out that it is not only the children who need containing. Carers need containment, too, 'since effective work requires the provision of a mental space in which it is possible to think about the meaning of a child's behaviour, and to respond accordingly, and in a co-ordinated way with other people in the child's life' (Sharpe 2008, p.49).

SENIOR CARE TEAM'S REFLECTIVE CASE DIARY

During a period where we had a number of children transition out of the programme and a significant number of new children entering the homes, a number of team members began to call in sick. With the changes in the homes we also had a number of children acting out. It certainly felt to me as if we were frantically running about trying to plug holes in a dam that was about to burst. We also started to notice that the instability was impacting on the wellbeing of carers and the children. In our senior care team meetings we worked on issues to do with illness and the quality of the 'holding environment' we were providing for staff and children. Concern had been expressed by a number of people that the working week is too frantic and there is little time for each other in a supportive way. It may be worthwhile for teams to consider how different meetings and supervision forums are being used, and really try to think whether the function is being used to achieve therapeutic aims or more defensively as a way of avoiding painful and difficult issues. For example, we may spend so much time in meetings to create a sense of being busy, or to convince ourselves that we are contributing, are in control, to avoid stopping and dealing with some of the more challenging and painful things we are facing.

Waddell (1989) talked about the dangers in social care work of becoming 'mindlessly' busy in doing things for those we work with. She calls this 'mindless servicing' as opposed to getting alongside those we work with and making ourselves emotionally available. Menzies Lyth (1979) in her paper, 'Staff Support Systems: Task and Anti-Task in Adolescent Institutions', argues that 'support systems' can work to improve 'task performance', or can be used as a way of defending against the anxieties involved. She states that the most supportive thing for a worker is to be enabled to get the satisfaction from doing one's job well. This reminds us that we are likely to be most supportive to each other when we focus on the difficulties we are facing and help each other to find positive solutions. Sometimes this might involve just sitting with discomfort in a non-judgemental way. At other times it might be finding a clear way forward, perhaps with a change of approach.

WORKING WITH ANXIETY

Working in a therapeutic residential setting with traumatized children that often presents a myriad of challenging behaviours can be extremely anxiety provoking for carers. As Keenan (2006, p.29) argues, 'Within the work of a therapeutic environment, I believe that understanding anxiety is a key ingredient. When unchecked or not contained, this can lead to intense feelings and panic which Winnicott called "unthinkable anxiety".' As well as the difficulties presented by the children, there are many factors that can contribute to the levels of anxiety: the carer's own experiences of trauma; the carer's own values, experience and expectations; their coping mechanisms and social networks; the amount of support that is available in the organization; the individual characteristics of the child; and the organization's structures and systems.

It can be very anxiety provoking to spend long periods of time in the presence of a child (or children) who is acutely distressed or disintegrating. One of the fears for both adults and other children who may be involved is that they might also begin to collapse into a fragile state. As Lanyado describes,

> Disintegration is catching – and the staff are prone to it too. At times staff may feel anxious that they too could collapse like a house of cards. This is an extreme situation – but I am sure there are few of us working in these settings who don't feel this way at times. The child's extreme anxieties can eventually threaten the integrity of their closest adults. (Lanyado 1989, p.140)

In the following diary the carer discusses work with a particular child during an especially challenging period. The carer considers how the expression of challenging behaviour may be linked to the recovery process. The importance of this and difficulty involved are highlighted by Black (1989): 'One needs to walk through the pain, Not over it, Not around it.'

CARER'S REFLECTIVE CASE DIARY

For a short period of time, following Jack's arrival, one of our homes felt 'upside down'. In clinical supervision with the in-house psychologist, I raised the issue of anxiety about Jack's arrival into the home. During the supervision session, the psychologist asked me what I was concerned about. At the time, I could not clearly articulate what the anxiety was about, other than that I felt unsafe in Jack's presence. It took two weeks and the next supervision session before I could begin to articulate what it was about Jack. Partly, I think it was the feeling of danger and fear that he could completely overwhelm me. Unfortunately for Jack there were other factors at the same time, which heightened our vulnerability collectively and individually. This included some misinformation about him through other carers, my own personal difficulties outside of the work (running on empty) and my feeling that I wasn't part of the decision-making process. However, our home recovered from being 'upside down' to the point where we were able to work on these matters, while holding on to and containing some very difficult and unpleasant feelings. In these circumstances it is clear how easy it is to lose patience and understanding, and react in a defensive way that goes against the basic grain of a therapeutic environment. Getting through the first few weeks was a difficult process, but once these issues were ironed out the therapeutic work was able to begin, which resulted in me being able to acknowledge the potential growth that could occur for myself and the child.

Effective support can help to make the pain bearable, not to take it away but somehow enable us not to be overwhelmed and therefore have the chance to think about it and understand the relevance to ourselves. If we can contain and think about our difficulties, then hopefully we can learn something about ourselves. From this position we can then make constructive decisions and take action that may help things to get better. If we can do this, the pain involved in this work has the potential for growth in it and the rewards that go with that. It probably is not stated strongly enough that it is the 'mother's' capacity for this process of containment, that enables the child to grow, to become integrated and to develop a strong rather than impoverished sense of self. Positive 'feeding' experiences can only be made real use of in this context.

Sometimes children who are especially challenging to work with do very well in the long term, despite of or maybe because of our worries about them. Meeting children who have left us, now young men, like David and Luke, certainly raises questions for me. David spent about two years with us and a lot of the time was extremely difficult – he was a typical storm centre, promoting group acting out at the slightest detection of any vulnerability in the environment, as well as extreme verbal and physical aggression towards women. He probably spent most of his time with us on the verge of having his placement ended. Since leaving a few years ago he has done very well, maintaining stable relationships, employment and has been able to remain in independent living arrangements. I found it almost unbelievable to hear how physically well and fit he is now, which is huge achievement as he was so overweight, preferred to live on junk food and he had no interest in exercise or being mobile. He seems to feel quite happy within himself now. His past carer keeps in regular contact and speaks very positively of him. He also remains connected to us through the outreach programme.

Luke was more emotionally integrated than David, but in some respects was more worrying in terms of his potential violence. After initially being seen as a threat by his carer, he had settled in well, and committed to a day programme that included a trade apprenticeship. He gives the impression of being happier within himself. These two examples draw attention to the ease with which we can believe certain myths about the work, without testing these in reality. We sometimes find out that children who we are not sure have benefited from our programme, seem to do well in the long term, while others who we were more hopeful about do not always fare so well.

COMMUNICATION CHALLENGES

To make and receive communication effectively and clearly requires a clear and receptive mind. Inevitably, in work with traumatized children we can become emotionally 'full up', which impacts on our capacity to communicate clearly, both with children and at all levels within the organization.

It is often felt within therapeutic communities that communication could be improved. Often there can be difficulty with different people feeling they haven't been consulted or informed about something, or by those attempting to send a communication that it hasn't been heard and acted upon. This can leave people feeling disempowered. Community psychology literature highlights that for a person to feel a sense of belonging and community, they have to feel that they have a level of influence. They have to feel that their needs are being met (integration of needs) within their system or community (McMillan and Chavis 1986). A system such as a therapeutic community, unconsciously as well as consciously regulates the flow of information across its boundaries to a level it can manage at that time. During times of stress, information that is felt to be of positive benefit to the system is more likely to be heard; that of neutral benefit may be ignored and that of negative benefit actively dismissed. The healthier and more open a system is, the more it will be able to use a diverse range of information to its benefit. Even 'bad' news can be used positively. The way in which communication is managed across the organization will give an indication of the general condition of the system. Often when there are problems with communication, it is more helpful to view this as a symptom and to consider why we might be having this difficulty, rather than only focusing on how communication can be improved.

The danger for systems that have become stressed and do not allow for reflective practice, and for opinions to be heard, is that they create an environment of mistrust and frustration, and unsurfaced anger can develop. This can result in unconscious and conscious undermining of the decision-making and other task-related processes. Bloom describes some of the qualities that are necessary to maintain open and reflective communication:

> For individuals and for systems this requires a rigorous process of self-examination and the development of a core system of meaning that will guide behavior, decision-making, problem-solving, and conflict resolution. Such a process involves the willingness to temporarily reflect on the past, create a culture of enquiry to examine the present, and commitment of sufficient time to engage in honest dialogue. Productive discourse, however, depends on good communication and recovering individuals need to learn how to listen and how to talk. Likewise, chronic systemic problems lead to communication breakdowns and the loss of feedback loops within organizations. As a result, an organization must learn how to reconnect and integrate with the various parts of itself. (Bloom 2005, p.65)

During times of stress and change, anxiety levels are heightened and the defence mechanisms of individuals are more easily triggered. Rigorous processes are required to ensure that the relationship dynamics within the organization are monitored closely, and the appropriate information, debriefing and opportunities to be heard are provided. One of the ways we do this on a daily basis is by ensuring that all group meetings have a space to focus on emotions and relationships. The 'I feel like saying' process in our meetings ensures that we constantly monitor the dynamics within our teams (see Chapter 8). It also provides an opportunity for reflective processes and for all participants to have an opportunity to voice how they are feeling about their work and the organization.

THERAPEUTIC SUPERVISION: WORKING WITH FEELINGS

The kind of emotional attention that traumatized children need could be regarded as a professional state of mind, similar to Winnicott's (1956a) description of a mother's primary maternal preoccupation with her infant. Although a child may need 'preoccupation', his sense of vulnerability and dependence will also be heightened, which can be frightening to him. The child who is not used to people thinking about him in a concerned way may find this extremely anxiety provoking, or may associate it with negative experiences where adults have only thought about him in terms of their own needs, however inappropriate. Our preoccupation or thinking may be constantly attacked or perceived as something else by the child, such as intrusion or abuse (Tomlinson 2005, p.45).

The actual process of thinking in itself can be very threatening to traumatized children. Their thoughts are predominantly associated with negative and painful emotions. Therefore, these children spend their energy on not thinking and for the same reason will also try to stop anyone else from thinking. From this it can be seen how it is possible that our positive intentions can be misconceived by children, tested, rejected and distorted. Being on the receiving end of this can raise doubts, anxieties and fears that are challenging to one's sense of self. We may feel we are being treated by a child as if we are someone else, often someone who has caused the child harm in the past. This is described, as we have mentioned, in psychodynamic terms as 'transference' and our feelings in response to it as 'countertransference'.

In work with traumatized children it is inevitable that strong feelings get aroused. This is partly because of what an emotionally disturbed child does to us and partly because of what they remind us of in our own childhoods, which we may have found painful. The genuine difficulty, risk and pain experienced by all involved create a strong potential for avoidance of the main issue and failure in treatment. As Maher (2003, p.280) states, 'Treatment is risky, difficult and painful for everyone involved – and often too risky, painful and difficult to attempt.' Sometimes our feelings are so strong we displace or distort them to make them feel safer. If we are made to feel 'useless', we may rather see that 'uselessness' in another team member or the organization, than in ourselves. If we feel furious with a child, to protect the child (and ourselves from feelings of guilt) we may direct that fury at someone in our team or outside it. It is essential that whatever feelings a person is carrying can be talked about and explored.

If we cannot explore the feelings we have, then rather than be understood in a way that can lead to change for ourselves and the children, the feelings are likely to be re-enacted in repetitive scenarios that don't improve anything.

CLINICAL SUPERVISOR'S REFLECTIVE CASE DIARY: DISPLACEMENT OF FEELINGS OF ANGER ASSOCIATED WITH LOSS

In individual clinical supervision, Sonia expressed anger over her experience during a couple of interactions with a manager, Thomas. One interaction was particularly distressing for her. She told me that Thomas was talking in a meeting about staff that had left the organization. He forgot to mention that the secondary carer in her home, Tara, had left. She felt that this was disrespectful and that Thomas did not care about Tara or appreciate what she had contributed to the organization. In processing the experience, Sonia was asked what assumptions she had made about Thomas. She told me that Thomas did not care about Tara who had left and that the organization in general did not care. Sonia was then asked what evidence she had about the way Thomas felt about Tara. This became a lot more difficult for Sonia to answer, as it was a feeling that she had and could not really provide any tangible evidence.

We moved on to processing Sonia's own experience of Tara's leaving. Sonia expressed feelings of loss and also anger towards Tara. Tara's leaving had activated a stress response in Sonia, and had also brought up some unconscious feelings of loss from her own childhood. She also experienced powerful emotions associated with loss, as she had a strong relationship with Tara. The home was functioning well in partnership with Tara and Sonia felt that she was now on her own caring for the children. In addition, she would have to build a new relationship with a stranger when a new secondary carer was recruited. When Sonia experienced these strong emotions the energy could have been directed in a number of directions.

1. Sonia could have blamed herself. Maybe she was not a good enough carer and Tara left because of her incompetence. This is a very difficult possibility to deal with.

2. Sonia could have directed the anger towards Tara who had left her and the children. This could have affected the potential for an ongoing friendship, and also Tara may not have been available to receive the directed anger.

3. The anger could have been directed towards the children. Sonia could have blamed them for being too challenging, which could have contributed to Tara leaving. This could have had a damaging impact on the children to have this level of anger and blame directed towards them.

4. The anger could have been directed towards Thomas. Thomas has the capacity as a clinician and in some ways it his role to deal with these transferences. He seems to be the most appropriate person to receive the displaced anger.

In this example, we can see a process where the anger associated with the loss of someone important is displaced onto a more appropriate 'container' until the feelings involved could be understood. Anna Freud (1986) refers to displacement as a defence mechanism in which there is an unconscious shift of emotions, affect or desires from an original object to a more acceptable or immediate substitute. The instinctual aim here is to protect one's own ego, but also to conform with higher social values. Sonia was unable to direct the anger towards herself as this would have been too painful for her. She could not direct it at Tara or the children, who were all directly involved in the process of Tara leaving. As a defence mechanism she displaced these feelings onto a more socially appropriate substitute. This example also highlights the importance of individual and peer supervision as an opportunity to process the emotionality of the work. It also averts the risk that carers may direct strong unresolved emotions towards the children, which could be extremely damaging to a traumatized child. It is much safer to displace or project feelings onto a clinical supervisor who can provide a holding space to work through and gain insight.

Whilst acknowledging the difficulties in our work it also important to acknowledge that it can be enjoyable and rewarding. First of all we must value ourselves and the capacity to enjoy our lives. To work effectively each individual needs to put themselves first at times. We need to strike a balance between putting ourselves fully into the work, but also finding the time and space to meet other needs away from work. Without this balance there is a danger that we become 'burnt out' with feelings of resentment towards the work. In work that is about looking after others, a dynamic can be created where the workers involved feel guilty about meeting their own needs and thinking about themselves. In this type of culture anyone who expresses something about their own needs may be questioned about their commitment. Self-care may be seen as a weakness, or not putting in for the team. We need to get the balance right. In this work, where we give so much in looking after others, it is important to preserve spaces where we look after ourselves, or are looked after. It can be misguided to imagine that the children only need us to think about *them* and not ourselves. One of their needs is that we are balanced people who can look after ourselves as well as them. We can only really be involved in our work and relationships if we value ourselves. It is positive role modelling for children, particularly those who have had to grow up too quickly and have had the responsibility of caring for others, rather than be cared for and nurtured in a way that a child needs.

Tom Main (1989) made an important point on this subject in his paper 'The Ailment'. This is regarded as a classic paper on therapeutic community work and how particularly challenging 'patients' can create major difficulties and splits in the staff team, amongst other things. 'Believing that sincerity in management is a sine qua non for the treatment of the patients I have described, I offer one piece of advice. If at any time you are impelled to give advice to others (to be less hostile and more loving than they can truly be) don't' (p.35). Main argued at length that sincerity amongst staff about what can and cannot be given with goodwill is the basis for the management of these patients. The same could be argued for a group of traumatized children. Main believed that insincere goodness is useless and potentially disastrous for the continuance of treatment. We need to be completely genuine in our work. For instance, if senior managers are not properly tuned into the reality of the carers' work, they will ask carers without much thought to try a bit harder and so on. The danger is then that the carers adopt a false caring persona, which cannot be trusted by the children who will see right through it. They will react to it causing even greater stress to the carers who will become demoralized. The carers need the opportunity to express their real feelings about the work, in supervision and other forums. If this helps to relieve the burden of feelings of anxiety and guilt that they aren't up to the job, they will then be able to work in a more genuine way. They will be more able to accept their feelings, such as guilt and anxiety, as part of the work rather than an indication they aren't working or trying hard enough.

One of the difficulties for children who have been so let down and experienced so much deception is that they can't trust what people say. So they try to read what is beneath the words. If they sense something not to be real they will test it. An additional difficulty is that they will often misread situations, people's words and actions. Helping a child to make real links with what is happening around them and in their relationships is an important task. Often in the past, the child may have said something or made an observation that was true, only to be told the opposite. It is important that we are honest and genuine and find ways to respond to uncomfortable and sometimes painful comments made by children, without dismissing what has been said or confusing children by denying reality. At the same time, being careful to not burden them inappropriately with our anxieties and worries.

CASE EXAMPLE: BEING GENUINE

A young teenage girl, Lucy, went to her carer, Gemma, one day in a very agitated state saying she had been 'told off' for suggesting to one of the other carers, Michelle, that she wasn't very happy that day. Michelle had reacted defensively and abruptly told Lucy she was fine. This developed into what Lucy considered to be an argument. Gemma suggested that the three of them talk about it. Gemma understood how Michelle was feeling, but could also see that Lucy had reason to be upset and the tension was escalating. Initially, Michelle continued to be defensive and felt criticized. Once Michelle could see that Gemma wasn't being critical the matter was resolved fairly quickly. Michelle acknowledged that she wasn't in the best of moods, but it was nothing that Lucy had done to her that made her feel like that, which was true. Gemma and Michelle found a few minutes to talk about a personal problem that had been worrying Michelle.

In this little vignette, there are a number of points that illustrate the importance but difficulty of sincere communication. Michelle was worried about something and took an accurate observation by Lucy as a criticism that she wasn't doing her job. She was possibly anxious that Lucy could see through her so clearly. Lucy, who was beginning to gain confidence in understanding her own and other people's emotions, felt frustrated because she was being told she was wrong. She may also have been worried that Michelle was unhappy with her, which Michelle clarified wasn't the case. There is little chance of making progress for children who struggle to be in touch with and make sense of external reality, unless we attempt to be clear and straightforward with them and ourselves.

CARER'S REFLECTIVE CASE DIARY

In our team meetings we have been focusing more on how we work together as a team and as individuals, rather than what the children project upon us. When work is very awkward it is easy to think it is because something isn't right and then feel frustrated about whatever or whoever it is. Then, when the heat has died down a bit we think more positively, that things can be so difficult because of our capacity to provide emotional holding. If we are providing a sense of safety, security and reliability we can expect children's difficulties to emerge and be expressed. I think this is relevant to working with others in a team, with children and our own issues. When the work gets close to what is really important it can be hard and unpleasant. Even though one can be prepared, it is still difficult not to take flight from the problem and displace it outside of ourselves. At these times we might find ourselves rationalizing why it would be right to stop working with a child, working with others in a team, and working on ourselves. It is at this point that sitting with this discomfort is important and taking the time to process feelings.

SAFETY AND CONTAINMENT

Children who have been traumatized and abused first of all need to feel safe before they can relax and become attached to anyone. This may take considerable time and it is vital that the programme allows for this time. As van der Kolk and Newman (2007, p.18) state, 'The foundation of treatment is the safety of the therapeutic relationship. If treatment focuses prematurely on exploration of the past, this will exacerbate rather than relieve traumatic intrusions.' Clear boundaries are an essential part of a safe relationship and safe environment. Establishing this for children who have had chaotic and traumatic experiences resulting in a complete lack of trust is a hard job. In essence, boundaries are limits and guidelines (a rule or set of rules giving guidance on how to behave in a situation). The adults need to role model how they live by the same guidelines and expectations. For example, it is not helpful to tell children not to shout and then to shout back at a child. Once the boundaries are understood it is most likely that they will be tested. The children we work with often believe that they are impossible to contain safely. They have experienced adults that are unable to hold firm boundaries, without becoming reactive, punitive or rejecting. Hills (2005, p.121) explains that, 'A child whose strategic repertoire is geared to anticipating and surviving loss, failure and rejection will recreate the familiarity of this drama with the unsuspecting carers.'

A boundary can also be a line between one thing or person and another. There may literally be a line, like a fence around a garden, or the line is metaphorical like the space between two people. There is normally a clear understanding between people about the limits of crossing a boundary. For instance, in entering someone else's home, you don't just walk in, but ring the bell, wait for an answer and permission to enter. The expectations or guidelines around boundaries are either made formally explicit or are understood and assimilated culturally. For instance, different cultures have different norms about what is considered appropriate physical space between people. To go closer to someone than the norm, without permission, would be considered an invasion of their space.

There are also personal boundaries concerning how we relate to one another. Shapiro and Carr, who look at child development within the family context, give a good explanation of how personal boundaries develop:

> In essence, when parents ask their child, 'what is your experience?' they authorize the child to have a separate experience and allow an implicit boundary to form between child and parent. On one side of this boundary is the child's experience of himself; on the other side are the parents' views of him. This stable personal boundary constitutes a key element in healthy growth and development, since secure self awareness allows the child to have flexible interactions with other people. (Carr 1991, p.12)

A strategy highlighted in *Parenting Effectiveness Training* (Thomas 2000) and which we use to establish a sense of personal boundaries is 'I' statements. 'I' statements provide the listener with personal information about the speaker. They are also a tool for integrating a sense of self into a communication. The statements can help prevent conflict as they imply personal accountability around experiences, which can help remove a sense of blame or antagonism. For instance, 'I' am feeling upset, rather than you are making me feel upset. They require some form of self-disclosure and often communicate emotion and vulnerability. In this way they can facilitate the formation of healthy open and honest relationships with children. The effective use of 'I' statements is an important skill to role model and for children to learn. An example of an 'I' statement is, 'I feel frustrated'. As a child develops more confidence and greater sense of self, the statements can evolve and provide more information about the experience for the child, such as, 'I feel frustrated when I hear raised voices, name calling and swearing, because I…'

To recognize the boundaries between people a person needs to realize that they are separate and different to others. Traumatized children have often internalized a model of boundaries that is confused and unclear; where personal boundaries have not been established appropriately. In addition, they are often emotionally immature and have not developed a clear sense of emotional separation from others. They may easily be confused about their feelings and other people's feelings. What belongs to me and what doesn't? Therefore, we can't expect them to recognize or understand things that we take for granted and that normally a young child would have learnt through experience. We need to explain things and will need to do this repeatedly.

To support the therapeutic task the whole organization will need to be clear about its boundaries. The larger and more complex the organization the more challenging this is. The whole boundary system of the organization will be experienced and internalized by everyone in the organization, including the children. The clearer the boundaries are between different roles and departments, the less confused everyone will be and more able to maintain clear and appropriate boundaries in the work with children. A clear structure of authority where it is understood exactly who is responsible for what is especially important. Boundaries need managing by people, and this involves the right to say yes or no, or to negotiate. The organizational culture and structure needs to be compatible with the treatment task. Miller (1993, p.4) describes how the 'holding environment' (taken from Winnicott's idea of what the mother provides for her infant) of an organization can promote psychological security for its staff, if it is effectively managed. Talking about organizations whose task is to provide care and treatment, he states that there is 'the need for a match between the holding environment that staff have to provide for their clients or patients and the holding environment that organisations and management provide for them' (p.4).

For example, a management structure that allows for little autonomy and responsibility in the staff is not likely to encourage the growth of autonomy and responsibility in the children. Balbernie and Miller (1984) explain the specific system of management developed in the Cotswold Community (a therapeutic community for emotionally disturbed boys) in their paper, 'The Cotswold Community: Management Implications of the Therapeutic Task'. An important point in this paper is that management isn't about managing a home, managing children or managing staff. It is about managing the boundary conditions within which individual homes, care team members and children manage themselves. Boundaries are established around a community, a home, and within a home that give individuals an appropriate amount of space within which to negotiate and make choices. A manager's task is to help establish effective boundaries and to manage the boundary between the home, the wider community and the outside world. Balbernie and Miller also emphasize the importance in the treatment task of providing role models. We work by the principle that we ask of ourselves what we ask of children, and that we lead by example. In our organization, we speak about all workers, whether in direct or indirect care, playing a part in role modelling appropriate emotional intelligence, relationships and boundaries. All of our team members, from administration to carers, are provided with the training and support required to develop healthy relationships with the children.

In reality, organizations that work with traumatized children can expect considerable difficulty in maintaining effective boundary management. There are a number of reasons for this. The work involves significant levels of anxiety that will impact on those working directly with children and the whole organization. Maintaining clear boundaries is particularly difficult when people are anxious and where boundaries are being continuously tested. Thinking becomes difficult and management can become reactive and too rigid, or on the other hand too permissive due to fear of negative reactions. In many ways, the dynamics of abuse, denial and secrecy can infiltrate the whole organization. There is always the danger that organizations can become closed systems much like those in which family abuse occurs. Farragher and Yanosy highlight how easy it is to become unthinkingly caught up in a re-enactment with a child:

> Here we have a little girl who has a history of being terribly abused at bedtime. She is scared and anxious and tries to imagine these emotions by building a barricade in her room at night. The staff are not attuned to the trauma history and view this behavior as disruptive and try to stop it. The child resists and ends up in a conflict with the staff. The situation escalates to the point that the staff restrain her and straddle her on the floor of the bedroom. When confronted with the reality that we were engaging in a reenactment with this

child and that nightly our 'treatment' program was retraumatizing this little girl, we were horrified… What we have found in our work thus far is that this compulsion to reenact the past on the part of children in care places extreme pressures on caregivers and on the system. If we are aware of what is happening, we stand a chance of responding appropriately. If, however, staff do not understand this dynamic, which is often the case, we are in big trouble. Even the most well-intentioned staff are at risk of re-injuring the children they are supposed to protect. (Farragher and Yanosy 2005, p.96)

When we are working with children traumatized by abuse, and in particular sexual abuse, being clear about things is often responded to by children as if it is abusive. This can lead to collusion as a way of avoiding the anxiety involved. The concept of 'tough love' can also be challenging for the organization to manage. Both providing care for some of society's most ill-treated and vulnerable children and also needing to be very firm and resilient in the work with them can sometimes feel like a conflict between care and control. Many people come into the work wanting to provide love and care for the children and find themselves being reacted to as if it is they are the ones doing the hurting and acting abusively. Workers can at times confuse collusion with actual caring, and don't realize the negative impact that it can have on children. The care team and the organization as a whole need to be consistent in their boundaries, to avoid confusion for the child.

Clemens Janzing, in 'One Foot in Hell: On Self Destructive Staff Dynamics', gives some advice on how to prevent destructive staff dynamics:

(i) The staff group and the unit it is leading should possess a clear, consistent and solid surface structure. There should exist a proper organisation and set of rules and regulations that is accepted and maintained by the workers. Thus strong leadership expresses itself in adequate functional authority; there is a consistent and logical division of tasks between the workers and, most important, each and every worker understands the aim of the treatment unit and the way treatment is done. In other words, there exists a sound and clear treatment philosophy.

(ii) Issues representing covert, hidden conflicts are recognised in time and understood by all staff members.

(iii) A free and open discussion is possible within clear boundaries of room and time during such meetings.

(iv) Staff group members must separate important topics from the less important ones, which means that there is a kind of mutually shared discipline regarding discussions.

(v) A conflict is considered as a means of achieving possible improvement of staff group functioning, not as a means of possible deterioration.

(vi) There exists a mutually shared culture in which realities and fantasies can be discussed but are kept apart.

(vii) There is a strong recognition of the fact that all existence of human beings is essentially interaction. This counts for staff group members as well and implies an acceptance of shared responsibilities regarding to all vicissitudes within the staff group. In other words, no one as a separate individual alone is to be blamed. Each staff member reflects on the part he plays in the fascinating realm of therapeutic community life. (Janzing 1991, p.11)

THE IMPACT OF TRAUMA WORK ON OUR OWN MEMORIES AND EXPERIENCES OF CHILDHOOD

When we are working with traumatized children our own memories and feelings, both conscious and unconscious, associated with our own childhood experiences, will be brought to the surface. This can be particularly painful if some of those memories are also associated with trauma. As Farragher and Yanosy (2005, p.97) write, 'Another contributing factor in this already toxic stew is that many staff bring with them their own history of loss and trauma, which may make them even more vulnerable.' However, discussing some of the reasons why we may go into this work, Clare Winnicott argues how this can also be beneficial:

> Some are in fact lonely and seek group living as a way of meeting their own needs. If the demands which such people are likely to make on their colleagues can be tolerated, many of them have much to offer to the children because they have a deep understanding of what it means to be lonely and to feel unwanted. It can happen that by giving to the children the adult conducts his/her own therapy and can establish self-confidence. (Winnicott 1968, p.4)

CASE EXAMPLE: WOUNDED HEALER

One of our trainers, Sheila, was running a half-day training event for around twenty residential carers. The aim of the training was to encourage psychodynamic thinking, to think about the meaning beneath children's behaviour and from that insight to consider appropriate responses. Sheila presented the following scenario to the group – one of the children, Luke, had disappeared from his home and a carer was looking for him. After a while the carer spotted him by a pond with what looked like a cat in the pond, attached to a long piece of string that Luke was holding. The group was asked what they thought was going on and what the carer should do immediately and in the longer term.

The carers did some work in small groups and then gave feedback. The general consensus was that the first thing that should be done was to make the situation safe, ensuring Luke was safe and the cat was rescued. Reasons for the behaviour were along the lines of: maybe Luke was angry and was taking it out on the cat; he might be treating the cat in a cruel and abusive way that was a re-enactment of how he had been treated. In terms of what to do the responses were: explore with Luke why he was doing that; make it clear to him that his behaviour was inappropriate; help Luke to put his feelings into words; use the situation as an opportunity to talk with Luke about his abuse in an empathic way.

As the discussion went on, one of the carers, Terry, who had been looking increasingly thoughtful, suggested that Luke might have been trying to save the cat. The group found this amusing and laughed a little. Interestingly, Sheila had taken the scenario from a child's case history and that was exactly what he was trying to do. The child had had a traumatic experience when he was younger – out playing unsupervised with his younger brother who fell into a pond and drowned. The child felt responsible for his brother's death and was blamed by his parents. He had a history of re-enacting this trauma in different ways in a desperate way to resolve it. He put the cat in the pond so he could save it, which he hadn't been able to do for his brother. Sheila explained this to the group who were surprised how Terry had made such an unexpected and insightful comment.

When the group took a break, Sheila approached Terry who had seemed very preoccupied and asked if he was OK. Terry said he had made the comment because when he was a child he had been with his younger brother who fell into a canal and drowned. Sheila empathized with the distress this exercise may have caused Terry, but also commented on how his own experience had given him the capacity for empathic insight. Terry then said that he had been physically abused by his mother as a child, and asked Sheila if she thought he would be able to do the work given his own experiences. Sheila suggested that it is very difficult to predict how our own experiences will either help us or hinder us in the work. On the one hand, if we have integrated our experiences into our life history, difficult experiences can help us provide empathy and understanding. On the other hand, the work may raise very painful feelings, some of which we may have repressed and things can feel overwhelming. She told Terry that the important thing was to talk about his feelings in supervision and other relevant forums, especially if something was particularly troubling. Terry actually turned out to be an excellent carer, showing great levels of patience and understanding with the children he worked with over a long period of time.

The key points of learning from this were: that a carer's own traumatic experiences can be useful in developing empathy and insight, if the person has integrated those experiences into their own history and identity. Luke had not been able, so far, to integrate the trauma of his brother's death and was compelled to re-enact it. Whenever we are working with trauma, talking or thinking about it, our own experiences will be brought closer to the surface. As van der Kolk and Newman (2007, p.6) said, 'In short, the study of trauma confronts one with the best and worst in human nature, and is bound to provoke a range of intense personal reactions in the people involved.' Sheila had not anticipated such an emotive exercise and was moved by the poignancy of it, which had an emotional impact on her. Working with trauma evokes powerful emotions and often when we least expect it. Terry showed how something constructive can come out of such awful experiences: how the capacity for healing can develop out of our own emotional wounds.

Some of the powerful and primitive feelings that are evoked in the work may be related to the kind of experiences we have described. Others may be more complex and deeply unconscious. The children's primitive behaviour will stir up our own deep-rooted primitive feelings and test the ways in which we manage these feelings. For instance, we might have angry feelings and impulses which are repressed. When faced with a child who seems to have no restraint in expressing her anger, we might find that very challenging without knowing why. If we are not conscious of our own repressed anger, we might identify with the child and gain some vicarious satisfaction out of her expression of anger. If our own anger is too threatening for us to contemplate we might try to control the child due to our own unconscious fears related to anger. If a worker does have repressed anger it is likely the child will sense this and push all of the worker's 'buttons' until the anger eventually surfaces. If the worker is not familiar with feeling angry, he may feel distressed and shocked to have such powerful feelings. Bettelheim explains how the level of personal integration that is sufficient for most of us to cope reasonably well in everyday life will be seriously challenged through working with emotionally disturbed children:

> These normal, well-adjusted individuals, who had sufficient ego strength to enter and do well in graduate school and in working with people, after living and working intimately with these unintegrated patients sooner or later appear to develop quite serious neurotic behavior. (Bettelheim 1974, p.360)

For example, the worker may become hostile towards the organization, the children or colleagues, or he may become withdrawn or highly defended emotionally. Bettelheim saw this as a normal response to a highly stressful situation, which is challenging the worker's emotional integration and causing internal turmoil. He also described in detail, how this requires the worker to change and reintegrate his personality in a way that will include the previously repressed feelings and aspects of himself. This is one of the motivations and potential rewards for the worker. The work requires him to change and to deal with unconscious and troubling aspects of his personality, which leads to a higher level of maturity and personal integration. Personal growth and development is one of the rewards involved in the work and this is often an unconscious motivation that attracts us to it. Bettelheim argues that,

> Work becomes meaningful only as we are convinced we gain something very special from it for ourselves. The skill demanded of the senior staff is the prime requirement for making the institution into a therapeutic milieu: they must be able to demonstrate to the rest of the staff how much they can gain for themselves from this work, and help them to do so. (Bettelheim 1974, p.447)

For the worker to be supported in thinking about and understanding the difficult feelings we have described, there needs to be specifically designed forums for this purpose. The forums, which can include supervision, team meetings, consultancy and training, will need to be clear in terms of boundaries and task. They will need to be reliable and consistent. In work with children who present such challenges to our emotions, thinking and ability to hold boundaries, and where staff have to deal with high levels of uncertainty, it is helpful that the key structures for staff support are reliable and provide an element of certainty.

CHAPTER 5

The Home Environment

When we talk of ending homelessness for children we don't just mean putting a roof over their heads. We mean ensuring that children live in a place that is the kind of home we will describe in this chapter. A place that feels cared for; a comfortable, loving and nurturing place to be. A place that the child feels part of, where they belong and where their uniqueness as an individual is reflected in the environment around them. Or, as Bettelheim (1974) put it with the title of his book on this subject – A Home for the Heart.

Historically, people working in therapeutic homes or communities for traumatized children have understood the importance of the environment in the therapeutic process (Bettelheim 1950; Rose 1990). This is so fundamental that the understanding almost feels intuitive and instinctive. We expect it is similar to the way that a parent knows how important the environment is for a young infant. It should be clean, soothing, not too noisy, the right temperature and so on. Unfortunately the traumatized children we work with were often deprived of these basic needs. Therefore, providing the right type of environment can be the beginning of the recovery process.

When asked the question of what home meant for them, a variety of children and carers at Lighthouse said that home is the following:

- a nurturing place, it's my foundations
- a safe place, it's a welcoming place
- walking in the door and everyone saying, 'Hi, how was your day?'
- shelter and love
- going to a place where there's actually someone there waiting for you

- being there at any given moment
- just being able to not worry about where you're going to stay
- trust
- community
- those long in-depth conversations and discussions
- love and support
- family
- where there are people who love you, they're there for you
- a place where I sleep, a place where I feel safe and secure, and a place where I feel loved
- doesn't matter where it is or what it is, it's about the people that are in it
- to build a good home it takes love and being there.

A healthy home environment reflects a family's values and mutual care for each other. Normally a home will be reasonably clean, safe and reflect the interests of those living in it. It will also give some sense of the family's history with mementos and photos of their time together. In this sense the home can be seen as reflecting back to everyone in it the way they are valued and cared for. For example, when a baby is born a space may be created for the baby that feels warm and nurturing. As the baby develops into a young child, playthings will be provided and hazards will be kept out of the way or made safe. The home environment evolves to meet the needs of everyone living in it. As Prilleltensky and Nelson (2000) state, 'Family wellness can be considered a state of affairs in which everybody's needs in the family are met. This requires that people reach a balance between pursuing personal aspirations, such as careers and studies, and contributing to the well-being of other family members.' For this to happen, the parents need to be attuned to the needs of their children. As the children grow up they also begin to value and care for their environment. 'While parents do most of the giving during the children's early years, children gradually develop the ability to reciprocate and contribute to family well-being in many ways' (Prilleltensky and Nelson 2000).

Child abuse and trauma often occurs within a wider context of neglect, where the environment the child lives in reflects the parent's lack of attunement to the child's needs. The home is often uncared for, unstimulating, chaotic and sometimes unsafe. Some children who are severely deprived have no concept of play and have never been provided with the kind of emotional interaction and stimulation necessary for play to develop. Additionally, because of the fear these children constantly live in, they become hypervigilant of everything around them, which also leaves little emotional space for any kind of relaxed, playful activity.

In the case of homeless children, they may have no expectation of a 'home' that respects and values them as individuals. These children often believe that the 'streets' are safer than any home. Whilst our aim is to care directly for the child, every aspect of the environment we provide for the child will give a message of how we feel about them. For some children, the mere fact that they can observe the environment we provide gives the first indication of whether we understand their needs. One child who was unable to trust the carers in his home and let them care for him in an intimate way, told us it took over a year before he could trust someone. But from the beginning, the way the home was cared for made him think that the adults really cared. He could see this from the way the adults looked after children's bedrooms, made their beds, made sure their clothes were clean, helped them personalize their space and looked after the home. A child might make a mess and see how much care is taken in cleaning it up, or break something and see how it gets repaired.

Children who have never had these things done for them in a reliable and caring way, will need to experience being cared for in this way before they can begin to look after and care for their own space. This is a very important point in work with traumatized children. Because of the mistrust these children rightfully have of all adults, due to the manner in which they have been neglected, deprived, let down and often abused, they will keep adults at a distance. Before a child might let an adult directly care for him in a way that feels personal and special, the child might begin to let the adult take care of an object of his, like a teddy or looking after a plant together.

CASE EXAMPLE: CRAIG

One sixteen-year-old boy we cared for, Craig, seemed to be completely unconcerned about turning his bedroom into an extremely chaotic and dirty environment. The extent of this was beyond the kind of mess we might ordinarily expect of a teenager. This was demanding for the adults working with him and sometimes they felt that he should be able to take better care of his room. Working with the adults and exploring his life history we could see that he had grown up in a chaotic and unhygienic environment. It was clear that he had no opportunity to internalize a sense of an ordered and cared for environment. It could also be hypothesized that he was recreating the familiarity of the only kind of environment he knew. It was meaningless for us to try to persuade him how he should look after his room or to take a punitive stance about the issue. He needed us to take responsibility for his environment and look after it in much the same way a parent would for an infant. We needed to continually tidy up and clean the mess he made.

This kind of repetitive cleaning up is normally something that goes on for the first few years of childhood and parents do it without expecting anything different. So we adopted a similar approach and after a few months it was clear that Craig began to enjoy the benefits of his cared-for environment. The repetitive cleaning and tidying of the adults also enabled him to feel that adults could be relied upon, and this basic level of care wasn't stopped because of his difficult behaviour or the mood of the adults. Once Craig began to feel these things he also began to help take care of things. Before Craig left us he had internalized a sense of being cared for and how this is reflected in the environment – not only did he value his own space but this extended to the whole home. He would help with jobs around the house and took a particular interest in looking after the garden.

This approach to work in a therapeutic environment means that many of the everyday and what can often seem like mundane things are crucially important in the therapeutic process. House cleaning, laundry and cooking are all central to this. As in infancy, these processes have huge symbolic as well as practical meaning. For instance, tidying up can feel like making order out of chaos, cleaning and taking care of a mess can feel like taking care of overwhelming feelings, and mending something can feel like repairing a feeling that is hurt or damaged. In these respects it is particularly important that a child's carer takes direct responsibility for as much of this as possible. It might take a while for a new worker to grasp the importance of this. It is not just that these things are done to a good standard, as it would be easy to create a clean and cared for home if that's all we wanted to do. It's that these things are done in a personal way with each child in mind. The carers who get to know how each child likes things make little adaptations to ordinary things that reflect their attunement to each child. For example, one child might like all their clean clothes put away and another might like a few left out ready for the next day.

We like to use the acronym PLACE to describe the type of home environment we try to create. This means the home is a playful, loving, accepting, curious and empathetic therapeutic environment, where children and carers can develop positive supportive relationships (Becker-Weidman and Shell 2005). It is a place where children can take comfort and respite from their daily challenges; a place where they can feel that their individual needs are recognized. The home is a secure base that enables children to grow, to try new things and to address their problems, all the while knowing that whatever challenges life may bring, they can always seek refuge in their home. For example, after a difficult day at school the child knows he will be able to go home, be welcomed and accepted for who he is, relax and be taken care of.

The home is a constant factor in the children's lives, providing them with a sense of permanence and stability. It forms part of a child's identity – a place where they feel connected to and belong. The sense of belonging is demonstrated in the way the home reflects each child's needs and interests as a person. It is a place where children feel welcome and are regularly reminded that their presence alone makes the home special.

The environment is warm, friendly, nurturing, calming and aesthetically pleasing. It contains facilities that can support and enrich a child's life. The home is a place for growth, development and a means of balancing the need for being sociable with privacy. It is a place where positive memories can be made and lifelong relationships established. Most importantly, the home is a safe place and sanctuary.

A central component to the Therapeutic Family Model of Care is that we don't have any locks on bedroom doors. The intentions of this are to emulate a 'normal' family home, to create opportunity for children to build trust and to demonstrate to them that they can be trusted. This is an important symbolic demonstration of trust. Many of the children have previously lived in institutional settings with internal security systems. This reinforces a belief that that those living in the home cannot be trusted. The absence of locks on bedroom doors and the message that the home is a safe place, slowly deconditions children out of their hypervigilance, allowing them to relax and engage with fellow children in a trusting way.

Children are encouraged to take responsibility for their home and on occasions when there are breaches of trust there are processes, such as 'family' meetings, where discussions about trust take place. The children are encouraged to decide what their home should be like. Over time, the home becomes a sanctuary and children develop a sense of trust for each other. If children can develop a sense that the home is safe, and that they can trust others because of the behaviours that others have demonstrated, they are also more capable of discerning trustworthy relationships in the outside world. We do not encourage children to lock themselves away from the world, or lock the world out. The locked doors in institutions can feel quite symbolic of this. The locks on doors are a short-term solution to the internal fear experienced by the child, which affects their interaction with the outside world. We work to assist children with internalizing a sense of safety instead through their experience of a trusting environment that validates their individual worth.

HOME AESTHETICS

The aesthetics of the environment children live in is extremely important for their psychological wellbeing. The children at one time or another can present with any number of psychological states that can be exacerbated by the look and feel of the environment they live in. A therapeutic home environment is created to promote a sense of order, safety and belonging, as well as a sense of pride. To facilitate a child's therapeutic development and an attachment to his home as a secure base, the following aesthetic aspects can be very helpful:

- bright, spacious and comfortable
- personalized
- positive and respectful (pictures, artefacts, etc. – positive and uplifting in nature)
- good quality furnishings
- a hygienic level of cleanliness
- mend things immediately.

Bright, spacious and comfortable

Ideally the home will be bright, light filled and well ventilated. Carefully chosen decoration, such as pastel colours, can help create a sense of space and light. It is helpful that homes are bright, as evidence suggests that low lit and dark environments can exacerbate depressive symptoms. It is important to create a balance between the presence of belongings, decorative items and furniture and the absence of unnecessary 'clutter'. Too much 'clutter' around the home can be a reminder of a chaotic environment and potentially exacerbate a child's sense of wellbeing and self-worth. The home should feel comfortable and cosy with furnishings that reflect this.

Personalized environment

Children and carers are encouraged to personalize their home with personal decorative items, photos and furnishings. Having personal pictures, photos, trophies and the like can greatly facilitate a child's attachment and sense of belonging to his home. In emulating a family home, we encourage the abundant display of 'family photos' that capture current children and carers. We encourage that family photos be continually updated when new children enter the home. Additionally, we encourage the display of photos of past carers and children, communicating a sense of history and permanent belonging to the home. Photos of past children in particular can ensure that children who have moved on can still feel they belong when returning for visits or respite stays.

Positive and respectful

When choosing decorative items, toys, games and books we ensure that all items are positive, respectful and not offensive to other members of the home. Ensure that the items:

- do not have sexual, alcohol or drug-related connotations
- do not promote, endorse or depict violence
- are not sexist or discriminating
- do not desecrate specific religious, racial or cultural values.

Good quality furnishings

An environment with good quality furnishings can have an immediate impact on how people feel about being in that environment. As Pughe and Philpot (2007, p.41) argue, 'The physical surrounding needs to be conducive to children's recovery.' Similarly, Mawson (2008, p.70) talking of his experience as a social entrepreneur involved in the regeneration of a rundown London community, states that, 'The environments we live, work and play in profoundly affect how we are as human beings and how we relate to each other.' He goes on to say that, 'When we are careful about the way we create a physical environment, when we pay attention to every detail of it, people begin to think of themselves and each other differently' (p.70). Conversely, an environment that looks worn out, shabby and uncared for may imply to people that 'they' are broken down or worn out or not worthy of a good quality environment. Homes fitted with good quality furnishings send the message 'I am worthy' to children. Additionally, the likelihood that these furnishings will be better cared for and respected by children will increase. As Mawson recognizes, this is a fundamental quality of human nature. In the community where he worked, local people helped to turn some wasteland into a park, for the whole community to use and enjoy. Unlike the previous history of vandalism in the community, this area remained remarkably free of such damage. A key component of the Therapeutic Family Model of Care is to show children the importance of nurturing and respecting everything connected to them.

A hygienic level of cleanliness

Children who have been deprived and traumatized have often experienced chaotic, uncared for and hazardous environments. Caring for their environment, ensuring it is clean, warm, safe and nurturing, is an essential form of provision for these children. As in the example of Craig (see p.137) we will need to understand the child's stage of development and take responsibility for his environment until he is ready to do so. At the same time, in our efforts to ensure the environment is cared for, clean and hygienic, we need to be careful not to communicate anxiety that a little mess is intolerable.

Mend things immediately

It is normal in all care environments that things inevitably become damaged or broken. In work with traumatized children this is especially common, and it can be seen to be symbolic of their damaged and broken lives. Sometimes a child may deliberately break something to show us how he is feeling, out of anger, frustration, carelessness or to see how we will respond. The child might not feel that he deserves good things and that he will lose them, so he damages things before anyone else can take them away from him. By repairing things immediately we show the child that we notice what has happened and that we care about it and him. It also gives the symbolic message that broken things can be mended and repaired. Where the child is able, involving him in the mending can also be a therapeutic reparative act. Where we don't mend things and allow them to remain broken, the child may feel we don't care or aren't attuned to him.

ENCOURAGING PLAY AND CURIOSITY

Play is central to child development and, as the American anthropologist George Dorsey (1868–1931) said, play is the beginning of knowledge.

Especially given the deprivation many traumatized children have experienced, the home should be an enriching environment, with a good selection of books, toys, games, sports equipment, computers and music, with a focus on learning and fun. Most importantly, the children need carers who understand the importance of play and who can encourage playfulness in their interactions with them. As Clifford-Poston (2001) claims, for children to develop they need a secure base and the permission to be curious. Traumatized children are often too fearful to express any curiosity and one of our tasks is to help stimulate their curiosity in appropriate ways. Therefore, we need to create an environment with interesting things around and where a child can explore and play. We need to allow them to experiment and not inhibit this by being too anxious about a little disorder or muddle. To facilitate curiosity and play, it is also important for the carers to be playful and get alongside children who may have had very little experience of playing with another. During infancy, a child needs someone to be with him while he tries things out, to make it safe and help him with the anxieties involved. Through her playful involvement with the infant, the adult reflects the infant's play back to him. This helps to hold the situation, enabling the infant to sustain, enjoy and make sense of his experience. Gradually through internalizing this experience, the infant is then able to play alone in the presence of another.

Whilst the home should be a stimulating environment, children who have been traumatized through abuse have often been extremely overstimulated. Rather than being introduced to the world 'in small doses', as Winnicott (1964) advises as being necessary for healthy development, they have often been exposed to things in everyday life long before they were emotionally ready to cope with such experiences. Winnicott describes this as an intolerable impingement on the child's ongoing sense of self. As a result, the child's stress responses are overstimulated, leading the child to be in a constant state of hyperarousal. These children need an environment that helps to calm and soothe them.

> During infancy a mother will protect the infant from impingement (excessive stimuli), so that the infant experiences a sense of continuing self without intolerable disruption. Infants need protection from excesses of emotional and physical stimulation. Infants that do not have adequate protection will develop reactions to impingement. (Tomlinson 2004, p.158)

To ensure that the home provides a general sense of calm and stability, careful attention needs to be paid to simple things like noise levels, the types of TV programmes watched, computer games played and magazines around the home.

Choice and participation

It is not the 'magical' creation of a positive environment that is most important, but the way in which the individuals, family and community are also involved in creating the environment – how choices are made and how everyone is involved in that. Clearly, adults in a parental role have to take responsibility for key things, but this can be done wherever possible by involving children in the process, for example, by taking into consideration children's interests, likes and preferences. Perry and Szalavitz (2006, p.70) explain the importance of this for children's development: 'To develop a self one must exercise choice and learn from the consequences of those choices; if the only thing you are taught is to comply, you have little way of knowing what you like and want.'

When one of us worked at the Cotswold Community in the 1980s, the concept of the 'X Factor' emerged (Miller 1986). We lived in what was like a small village with a working farm as our immediate environment. In the days before many of our present health and safety regulations, there were many farm, building and maintenance projects for everyone to get involved in. We noticed the difference it made to the therapeutic climate of a home when people were involved in working together on a shared project or X Factor, compared to times when nothing much was going on. An X Factor creates the opportunity for two or more people to work on a shared external factor. This then helps to reduce the intensity and head-on nature of relationships and can be especially helpful in an environment where relationships tend to become highly emotionally charged. There is also something deeply satisfying in transforming an environment, which can be seen by the popularity of makeover TV programmes. Especially for traumatized children, creating something positive, and mending and rejuvenating things can have a very significant symbolic meaning. As with trauma, something that has been damaged can be repaired. This kind of work is an important component of a child's treatment. And as Best (2009) stated, 'When repairs to the fabric are carried out at once, and as often as it takes, it is a sign of survival and restored hope for the whole community' (p.3).

A therapeutic environment and everything that happens within it can be healing. The importance of this needs to be looked at alongside work that is more to do with verbal communication and talking about a child's problems. Perry and Szalavitz (2006, p.231) support this point of view: 'But while emerging therapeutic models like the neurosequential approach hold great promise, my experience as well as the research suggests that the most important healing experiences in the lives of traumatized children do not occur in therapy itself.' They do occur, they go on to explain, in exactly the situations we have described in this chapter.

PRIVACY AND SECURITY

A starting point for any therapeutic service for traumatized children is that it must provide safety for the children. Only when the children feel safe can they begin to relax, calm their overloaded stress response systems and begin to engage. So, first and foremost, children in out of home care need to be protected from further abuse and exploitation. This standard can be measured by 'the ways that out of home care services implement effective safeguarding children policies and procedures; the number and scope of abuse in care allegations; and the ways in which allegations of abuse in care are identified, investigated and responded to' (Tucci *et al.* 2010). However, the general emotional climate of the home is also a good indicator of how safe the children feel. Often traumatized children pick up the slightest warning sign that there is a potential danger. Rather than talk about this, they display their anxiety through their behaviour. Our attunement to this can help us be aware of anything potentially harmful that may be developing. For instance, one child may be covertly bullying or trying to inappropriately involve another child in sexual activity. As many of the children are so familiar with abuse and exploitation that they think it's normal, we have to continually role model healthy ways of relating to each other, by always treating each other with dignity, respect and appropriate confidentiality. We need to continually demonstrate our expectation that everyone in the home should consider and respect the safety and security of all children and staff and not involve themselves in behaviour likely to endanger others.

Bedrooms as private spaces and sanctuary

Bedrooms are an individual's personal space. They are a place where children and carers can seek time out from the ebb and flow of normal busy family life. We acknowledge that carers' and children's privacy is of the utmost importance in ensuring that all individuals feel comfortable and safe in the home. Particular respect and attention should be paid to entering a child's bedroom. This can be especially important to children who have been abused, with the abuse often taking place in their bedroom. Child abuse inevitably involves the inappropriate breaking of personal boundaries. Creating clear boundaries in this area can help establish, for the child, the sense that he has a personal boundary. This should always be supported and respected by adults, rather than crossed.

Affirming environment

We acknowledge that an individual's bedroom is their personal space. Children have the freedom to decorate their room to their own personal tastes, within a reasonable range of options and a personally selected standard of order and cleanliness. However, in creating and role modelling an appropriate and hygienic environment for children, they may need to be supported in maintaining this in their own environment. The bedroom can be a reflection of one's own internal and external world. The children's environment should be one that is affirming and that promotes a positive sense of self and world view, a sense of safety and love. We encourage the children to have photos of loved ones, images of positive role models, and any other articles that promote this. It is especially important that the room looks very well cared for when the child arrives, to give the message that this is what they deserve. Once the child arrives we should quickly help him settle in. We make sure we help him unpack and personalize his bedroom. We give the clear message that this is a permanent home, rather than somewhere in which he is going to live temporarily out of a bag.

CHAPTER 6

The Holding Environment and Daily Routines

When working with children who have been severely deprived and traumatized, we need to plan each day and week to provide a high level of continuity and consistency. 'I also cannot emphasize enough how important routine and repetition are to recovery. The brain changes in response to patterned, repetitive experiences: the more you repeat something, the more engrained it becomes' (Perry and Szalavitz 2006, p.245).

Traumatized children have often suffered severe deprivation resulting from chaotic and unpredictable environments. It is essential we do everything possible to provide an experience of the consistency, predictability and 'illusion' of stability which they need and have never had enough of. This concept of 'illusion' is related to the way in which parents provide a level of consistency for young children, enabling them to believe that the world is a predictable and secure place. To some degree, this is an illusion that the parent creates for the child, until she has the emotional resources to begin coping with the disillusion, of realizing the more unpredictable and insecure realities of her own life and the world around her. For example, in the USA following 9/11 there was a huge debate in schools, religious and other groups about what to tell young children. Some groups felt strongly that children should not be given much detail, while others felt children needed to know what had happened – obviously taking into account age differences. Whatever the answer to these questions the thoughtfulness involved is something that traumatized children have often never experienced.

Most of the children we work with who may be in their teens have suffered a complete lack of protection from overwhelming experiences. One such example is a two-year-old child witnessing regular violence between her parents. This would have felt overwhelming, traumatic and something the child would not have been able to make sense of. The result would be that the child becomes highly anxious, fearful and hyperaroused and therefore less able to make use of the kind of nurture and nourishment necessary for development. So, these children who may be chronologically much older than an infant need the security of a calm, predictable environment. They need to reduce their states of hyperarousal and enjoy the kind of experiences that are necessary for their recovery. This also gives the child an experience of being cared for in a way that puts her needs first and where the carers manage the environment around her appropriately. Before a child can successfully manage the realities of the external world she needs to internalize the experience of carers doing this for her.

The starting point for each staff team is its resources and how to organize them. This provides a basic structure or framework. The following two principles are important:

1. Have consistency in the numbers, experience and gender of staff working each day. Boys and girls should have as much opportunity as possible to relate to adults of both genders.

2. Minimize the number of staff handovers each day, of management changes and general comings and goings. It is very helpful for the children to know exactly who they can expect to be in the home each day, especially who will be putting them to bed and waking them up. This is something a young child would normally take for granted and not have to worry about. It can be hugely reassuring for traumatized children when this is clear and reliable. At Lighthouse each child has a primary and a secondary carer, who are the only rostered workers in the home. When a carer is on leave, they will have a respite carer that is attached to the home and has regular contact with the children. The child has an established long-term predictable relationship with the carers.

These are just basic structures to do with the day-to-day running of the home. However, they are an essential starting point in providing the children with a reliable sense of who is going to be with them from one day to the next and how changes will be managed. Once children are clear about these basic things, it is then possible to stop worrying about 'who's going to be in today?' or 'who's waking me up?' and to move on to the next level of expectations like 'what's for dinner today?'

ROUTINES, LIMITS AND ANCHOR POINTS

In 1956, John Brown, who had founded the Browndale Community in Canada, for emotionally disturbed children, published a handbook, *Routines, Limits and Anchor Points*. He said it was for the management of the child in the therapeutic family throughout the day. Much of what was written remains essential today, when trying to establish a therapeutic healing environment. We shall draw upon his ideas in this section.

Routines

Every children's home and family home will have its own culture that includes norms and expectations, based around the daily routine. Routines are the way in which the home manages everyday events such as eating, waking and sleeping. A consistent routine is especially important for children as it provides them with a sense of security, knowing what is happening and what to expect. It gives a degree of predictability and reliability to their world. It is also necessary for basic physical health to have regular patterns of eating, sleeping and general hygiene, which in turn supports healthy brain development.

The degree of routine and structure to each day will vary from family to family and the needs of the children. For instance, infants are likely to have a higher level of routine, and more flexibility is built in as children mature. At one end of the spectrum, there is a complete lack of routine which feels chaotic and insecure. At the other end, such rigidity in the daily routine might feel excessively controlling and inhibiting of individual growth. When working with traumatized children we need to strike the right balance. A sense of routine for these children is especially important as they have often lived in chaotic, unpredictable and unsafe environments, which has disrupted their emotional and cognitive development. For recovery to take place, Perry and Szalavitz (2006) argue that the most important ingredients are time and patience, and repetition, repetition, repetition! So for example, it is helpful to have regular times for meals, bedtimes, meetings and so on. For many traumatized and deprived children it may never have been clear when they would next eat, what they would have to eat, what would happen at bedtime and waking up time. So these particular aspects of the routine may have additional anxiety for them. Therefore, if they know as much as possible about what to expect their anxiety levels can be significantly reduced. It is only when the child's anxiety levels are reduced and she feels safe, that she will be able to begin forming attachments with those close to her. van der Kolk, van der Hart and Marmar (2007, p.321) explain the importance of routine for traumatized people who disassociate:

'Since disassociation involves the loss of a continuous sense of time, schedules, regular appointments, and routines are essential. Because fatigue and stress probably exacerbate dissociative episodes, establishing regular sleep-wake cycles, activity-rest schedules, and mealtimes is important.'

Limits

Limits are the rules of the home that must not be crossed, and normally relate to safety. These are non-negotiable and need to be clearly understood by everyone. An example of a limit might be that hitting another is unacceptable. It is possible that limits are quite variable from a cultural point of view. In some ordinary family homes swearing or blaspheming might be considered a limit, whereas in other homes these issues might be dealt with more lightly. Young children and traumatized children need limits to be consistent and easy to understand. This helps them to know where they stand and to feel secure. Hannon *et al.* emphasize the importance of clear and consistent boundaries for positive child development:

> However, as Diana Baumrind (1991) has highlighted, responsiveness is only one-half of the picture; the parenting that contributes best to children's development must combine attachment with 'demandingness', which refers to a parent's ability to impose consistent rules... Empirical studies show that children who were raised by *authoritative* parents consistently had better social skills, a stronger sense of agency, and were more cognitively advanced. (Hannon *et al.* 2010, p.74)

As with routines, traumatized children have often experienced wildly unpredictable limits due to the instability of their parents. An example of this is a small misdemeanour going unnoticed one day and then severely punished the next, depending upon the parent's mood. It is often this kind of experience that causes the child to become hypervigilant, looking for the slightest change in the parent's mood. As we have discussed, these children may also tend to become withdrawn or 'frozen' through fear that anything they do may meet with severe disapproval, punishment or abuse. Stien and Kendall explain the difficulty that can be involved in limit setting and give some useful advice on how we might approach this:

> most abused children need external control to fortify their internal controls. Limits, however, are frightening to them because of fears about being out of control. In their minds, the exercise of parental power usually means abuse and humiliation. If parents are able to communicate empathy for the child's perspective, a traumatized child will be less likely to interpret the limits as

simply a way to dominate and exploit. Thus, empathic limit setting requires a two part statement. In the first part, convey an understanding of the child's feelings to show you are on her side. In the second part, make sure to state the boundary that the child has crossed (Chu 1998). (Stien and Kendall 2004, p.152)

Anchor points

Anchor points are the expectations of how everyday events in the home will be conducted. An example of a routine might be that everyone will have an evening meal together and an anchor point might be that hands will be washed before the meal, or people won't rock backwards on their chairs. Some homes have anchor points around things like wearing dressing gowns at bedtimes or not wearing outdoor shoes in the home. The precise nature of these is not especially important. The important thing is that each home has some anchor points that are understood by everyone. The benefits of anchor points are that they provide a regular opportunity to remind everyone in the home of expectations. They also provide an effective way of gauging children's moods. Certainly in work with children who can be challenging, the first thing to be tested is often an anchor point. So, a little battle takes place about whether the child is going to wash her hands. If this becomes difficult then it is often an indication that there is an underlying problem for the child that needs addressing. The effective use of anchor points allows difficult feelings to be picked up and worked with before they escalate to a child breaking a limit. Sometimes children need their feelings to be noticed and can only do this by being a little challenging. Without everyday anchor points they are more likely to become extreme in their behaviour as a way of seeking attention.

DAILY PROGRAMME

It is important to consider all aspects of daily activities that happen in and out of the home, including the provision of activities that are developmentally appropriate, aimed at building a sense of self-worth, skills and relationships. van der Kolk and Newman state the importance of this in treating trauma:

the first task of treatment is for patients to regain a sense of safety in their bodies. For most individuals, this requires active engagement in challenges that can help them deal with issues of passivity and helplessness: play and exploration, artistic and creative pursuits, and some form of involvement with others. (van der Kolk and Newman 2007, p.18)

Activities can also be chosen that help children to become involved and connected to the local community, hence widening their social networks. Activities should be individual, as well as group focused. An understanding of the child's emotional development and the impact trauma has had on this, will help determine the kind of activity that will be most appropriate for each child.

Children in out of home care need to be supported to positively engage with an education programme and/or school. It is acknowledged that good quality educational experiences and attainments can be especially important for children in achieving positive long-term outcomes. As well as supporting the children with their school work we should also ensure the home environment offers opportunities for learning in a general sense. For many of the children, this needs to be at a level where they are learning things like the sequence and pattern of daily events, how one thing leads to another, as well as the causes and consequences of events in their daily life. Perry and Szalavitz emphasize the importance for traumatized children of learning about cause and effect:

> children who develop severe behavior problems often lack this ability to link cause and effect. The early chaos of their environments doesn't make these connections clear and visible. There are too many anomalies, too many inconsistencies. A child of average or below average intelligence won't be able to learn without constant repetitions. (Perry and Szalavitz 2010, p.153)

USE OF TELEVISION AND COMPUTERS

The use of television and computers is an important part of daily life. Both can be used educationally and for relaxation. Computers in particular offer a wide range of possibilities in terms of play and learning. However, if used excessively both can also be negative, sometimes being used as a way of avoiding relating to others or of completely switching off from the world. Therefore, limits should be set around the time spent watching television and on computers. We also need to ensure there is time for bonding as a 'family', general communication, relationship building, and shared experiences. In role modelling good parenting, we need to be careful not to use television and computers as a form of pacifier, as a way of avoiding the challenging therapeutic work. Managing the use of television is also a way of preventing impingement as it can lead to overstimulation, particularly prior to bedtime.

With the ease of access to inappropriate material on the internet and TV, both also need careful monitoring. Watching a TV programme together is important, so that the carers are tuned into anything the programme might raise for the child. Some TV programmes may provide opportunities to have discussions about a theme that is relevant to the child. Talking about things in this way, about a TV character or theme can feel once removed and easier to talk about, for instance, exploring choices a character has made, why they did something and what else they could have done. Some programmes might be particularly enjoyable to watch together as a group, like a good comedy. This can help to build positive shared experiences. A weekly pattern around TV programmes watched also helps to provide structure to the daily routine and expectations.

FREE TIME

Whilst it is important to create a stimulating home environment with a variety of interesting activities it is also necessary to make sure children have enough time just to be. Too much activity can be used as a way of avoiding feelings by busying ourselves so much we don't have time to feel anything. Children also need time just to relax, do nothing much and have time to spontaneously follow an interest, such as reading, listening to music or chatting. These simple pastimes can be a way for a child to explore, think and gain insights about herself, others and the world around her. As one boy in a therapeutic community put it, when asked by a visitor, 'what do you do all day?' – 'I don't know what we do, but it's a fine place to be in' (Harvey 2006, p.56).

THE IMPORTANCE OF FOOD IN THE HEALING PROCESS

Food represents one of the child's earliest contacts with the external world. It is the activity around which personal relationships first develop and around which they may first break down, with the most dangerous and far-reaching of consequences.

Bettelheim 1950, p.180

Through our therapeutic work with children, mealtimes and food provision gives workers a crucial tool in combating emotional trauma that children may have suffered.

Keenan 2006, p.83

Our first experience of food is normally within the context of a loving relationship with a parent. The baby who is being fed receives the nourishment of milk but ideally far more than that. Some studies have shown that the physical warmth and contact in the earliest feeding experiences are as important as the feeding itself. The 'mother' not only holds and feeds her baby but she is also emotionally attuned at a deep level, responding to small changes in the baby's feelings. The experience of feeling emotionally held in this way and its association with food will help, it is hoped, the young infant to develop a positive relationship with food and feeding – as something satisfying, enjoyable and nourishing. From this positive beginning the infant is then able to become sociable around mealtimes, as she moves from being fed to sitting and feeding herself. Her first family meals, with parents and siblings may become a focal point for the family where they enjoy each other's company. Bettelheim (1950) captured the importance of food in the process of becoming a sociable person, by titling a chapter in his book *Love is not Enough* – 'Food the Great Socializer'.

Rather than associating food with positive experiences, children who have suffered deprivation, trauma and abuse are normally very anxious in relation to food. Their anxieties can range from feeling there won't be enough food for them to a genuine fear that the food might be contaminated or even poisoned. Some children may act very suspiciously of food and eat very little. They may need to feel in control of what they eat and may only be happy to eat very specific foods, until they feel safe enough to try new foods. Other children might always appear to be hungry and eat excessively. This may be related to anxiety and constantly eating as a way of trying to keep difficult feelings at bay or a form of self-soothing. Deprived children and in particular children who have been homeless are used to fending for themselves. This kind of self-provision can make it hard for them to accept food from someone within the context of a relationship or social situation. Some traumatized children may be extremely mistrustful and rejecting of our efforts to provide food. This can be difficult for us to manage as Keenan describes:

> As caring adults, children not eating can cause adults distress, creating an anxious pre-occupation… Like the mother feeling rejected by a child who spits out her milk (McMahon 2003), the worker may feel personally rejected by the child who won't eat the food provided, leading to strong feelings. (Keenan 2006)

In some cases, where it seems that the child may be developing an eating disorder these anxieties are especially challenging. Careful attention does need to be paid to this and whether there are any signs that a child has a specific eating disorder.

As food is so symbolic of early provision and everything that hopefully goes with it, like a parent's love and care for his or her infant, it can become the focal point where feelings about relationships in the present and past are expressed. Food can be perceived by a child to represent our care or lack of care for her. Therefore, a child who accepts food happily from an adult may be conveying a message that she also accepts the relationship with that adult. Conversely, by rejecting or 'rubbishing' the food it can feel like she is rejecting the adult's care. In reality, both scenarios may hide more complex issues and we need to be careful to maintain a thoughtful response. For example, a child may be rejecting the food and hence the adult's care as a form of testing:

> he is trying to breach what he may perceive as the grown-up's caring façade. He will want to get beneath this façade and prove that she shares his perception of himself as worthless and unlovable. Once again the carer needs to develop a kind of 'therapeutic stubbornness' whereby she continues to provide the opportunity for a good experience despite being shown by the child that she is completely hopeless. (Hamil 2004, p.7)

Paradoxically, a child who is behaving like this may be more engaged with the adult than a child who appears to be more readily accepting, but may also have learnt to please adults to protect herself from potential harm and to keep an emotional distance.

Often traumatized children who feel an emotional emptiness are unable to trust anyone to provide for them. They may try to fill this emptiness through comfort eating, or sometimes through delinquent activity where the feelings of excitement replace the feelings of emptiness. However, these attempts by the child to ward off feelings of emptiness are ultimately unsatisfying. They tend to lead to a habitual but ineffective pattern. If a traumatized child begins to form an attachment and to feel safe and secure, she may begin to feel that her needs for nourishment can be met in the context of a caring relationship. At this point the child may become hugely demanding of her carers to fill her emotional gaps. In essence, this is a healthy development but can be misunderstood because it might appear that the child is becoming excessively demanding and 'greedy'. Dockar-Drysdale (1990a, p.82) has talked of how delinquent excitement can be replaced by oral greed, 'part of the therapeutic process is to help the child to find his lost infantile greed, which has been displaced into delinquent excitement.' The key factor is that the greed, which is really a wish to have needs met, takes place in the context of a relationship rather than self-provision, such as mealtimes provided by carers. Though it may be necessary to have some reasonable control over how much the child eats, it is not helpful to respond in a critical or punitive way. Often children who have been deprived expect that their ordinary needs are a burden to their carers. They are used to being punished for expressing any kind of need. As a result they may feel that their needs and desires are 'bad' and 'greedy'. An empathic response would be to recognize that the young person has a genuine need and to ensure this is met by positive and enjoyable experiences around food. As the child begins to realize that the provision is reliable, the feelings of greed normally subside.

Whether our feelings about the child's attitude towards food are to do with eating 'too much' or 'too little', it is likely that we are affected by both the child's own feelings and our experiences in relation to food. On the one hand, the child may be 'projecting' her own feelings about food and everything it entails for her. On the other, as food is an emotionally laden subject for many of us, our own feelings and experiences are stirred up. We may remember being told we were greedy; anxious there wasn't enough food; made to eat food we didn't like; or being criticized for not having good table manners. If we had largely positive experiences we might feel particularly frustrated if the child can't enjoy the food we offer and feel appreciative. Keenan (2006, p.44) wrote about how demanding it can be for us to manage our own anxieties and responses around food, 'As a therapeutic worker, it is vital to be as in touch as possible with our selves so that we can work objectively with the children, not using them to relive our histories.'

The children's attitudes around food and eating habits provide us with valuable insights into their emotional states and their experiences. In therapeutic work with traumatized children, it is particularly important that we recognize both the emotional as well as the physical and nutritional aspects of food. Dockar-Drysdale, in 'The Difference Between Child Care and Therapeutic Management', wrote that,

> The differences between child care and therapeutic involvement are best seen by comparing the two kinds of work within the framework of everyday life. For example, child care workers know a lot about food and just what children need to keep them well, therapeutic workers…, while they are aiming to provide a balanced diet, are tuned into the emotional needs of the child where food is under consideration. (Dockar-Drysdale 1988, p.8)

Whitwell gives an example to illustrate this point:

> a child who has a problem with sharing, linked to an anxiety as to whether there will be enough, could have a negative reaction to a cake being divided into slices. A whole, small cake may be a more complete, emotionally satisfying experience for this child. (Whitwell 2010)

This can also be seen to be what Dockar-Drysdale refers to as a 'complete experience'. She describes the importance of such experiences for traumatized and deprived children:

> Finally, I want to draw our attention to the concept of 'the complete experience' which is important for both child care workers and those who are trying to provide therapeutic management. Deprived children have had endless incomplete or interrupted emotional experiences. People have come and gone in their lives with little realization of the awfulness of this coming and going

for the child. The ordinary devoted mother sees to it that the experiences which she gives her children are complete – with a beginning, a middle and an end. She does this intuitively – it does not have to be thought out. (Dockar-Drysdale 1988, p.12)

The way we provide food for children, whether individually or in a group mealtime is one of the most effective ways we can provide 'complete experiences'.

Meal preparation

This begins with the making of a meal plan and shopping for the food. The way this is done needs careful thought and with as much involvement of the children as possible. A good starting point is to discuss the children's likes and dislikes and to ensure that there are meals that everyone likes on the menu. This way each child will have particular meals they look forward to, which helps on the days when they aren't so enthusiastic about a particular meal. Involving children with food shopping, as well as helping them to feel confident about the food and where it has come from also helps them to learn the practicalities of shopping and creative budgeting.

As we have discussed earlier, it is not just the food that the child takes in for nourishment. Equally important is the emotional care and love that is provided. For children who have not internalized this kind of experience we need to use the opportunity to ensure that food is provided in a caring and thoughtful way. The more care and effort that is put into preparing and cooking a meal the more the child will feel that the food is being provided by someone who cares about her. A quick meal out of a packet provided in an impersonal way will not help the child to feel cared about. This means that time needs to be put aside for cooking, wherever possible using fresh ingredients and making a meal. It will be helpful for children to be able to observe and ideally help in preparing food. Seeing the food that is being used will help reduce anxieties about what might be in the food. It is also a good opportunity to learn about food, develop cooking skills and to experience the pleasure of providing a meal. At Lighthouse we were lucky enough through a partnership to receive cooked meals from a five star reception. It was very successful in terms of reducing the workload for carers. However, we found that it started to have an impact on the development needs of the children to be part of the cooking process and the internalization of the experience of being cared for. We have had to find a balance to ensure that the carers are supported with pre-prepared foods, but also that there are opportunities for carers and children to prepare meals together. This is an important element of family modelled care.

Ideally, carers prepare meals with the involvement of at least one child. Often children will gravitate around the kitchen when a meal is being prepared, observant and curious to see what is happening. Some children may be anxious to see exactly what is going into the meal so they can be sure that it is safe to eat. Where appropriate, carers may support a child in taking responsibility for preparing a meal. It may be one of the ways an older child contributes to the running of the home. This expectation of a child is based upon their stage of development. As discussed earlier, children need to experience being provided for before they are able to do it for others.

Meals prepared for children need to have a high nutritional value. The types of food the children eat will also have an impact on their physical, mental and emotional wellbeing. We need to be sensitive and supportive towards specific needs and preferences, such as those related to culture and religion. Some foods might trigger positive memories while others may be associated with abuse and trauma. One child reacted with panic when simply asked to finish his breakfast as it was time for school. He became out of control with panic and it was difficult to understand why. When we later searched his case history, we found that on an occasion when his mother asked him to finish his breakfast and he didn't, she hit him on the head so severely with a stick that he needed admitting to hospital.

Mealtime

Mealtime is also a setting which permits us to provide children easily and casually with those infantile pleasures they are anxious to receive but afraid to ask for directly.

Bettelheim 1950, p.200

Mealtime is an important aspect of daily life for children and ideally as many of the daily meals as possible should be shared together as a 'family' group. Having set mealtimes adds structure to a child's life and reduces the level of anxiety they experience. Mealtimes are a good opportunity to set clear expectations around behaviour and to create a sociable culture in the home. In terms of predictability, it can be helpful for everyone to have their own place in which they sit for all meals. Being clear about how the food is served will also help. Sometimes if this isn't clear, anxiety can escalate with children worried that they won't get a fair share.

We should consider the kind of things that are discussed at mealtimes. How do we ensure that conversations are positive, interesting and fun? To make the occasion as enjoyable and anxiety free, potentially difficult discussions should also be avoided. Disruptions should also be avoided, such as answering a mobile or sending text messages! How is the table cleared at the end of the meal? Does everyone help together or do children take it in turns to help? It can be seen from these examples, how many anchor points are involved in a mealtime. Not only do these anchor points help to provide the clarity and consistency the children need – they also act as something children may push against or test, which lets us know how they might be feeling before things escalate to a more serious level. Coming together in this way on a daily basis is an excellent way for everyone to connect with each other and be tuned in to the mood of the group.

It is often said in therapeutic residential care that the start of the day is the most important time of the day. The way children are woken and provided with their first meal of the day can often determine how the rest of the day goes. An appetizing breakfast provides a positive incentive at the start of the day. An enjoyable experience will help a child feel nourished physically, socially and emotionally. Through the routine at the start of the day any worries and anxieties a child has can also be picked up on and worked with before they embark on the rest of the day.

Snacks and food in-between mealtimes

As well as the regular mealtime, consideration needs to be given to how snacks are provided. It is normal for children to want a snack between meals. The medical advice on eating would also suggest that eating a little, regularly and often is good for the digestive and metabolic system. However, there are potential problems if this isn't handled thoughtfully. Bettelheim (1950) argues that making food freely available avoids the distraction of feelings of hunger in children. It makes mealtimes a social rather than a purely physical event and symbolizes emotional care for many children. Where food has been a bargaining tool or children have been more generally deprived, they have to experience it as freely given before they can begin to enter into normal relationships with people. Some may need to eat alone with a carer at first because they cannot enjoy a shared meal. Certainly for some children, who may be especially anxious about eating in a group, knowing they can have a snack before or after the meal can help to relieve their anxiety about having something to eat. However, we need to be careful at the same time that we don't reinforce the idea that children can provide everything for themselves. For deprived children, and especially in the case of homeless children, becoming self-sufficient in this way can be a way of avoiding relationships and the need to be reliant on another. One way around this is to make snacks available in-between mealtimes but to expect children to ask an adult if they can have a snack, rather than just help themselves. This can be done in a casual way but it at least connects the provision to an adult in a small way. Dockar-Drysdale (1969, p.63) argues that, 'the food, in my view, should always *be given by somebody*, rather than be collected by the child from the larder.'

Another issue can be the type of snacks that are provided and making sure a balance is kept between making healthy snacks available, such as fruit and less healthy snacks. Patience is needed with this, as many children are only used to eating 'junk food' that is laden with carbohydrates, preservatives and sugars. Making a shift from this type of food and eating to a more balanced diet is not easy due to the addictive nature of 'junk foods'. In some cases, the food a child enjoys may be used as a form of self-soothing. To some extent, this soothing is a substitute for the kind of soothing a child would normally receive from a parent. We can't expect that a child will just be able to give this up. However, as they become attached to a carer and find other ways of feeling soothed they may become less reliant on food for comfort.

Food and individual provision

Where children who have been deprived of the most important and formative provision – that which is provided within the context of a primary attachment relationship, careful consideration should be given to individual experiences connected to food as well as the group experiences. As a child develops an attachment relationship with a carer she will need experiences within this relationship that help to fill some of her developmental gaps. The provision of a special food experience between the child and carer can be especially nurturing and symbolic of the kind of provision she has missed. How this is done can be explored with the child in a casual way. For example, 'maybe there is a special kind of food or drink that you would like me to give you, when we have time together on our own.' At Lighthouse the structured one-to-one time between the primary carer and the child, provides an opportunity for this kind of provision to develop.

It is quite usual when a deprived child is offered this opportunity within a trusting relationship, that she will ask for something that has a quality to it that is similar to the kind of provision of you would provide for a young infant – quite often something that is warm and easy to eat. Dockar-Drysdale (1961) called this adaptation to need and symbolic provision. If this kind of provision is made, because it is symbolic of the very important primary provision that the child either never had or was disrupted before they had had enough, it is essential that the provision is made reliably. Because the provision is symbolic it is especially meaningful and doesn't need to be made all the time.

The important thing is that it is reliably provided by the child's primary carer, for example, on two or three evenings per week (as discussed in the Robert case example on p.95). The experience can go on for as long as the child needs it. Normally when the child has had enough so that she has internalized the experience, she will let the adult know she doesn't need it anymore. The symbolic aspect of this provision is important, in that it symbolically represents early experience rather than acts as a direct substitute. A cup of warm milk with a biscuit dipped in it may be symbolic of early feeding, whereas giving a child a baby's bottle would be a concrete substitute and potentially confusing for the child. It might imply that the child can really be an infant again, rather than she can have experiences that are symbolically reminiscent of being an infant.

Grappling with this issue is very important as severely deprived children cannot progress developmentally without having the kind of experiences they missed as an infant. As Perry and Szalavitz (2006, p.138) have illustrated, 'these children need patterned, repetitive experiences appropriate to their developmental needs, needs that reflect the age at which they'd missed important stimuli or had been traumatized, not their current chronological age.' Similarly, Dockar-Drysdale refers to this as returning to the point of failure:

> Winnicott described this kind of regression as taking the patient back to the point of failure on the part of the mother towards her baby. The patient may now be a fourteen- or fifteen-year-old, a delinquent hero who certainly does not seem to accept *any* provision from us. The point of failure is nearly always somewhere in the course of the first year, so that it is to this crucial period that the adolescent must return. (Dockar-Drysdale 1990a, p.29)

We have discussed how some of these early needs can be met through the provision of food. There are also many opportunities throughout the daily routine, such as the way we end and begin each day.

BEDTIME AND WAKING ROUTINES

For many reasons these times of the day are often particularly difficult for children who have been deprived, traumatized and abused. Night-time means being on your own and many of the children will have little emotional capacity to manage the feelings of separation, the anxieties involved or being left with their own thoughts. In addition, if they were abused, this would often have happened at night-time and their fears and memories may easily be triggered at this time. Mornings and waking require the child to start a new day, when she might feel anxious and worried about the kind of day she can expect. She might not have slept peacefully and it is possible she may have had nightmares.

As we have emphasized, the starting point for reducing the child's anxiety is to provide a calm, consistent and predictable environment. The routines and expectations around bedtimes and waking times need to be especially clear and reliable, for instance, the times for going to bed and waking up, who will put the child to bed and wake her and the details of exactly what happens at these times.

It can work well before bedtime for the group to spend some time together doing something relaxing and enjoyable, like sharing stories around a small supper. The familiarity and sense the whole group has of going through another day together can be reassuring. After finishing the day as a group each child will need individual attention before they settle to sleep. This might include help with making sure they are washed and have cleaned their teeth. The privacy of a bedtime might be a time when the children can enjoy some individual provision and nurture from their carer. Children who are in their teens and who have unmet infantile needs, but at the same time have had to fend for themselves and, in the case of homeless children, literally become 'streetwise', may only feel safe enough to let down their 'tough' exterior when they are away from other children.

Generally, bedtime should be a time for relaxing and not raising difficult issues. However, if the child wants to discuss something so she can resolve it before going to sleep, this can be helpful and she will feel in control as she has chosen to raise the issue rather than having it unexpectedly brought up. Thinking ahead a little to the next day can also be helpful to give a sense of continuity and perhaps make the next day seem manageable. One example is by making sure that clothes are ready for the morning along with anything the child might need for school. The carers should become attuned to the specific way each child likes things to be done at these times. This is another way of making adaptation to individual needs and doing things in a child centred rather than impersonal way. It can make a huge difference to how the child feels cared for, understood and valued. On a basic level, clear and enjoyable bedtime and waking routines that enable a child to sleep are especially helpful to traumatized children, because being rested is strongly associated with reducing stress throughout the day. Children who are rested, like all of us, are less reactive to potentially stressful triggers.

PLAY

The daily routine must allow the space and time for children to play. Some of the play will be structured and organized but there also needs to be free time for spontaneous play. Deprived and traumatized children will have missed many of the normal developmental play experiences. The opportunity to play, and fill some of the gaps in this way is particularly important. To understand the type of experience a child might need, first of all we need to understand the role of play in normal child development.

Play has been referred to as children's work. On the one hand, we do not think of play as work, but for children it is the way they form relationships, work things out, learn and develop skills. Starting with infancy, a baby learns to play through the interactions with the mother and other carers. To start with this is a simple kind of play: making baby noises and getting a similar response back, playing with an object, giving it and taking it back, dropping something for it to be picked up and dropped again! We are familiar with this type of play and we know the baby's smile of delight as we engage with the play. This play has a kind of rhythm to it and the baby's carer is attuned to the baby, mirroring her gestures. The baby is learning about a reciprocal playful relationship, where both contribute to the enjoyment.

Playful routines develop between the carer around daily activities such as feeding and nappy changes. Through this play the baby is also learning about herself, what she likes and enjoys and what she doesn't. As the baby develops and the attachment between the baby and carer feels secure, the baby or young infant begins to play on her own. Winnicott (1958) refers to this stage of development as the 'capacity to play alone in the presence of another'. The infant will enjoy playing with her carer but now has an interest in exploring and trying things out for herself. She might feel curious about different things she sees around her. As the infant becomes mobile, she moves around to pick up various objects, look at them, see what they can do, and so on. She is learning about the quality of things and how they work. Normally, at this stage there is also plenty of teaching from the carer, about how things work, what is safe and what isn't. The infant will be provided with toys that are designed to stimulate her interest and development. Often these toys show cause and effect – press this and see what noise it makes, shake this and see what happens, see how these bits fit together.

By the age of two to three the infant has normally had a rich experience of play and has learnt a great deal. The brain develops most rapidly at this age. Her experiences will be internalized and this forms her 'inner world'. The inner world consists of the infant's experiences, relationships and feelings. Her inner world is organized unconsciously and symbolically. So, a symbolic object will be associated with a particular experience. For example, a monster might represent bad feelings and a teddy might be symbolic of the carer's nurture. Often an infant will use an object, such as a teddy, to help her manage feelings of separation during the temporary absence of the carer.

She will use the object in the temporary absence of the carer. The carer is out of the room for a short period and the infant holds on to the object, which symbolically represents the carer. An object used in this way is a 'transitional object' (Winnicott 1953). It is invested with meaning by both the infant and the carer and it acts as something that is between them. The carer will know how important this object is and if it is lost temporarily, we know how upset and distressed an infant can feel.

As the infant's inner world develops she begins to play in a symbolic way – organizing toys like play figures and animals, acting out various scenarios. If this type of play is observed closely it can be seen that the infant is often completely absorbed and busy working something out. She might be trying to resolve something that is difficult or replaying a pleasurable experience. At the same stage of development she might also enjoy playing more complex games, where she has to make something and master new skills. As the infant develops into a young child she is increasingly able to play at a complex level and to involve a variety of other people in this, such as siblings and other young children. The play becomes a social event where the child is learning about making relationships, sharing, taking turns, negotiating and compromising. There are often many tears at this stage as the child experiences some of the challenges involved. In a healthy environment the carer allows the child to experience some of the difficulties but doesn't allow things to become too overwhelming. The carer allows the child to experience at the right pace, offering support and guidance, and helping the child to learn and think about things.

As the young child begins school she will learn to play in large groups in a structured way, like team games and sports. This type of play will have an emphasis on rules, expectations and playing together. In this situation, she is learning about play in a wider social context and this continues throughout the school years. Increasingly, the child is learning to master new skills and test herself in a social context, learning what she is capable of.

One of the challenges in a residential care setting is how to provide a range of opportunities for play that meet the various developmental needs we have described. This is especially so with teenage children who have developed a defensive stance, sometimes as a way of coping with the hurt of what they have lost before they had had enough. They might be disparaging towards their more infantile needs in general, perhaps referring to such needs as babyish. Allowing the fulfilment of their needs involves the risk of being vulnerable, hurt and rejected.

To create opportunities for play, the culture of the home needs to be a playful one and this begins with the carers. If the carers adopt a playful attitude in their day-to-day interactions, this will help the children to relax and enjoy playful relationships. After a while it will give them the message that it is OK to play. A playful attitude is one that encourages relationships to be fun and acknowledges the children's interests and personalities in an affirming way. This encourages the use of imagination. To do this the carers need to feel comfortable playing. This may be one of the most important qualities for a carer. Can they get alongside a child and play? Can they allow themselves to feel a little childish? For instance, some carers are excellent with messy play and join in with it enthusiastically, while others might feel inhibited and anxious about the mess. It doesn't matter that every carer is comfortable with all types of play, but it is important to find some area of play that can be enjoyed with the children. If carers have a playful attitude, many spontaneous opportunities can be found with the children, and an abundance of play materials and games is not necessary. Too many play things around may even be intimidating and too much for the children.

CASE EXAMPLE: EMMA

One group of four girls we were working with, between the ages of sixteen and seventeen had experienced much deprivation in their lives and had a great need for early nurturing experiences. We worked on building some of this into one-to-one times with their carers, such as by providing the kind of bedtime experiences we have discussed earlier. However, the general home environment felt a bit cold and not facilitating of play. Picking up on some comments from the girls that there was nothing to do in the house, we discussed if there were any kind of toys they would like that we didn't have. In exploring this it was clear that some of the girls were worried about appearing babyish and one girl, Emma, who was more keen on the idea soon dropped it to keep face.

As a care team, we felt strongly there was a need for play and we needed to be creative in how to provide for it. The girls generally enjoyed their bath times, so we decided to get some bath toys and just put them in the bathroom. When this was done, Emma immediately noticed and asked what we had put them in there for. We said that the bathroom seemed a bit empty and we thought it would be nice – we didn't expect that all the girls would be interested but it helped to brighten things up. The next day Emma suggested she would like to choose a few more bath toys, rubber ducks and other squeezy toys. She said she was looking forward to her next bath and asked her carer if she would mind sitting outside the bathroom and read her a story while she had a bath. Given Emma's age this was as close she could get to enjoying a nurturing kind of bathing experience – she played with the toys and her carer read to her. It was clear by her excitement and pleasure in this experience and the way she involved her carer that it met an important need, and was symbolic of experiences she had missed.

To provide these types of opportunity the carers need to be able to recognize the children's needs, give positive messages about play and some materials and toys should be available that can be used playfully. There is also the need for the organization to have an understanding of the psychosocial development of traumatized children, and to not judge this behaviour as being inappropriate due to the chronological age of the child. Training and supervision must ensure that the workers are supported in understanding and meeting the developmental needs of the children.

Some types of play that have an infantile quality to them, like messy play with clay, also have a more universal appeal associated with art and creativity. These can also be excellent ways of meeting some of the earlier needs in a way that is non-threatening. Other types of play, including music, building and making things, can meet a variety of needs including the development of new skills. This can help a child to develop a stronger identity and self-esteem. Some of these activities might also include a strong social aspect, for example playing a piece of music or making something together.

Recreational activities

These can be a great way of providing children with respite from dealing with their day-to-day issues. It can be a mistake to assume that talking about difficulties is always the only or the best way to improve how a child feels. Taking part in an activity that gives an opportunity for physical mastery can be very restorative and help to balance negative emotional feelings. We know ourselves through the satisfaction we might gain from such activities as walking together, gardening, building something and playing sport. After these experiences we often feel rejuvenated and ready to tackle something that might be emotionally challenging. Research in recent years has shown how exercise also increases the flow of various chemicals and hormones in the body, such as endorphins, which enhance our sense of wellbeing and alleviate the build-up of depressive feelings.

Sharing positive enjoyable experiences together is an excellent way to foster connections between children. It can provide a solid basis for relationship development. Activities like group outings, sporting games, indoor games, birthday celebrations, watching each other's performances can greatly facilitate a sense of belonging, identity and normality to a child's life. These activities can also provide an opportunity to develop networks with the wider community, and help address a child's social isolation.

Common goal (team building) activities

Group activities and team building activities that see children working together towards a common goal can greatly enhance relationships and create connections between children. Overcoming challenges and solving problems together help counteract the experience of an isolating and antagonistic world where 'everyone is against me', by creating an experience of collaboration, cooperation and shared success (as with the X Factor, described on p.144). When engaging in common goal activities it is helpful that: children have the opportunity to rely on each other; each child feels that his or her opinions and contributions are valued; each child has a role to play; and that a safe environment exists where children feel comfortable sharing ideas, taking risks and making mistakes. It is also important that the child is developmentally able to be involved in this type of play, as the possibility of not being able to keep up with the other children can raise feelings of failure and rejection.

Community activities

Where an organization has a number of homes, this can provide opportunities for similar types of recreational group opportunities that might take place in a school, for instance competing against another home in a sporting game or other recreational activity. This can be an effective way to create a sense of identity and belonging to a child's home and also the wider organization. Children competing on behalf of their home can also imbue a feeling of pride and responsibility in representing their home. All children should be given an opportunity to participate in such activities regardless of their skills and good 'sportsmanship' should consistently be encouraged. Competitions may be ad hoc, such as a game of backyard cricket, or more formalized competitions between homes with prizes for the winning home.

Other cultural events can also be an opportunity for the wider group to come together and share a positive experience – a celebration, or a musical or theatrical performance. The nature of these will vary according to the particular cultural context and the way the organization builds its own culture. It can be particularly helpful for many traumatized children to have events that are associated with the yearly calendar and seasons. These events help to provide a marker that breaks the year into manageable time periods, and also reminds them of the length of their involvement in the programme. As adults we can recall childhood memories of how special times of the year and things we did were associated with the seasons. Living in a multi-cultural society provides an increasingly wide variety of opportunities for cultural development. It can also be a fun and educational way of learning about other cultures and customs. For children that have developed polarized thinking as a defence mechanism it can also be a way of starting to see the grey areas.

CELEBRATIONS AS A SENSE OF BELONGING

Celebrations are a significant component of a child's experience. Many traumatized children have had limited positive experiences of celebrating events such as birthdays or Christmas. In some cases, their experiences will have been especially negative. We promote the view that 'life is to be celebrated' and recommend celebrations wherever possible. Whether it is a child passing an exam or going to school consistently for a month, we encourage the celebration of all children's milestones and achievements. The sense of being valued and affirmed in this way is hugely beneficial for children who have received so much devaluing of their self-worth. For events such as birthday and Christmas, we make sure that as many children as possible celebrate together.

Whilst this is a worthy aim, we need to understand that children who have such low self-esteem and who have suffered so much rejection, may not always respond positively to our efforts to celebrate their achievements, birthdays and cultural events. The child may feel that she is undeserving of positive acknowledgements and may react negatively to spoil our efforts. The new experience of being valued might raise difficult feelings about her past experiences. If she accepts our appreciation of her she may fear that this will only lead to further rejection at some point in the future. Allowing herself to trust that adults can really care for and value her will raise anxiety about being let down again. We need to be thoughtful about how we introduce celebrations into their lives, so that we can contain the associated anxieties.

Christmas

Whilst we are writing about Christmas, because it is part of our own cultural experience, the issues we refer to may also apply to other cultural celebrations. Christmas can be a particularly distressing time for children who have come from backgrounds of deprivation, abuse and trauma. The mere fact of living in care is a painful reminder that they don't have a birth family they can be with, at a time of year where there are so many messages about the positive aspects of families sharing special times together. In addition, our own emotions and feelings about these times will also be raised and be part of the emotional mix.

CARER'S REFLECTIVE CASE DIARY

At the beginning of December a number of children talked of being abused at Christmas, of family conflict and having presents taken off them as a punishment. Although it seemed important to explain a number of times what would happen here, this seemed to have little effect on some of them. I found myself very preoccupied with the children I look after and trying to understand their feelings about Christmas. David couldn't openly respond in a positive way to anything I gave him. After continually acting out these feelings by ignoring or rejecting my efforts, it was quite a relief when he eventually muttered to me that he 'didn't like Christmas'. The emphasis in our team meetings had been to do with thinking about our feelings connected with Christmas, trying to understand the children's feelings and attempting to respond appropriately to these feelings. The idea of providing a 'good experience' is still relevant but not so prominent. This reduces the pressure on us to ensure a good experience, perhaps allowing more space for empathy to develop. For instance, Daniel said he hated Christmas and that his present was rubbish. The next day he was enjoying playing with his present. Tony also needed to 'rubbish' his present and for this to be accepted before he could enjoy it. It can be easy for us to expect a child to be thankful, especially after all of the effort and thought we have put in. It can feel very hurtful in a way that feels quite personal when a child doesn't respond as we would wish.

The essential thing seemed to be to contain enough of our own and children's anxieties to enable us to provide a good Christmas. I think we did this. Hopefully the children's experience this year will enable them to feel a bit more 'Christmassy' next year. This is similar to providing Christmas for toddlers – the excited anticipation and Christmassy feeling can only come when they have experienced a good Christmas. Before that, adults provide all the enthusiasm. That is very difficult when the children not only 'have not' experienced, but have had awful experiences.

At our Christmas meal I don't think the adults felt too anxious about how much would be eaten. If children feel they need to eat to make us feel good, I'm sure that tension could cause considerable problems. As it turned out the whole experience was really positive and in some ways surprised me. Maybe surprises are important in this work. Important changes or happenings are often ones where we surprise ourselves, or which come unexpectedly. Perhaps the endless hard work, wondering if you are getting anywhere, is what enables this to happen.

CHAPTER 7

The Organization and Community

Recovery from injuries perpetrated in a social context must occur in a social context. These centers, responsible for healing, must become therapeutic communities where recovering is more important than control, and compassion and empathy drive out fear and coercion.

Farragher and Yanosy 2005, p.100

Abuse and neglect suffered by children occurs within the context of a social environment. Even when the abuse is largely carried out by one person, it is often a symptom of dysfunctional dynamics within the family system and sometimes the wider community. For example, abuse perpetrated by one person may be condoned or colluded with by others. Though a child may have suffered abuse primarily from a parent, the fact that no one within the family, the extended family or the wider community prevented it, means the child will have experienced the environment as a whole to have failed them. As a result, they will not only be fearful of any individual's capacity to take care of and protect them, but also of the whole environment. The internalization by the child of the dysfunctional system is especially damaging for their future roles and relationships with others, whether within close relationships, families, employment or society.

Therapeutic communities were developed to create the possibility of a healthy and functional rather than dysfunctional system. The belief was that this could then be internalized over time, by everyone in it, leading to personal growth, development and the modification of previous internalized models. As a reflection of the emphasis on the whole organization or community in the healing process, the phrase 'organization as therapist' is sometimes used. As Bloom (2003, p.7) argues,

Creating a safe social environment requires a shift in perspective away from viewing only the individual, towards viewing the individual-in-context. In doing so, the entire community serves as a model of 'organisation as therapist' (Whitwell, 1998[a]) so that all of the chaotic, impulsive, and painful feelings of the members can be safely contained and defused.

This means that the whole organization, as in a healthy family and community, needs to be attuned to the needs of the children and the role everyone plays in supporting their development.

For instance, a child may be settling into a new home and getting to know the carers. As things progress, the child is likely to challenge and test those closest to him. Therefore, the team working with the child are all involved in responding to this, to ensure that any developing attachments for the child take place within a safe and emotionally containing environment. The child will test the team's capacity to work in a safe, effective and reliable way. Traumatized children are familiar with chaotic, fragmented and conflict-ridden environments and they will try to recreate this dynamic amongst the team. 'Splitting' is common, where the child plays one team member off against another, by treating one carer as if she is useless and 'bad' and another as if she is wonderful and 'good'. The reality of working with this behaviour is hugely challenging on an emotional level for everyone in the team. There is a strong likelihood that team members begin to take on aspects of the role the child has given them. Therefore, it is essential that the care team's work is understood and supported by the organization as a whole. This may happen in the form of supervision, consultancy, training and practical support. The team will need supervisory help, both on an individual and group level, on making sense of the children's behaviour; training which helps to make links about the impact of trauma on child development, as well as on the therapeutic approach; and practical support to help keep on top of things in general. This might involve all departments of the organization, such as human resources, marketing and fundraising, finance and maintenance. If the staff in these departments don't understand the complexity of the therapeutic task, it can lead to a judgmental attitude and a frustration as to why the carers are not managing things better. This is likely to be unhelpful for the children and will exacerbate the carers' feelings of being inadequate and failing, leading to further isolation and demoralization.

THE LANGUAGE OF THE ORGANIZATION

The trauma of the children will have an impact on everyone in the organization, both directly and indirectly, and everyone will have an emotional response to this. In the same way, everyone's response will have an impact on the children, directly or indirectly. The organization as a whole provides a therapeutic milieu, which is about recovery from trauma. As Bloom (2003, p.13) explains, 'This means that every member of the staff and patient community plays a role in creating or failing to create a non-violent, health-promoting atmosphere.' Therefore, it is important for the organization to have a shared language and understanding related to trauma.

> Armed with the words to describe the behaviors they were seeing and a greater understanding of their own responses, staff were better able to communicate with each other and with the children. With everyone using the same words and concepts, it becomes easier to talk about problems and formulate solutions, rather than blame each other for bad outcomes or ignore them altogether. All members of the milieu are on a level playing field and all understand what we are trying to accomplish together. (Farragher and Yanosy 2005, p.101)

The language of the organization needs to be embedded within a trauma-informed culture. Bennington-Davis and Murphy describe their experience of establishing a trauma-informed culture:

> The cornerstone of our cultural change was being trauma-informed: understanding the prevalence of trauma in the lives of the people we served, the neurobiology of young exposure to trauma, and the subsequent way these folks perceive their surroundings, and in turn, how staff react to these features. Staff members used to interpret the things we saw – aggression, power struggles, disengagement, catastrophic reactions – as people being contrary, manipulative, threatening, and predatory. With the lens of trauma information, we learned that these characteristics are in fact important survival tools. (We also learned a lot about how language and vocabulary influenced our thinking!) The lens of trauma information, in other words, changed all of our basic assumptions about those we were serving, and led us to the conviction that a change in the environment and in ourselves could produce a change in behavior. We figured out that we could use the environment itself (both the physical and the social environment) to help people remain physiologically calm, to avoid triggering the survival mechanism, and to keep people's brains engaged in complex thinking and problem solving. But first we had to work on Recovery for staff! Changing practices required a leap of faith – and that required an optimism and belief in recovery that wasn't necessarily present when we began. (Bennington-Davis and Murphy 2005)

Whilst the language of the organization needs to be trauma-informed, the specific detail of the language and how it is used will emerge out of the organization's own process. This is because there are often many different professional disciplines involved in the work – carers, therapists, youth workers, social workers, psychologists and teachers. In addition, other workers in the organization often have a supportive role. It is necessary for everyone to have some understanding of trauma, its impact on children's development and what is involved in the recovery process. If the organization doesn't create its own language, the language of one particular discipline tends to rise to the top of the hierarchy. This puts staff who have not had training in that discipline at a disadvantage and it often puts the staff from that discipline in a 'pseudo' leadership role. The language can also become overtechnical in a way that can be alienating, mystifying and exclusive, which can lead to a rivalrous attitude between different disciplines. Bloom (2005, p.68) refers to the importance of this: 'The accessible language demystifies what sometimes is seen as confusing and even insulting clinical or psychological aspects of pathological adjustment that pose the greatest problems for any treatment environment.'

The organization needs to have a clear understanding of child development, trauma and recovery. Clearly, there are theoretical variations on these themes; therefore a consensus of the core theoretical foundations, organizational beliefs and therapeutic approaches needs to be agreed. Once the underpinning theory has been mapped out, it needs converting into straightforward language that is understandable to everyone. This can then be incorporated into training, daily interactions, supervision and other processes. It can be particularly helpful in establishing a common language, to have a process that is central to the work with children and which involves the different disciplines. One such example is a child assessment process that is underpinned by theory, but designed using straightforward language and which can be used by carers, therapists and other disciplines (Tomlinson and Philpot 2008). This helps everyone to practise using the shared language on a regular basis until it becomes engrained into the organization's culture.

Another important element of having straightforward and child-centred language is that it provides a different experience for young people who may be used to institutionalized language that can inhibit the recovery process. At Lighthouse we ensure that the language used is consistent with that of a family environment. We don't use words such as clients or patients when we talk about children, and when talking about the home, we don't use terms such as units. These are just a few examples of the importance of language in promoting a sense of home and belonging. In some ways the recovery process for children is a process of de-institutionalization.

TRAUMA RE-ENACTMENT AND ITS IMPACT ON THE ORGANIZATION

As Bloom states,

> Traumatic events – and chronic stress – can produce a similar impact on organizations. Without intending to do so, without recognizing that it has happened, entire systems can become 'trauma–organized'. A traumatized organization, like a traumatized person, tends to repeat patterns of behavior in a way that prevents learning, growing, and changing (Bentovim 1992). And like individual trauma survivors, systems find it very difficult to see their own patterns. They resist the pain it takes to grow and change, to thaw their frozen parts and reclaim movement. (Bloom 2005, p.63)

For the organization to be effective in its work of enabling traumatized children to recover, it needs to be especially aware of the way in which trauma tends to be re-enacted. Traumatized children will try to create re-enactments of their experiences for various reasons. One simple reason is that it is familiar to them, and therefore reassuring in some way even though the consequences can be destructive. These children are especially fearful of change. Even though we are trying to provide a healthy environment for them, it is new and unfamiliar, and therefore potentially threatening. A traumatized child may feel that a return to a chaotic and abusive environment is inevitable, so rather than wait for it to happen he takes control and tries to provoke it to make things feel more predictable. On the other hand, if the child is able to identify the new environment as potentially positive and hopeful, this will then raise anxieties about being let down and rejected. The child will challenge, test and attack the new environment to see how reliable and trustworthy it is.

Another more benign reason why the children will create re-enactments is as an attempt to resolve their specific traumatic experiences. A child who has been traumatized may feel compelled to act out continuously the trauma with those around him, as an attempt to find a better outcome. The child may not be able to put his experience into words or to play in a way which can work things out symbolically. Particularly when the trauma occurred at a pre-verbal stage of development, he may only be able to act things out in a very literal way, by using other people as 'players' in the traumatic scenario. It is as if a 'script' is developed, and the actors or players may take on the role of 'objects' from the past, such as father, mother or brother. These can be 'good' or 'bad' objects. By reliving the trauma through this script in the present, the past traumatic experience can be recreated, and different outcomes can potentially be achieved, or in the worst scenario reinforced. Lindy (2007, p.526) describes how the child's re-enactment can be a positive process when it happens within the context of a safe therapeutic relationship: 'usually it is only gradually that reenactment becomes amenable to the therapeutic process, as a therapeutic alliance develops and as the treatment becomes a secure enough holding environment for the trauma to be expressed and worked on within the alliance.'

Whilst we need to be careful not to get caught up in a re-enactment to the point that we literally take on and act out a negative role, to some degree it is inevitable that we do get 'caught up'. This is due to the unconscious and powerful processes at work. The important thing is that we maintain the capacity to observe ourselves and reflect on the positions we find ourselves in. In this way we are able to gain insights into the roles we are unconsciously being asked by a child to take on and how this is related to their past experiences. When we are unable to do this directly in a situation with a child, this becomes a crucial feature of supervision. As Ruch argues,

> What makes it complicated is that because these patterns develop unconsciously, we are not likely to be aware of them as they are happening, although we may be able to make them more 'visible' through later reflection or supervision – which is one reason why supervision is important. (Ruch 2010, p.35)

In a similar way, the supervisor uses her own feelings during the supervision process to gain insight into what may be happening for the supervisee in her work. Mattinson (1970) refers to this as 'mirroring', whereby the dynamics taking place in the supervisee's work are played out or mirrored in supervision. So, a supervisor who finds herself feeling irritated with the supervisee may be experiencing unconscious feelings that the supervisee has towards someone he is working with. From this example, it is easy to see how the child's trauma first of all impacts on those directly working with him, followed by those who are indirectly involved and then potentially the wider organization.

Trauma-informed theories on working with traumatized children can be seen to have an emphasis in the following descending order – the impact of trauma on the children, the impact through vicarious trauma on those who work with them, and finally the impact on the organization that provides the service. Farragher and Yanosy highlight the potential implications of this:

> It is our assumption that readers have had at least some orientation to trauma theory and the impact trauma has on children. What might be less common knowledge, however, is the impact trauma has on every level of the organization and why organizations that fail to grapple with this issue do so at their own peril. (Farragher and Yanosy 2005, p.94)

The difficulties facing the organization as a whole can often be underestimated. As a result, the organization may fail to put in place the measures and processes we have described above, that are necessary to support and sustain the work.

MANAGEMENT AND THE THERAPEUTIC TASK

As well as establishing appropriate processes and structures, the management of the organization is also about creating and leading a culture that runs through the organization – one that influences the way everyone thinks and works together on a day-to-day basis. Processes and therapeutic approaches, however sophisticated, will be of limited value unless they are embedded within a culture that reflects their core aims and values. Within this culture, thoughtfulness and communication are central. 'The culture must be an open one, where within appropriate boundaries communication and thinking is encouraged rather than censured or dismissed' (Tomlinson 2005, p.51). A culture that encourages, thoughtfulness will support the work taking place with the children. As Lanyado highlights,

> There is a danger when working with disturbed children not to hold onto the 'thinking' part of containing anxieties. Thoughtful communication between the team members supports them in their emotional experience of a child and enables them to think about this in a way which moderates the anxieties raised. The staff are doing the work on themselves in order to feedback a more coherent and digestible response to the children. (Lanyado 1988, p.46)

For open communication to take place, boundaries need to be clear, consistent and reliable. There are two key reasons for this – clear boundaries enable everyone to know: (1) where they stand, how things work and what is expected. This reduces anxiety and distraction and enables everyone to focus on the therapeutic work in hand; (2) where the appropriate place is to communicate about various issues and concerns.

Without this clarity there is tendency for feelings to spill out in various forums, in a way which takes the work off task. On the one hand, clarity of purpose and task can reduce anxiety and provide emotional security. On the other, there needs to be the opportunity for anxieties to be communicated. It is important that organizations provide the meeting spaces for team members to work through the emotionality of the work. Even when a meeting is task focused, there also needs to be the opportunity for emotional processing. Without this the task focus can be easily taken over by repressed emotions associated with the work. This can result in team members presenting with primitive defence mechanisms that derail any form of constructive work. The success of 'operations' depends upon the emotional wellbeing of team members.

Bion (1962) has described how, when a group of people are working together on a specific task, there are parallel conscious and unconscious processes within the group. Consciously the group may be focused on the task and applying their skills and abilities to achieve successful outcomes. Bion refers to this as the 'work group'. At the same time, there will be unconscious processes related to the anxieties inherent in the task. If the anxieties become overwhelming, the work group will struggle to keep focused on the task and may regress, to what Bion calls the 'basic assumption' group. The basic assumption group attempts to find solutions to the problem, based on the unconscious defence mechanisms of fight/flight, dependency and pairing. The group gives up on finding rational solutions based in reality, and increasingly becomes focused on its own dynamics as a way of relieving itself of primitive anxiety. In the fight/flight mode the group may perceive an external threat, which needs to be fought or defended against; in the dependency mode the group looks for an omnipotent leader who will solve everything and save it; and in the pairing mode the group wishes for a couple who will magically produce the answers.

These unconscious solutions are disconnected from reality and are likely to lead to a spiral of further difficulties, higher levels of anxiety, and increasingly desperate dynamics. The more primitive and extreme the anxieties involved in the task of the work group, the greater the likelihood that the group will slip into a basic assumption mode. This cannot necessarily always be prevented, though clarity of task and boundaries, and an awareness of this tendency, will help identify when a group is regressing into this mode of functioning. This can then be seen as a symptom and something to be worked on, to uncover the possible underlying causes – lack of task clarity, leadership problems, anxieties that are not being communicated and processed. Traumatized children have often experienced multiple failures in efforts to help them, so the task can feel almost beyond rational human effort. Coupled with this, the responsibility involved in the work and the consequences of further failure can be so overwhelming, it is no wonder that those involved can become particularly prone to unconsciously wishing for 'magical' solutions or quick fixes.

For the organization to stay on task, clear management and leadership are essential. As Whitwell (2009) stated, 'Therapeutic communities need to have leaders who are clear about the primary task and are knowledgeable about therapeutic work with emotionally disturbed children' (p.3).

Achieving the appropriate level of clarity is one of the biggest challenges for organizations working with traumatized children. There is a danger that management and therapy are perceived to be in conflict with each other, rather than two complementary aspects of the treatment environment for children. Children who have been traumatized from an early age need an environment that is well managed and emotionally containing. This is in the same way as an infant needs appropriate handling, as well as attunement to his emotions. At times, effective management can also be the most therapeutic intervention. As Menzies Lyth (1979) has stated, it is possible to have management without therapy, but not therapy without management. Management includes safety, boundaries and all aspects of the organizational structure. Without these conditions, traumatized children will not be able to make use of therapeutic work. Feelings of insecurity, anxiety and mistrust are likely to be overwhelming.

In a similar way, there is sometimes a split between 'business' and care. This is characterized by carers perceiving senior managers to only be concerned with the business and financial side of things and not caring enough about the children. Senior managers, on the other hand, perceive carers to have unrealistic expectations of what can be provided and not understanding the importance of the business. In a well run organization both are compatible and integral to the task of the organization. Without good quality care and sound business management the organization will not be viable in the long term. The challenge is how we make the best use of our resources within the limits that we are working in. The way this is managed and getting the balance right, potentially serves as an excellent role model for children who in the future will need to make the best of things within the reality of limited resources. A culture where those responsible for managing children's homes are given the authority to manage budgets and make decisions can help prevent this split from developing. As far as possible, the running of the home should reflect a typical family situation, with carers having the same kind of responsibility that parents have. It is also vital that those responsible for the business management of the organization have an understanding of the challenges of managing a home.

Parents with an infant strike a balance between attending to the management of the environment and focusing on the infant's emotional/physical state. Keenan (2006, p.33) refers to Winnicott's conceptualization of these two functions that are both necessary to 'hold' the child:

> The object-mother is the mother as the object of her infant's desires, the one who can satisfy the baby's needs... The environment mother is the mother in the role of 'the person who wards off the unpredictable and who actively provides care in handling and in general management' (Jacobs 1995, p.49). (Keenan 2006, p.33)

Sometimes the parent may become so caught up with the infant on an emotional level that other issues are neglected, such as shopping, housework, paying bills. At other times the parent may be so busy with these things that the infant's emotional cues aren't noticed. Holding the two together is a challenge that ebbs and flows, and unless things become extreme in one way or another, the overall experience for the infant will be 'good enough'. From this example, it can be seen how all these aspects of the infant's environment are connected to his overall sense of wellbeing. It would be no use to have emotional needs met within the context of an environment that is not being well managed. The consequences of the lack of management would soon lead to a deterioration that would cause stress for the parents and potential hazards in the environment, which would impact negatively on the infant. The same applies in organizations and it could be argued that effective management provides the container in which therapy can take place.

Central to the challenges involved in achieving a healthy balance is the way anxieties are managed. At times, anxiety related to both the work with children and managing the environment can become overwhelming. For instance, the children's needs and demands may be extreme and other pressures like the need to keep up with day-to-day tasks can also be challenging. Rather than try to hold both together, a defensive solution may be to see them as 'either/or' options, focusing on one and ignoring the other. For example, ensuring a home is run perfectly can be a way of avoiding anxieties related to the work with children. Focusing entirely on the children can be a way of avoiding management responsibilities. The two become polarized and a split between management and therapy or care can develop.

Keeping the management of the organization on task with clear boundaries is by its very nature hugely difficult – partly because it keeps everyone in touch with the trauma we are working with. As described, appropriately clear management can be perceived to be harsh and abusive. When we are working with children who have been traumatized by abuse, and in particular sexual abuse, being clear about things is often responded to as if it is abusive. Boundaries and roles in abusive scenarios are muddled and blurred – who is the adult and who the child? Therefore, in our work situation, an adult who is clear about her boundaries and stays appropriately in role is facing the abused child with the reality, that what happened was inappropriate. There is likely to be huge pressure to muddle this reality and blur boundaries. This will come from the children, those working directly with them, the organization, children's workers, parents and others, as the reality of abuse is painful with ramifications for everyone involved. This pressure will continually push itself into the organization so that, at all levels, there will be a tendency for things to become unclear and muddled (Tomlinson 2005). Menzies Lyth (1979) also points out how there is a specific danger in the caring organizations that systems, and particularly the managerial structure, become excessively infiltrated by attitudes and behaviour derived from professional attitudes to therapy. So, for various reasons there is the possibility of management and boundaries becoming unclear.

There is also the possibility that management and boundaries become excessively rigid and inflexible. As Farragher and Yanosy argue,

> Leaders in residential centers become extremely risk aversive. In most cases they are operating in or near the financial margins, and one bad incident or unflattering newspaper exposé can push an already challenged system over the edge. The stress caused by troubled and sometimes scary children on one end and a threatening and hostile financial and political environment on the other generates consistently high levels of stress. Systems that are this stressed respond in much the same way as the traumatized children they treat. They become reactive, overly controlling, fragmented, rigid, hypervigilant and helpless. The treatment center often becomes less about treatment and recovery and more about control and coercion. The facility slowly becomes more concerned about self-preservation than about actually accomplishing its stated mission. (Farragher and Yanosy 2005, p.99)

The dilemmas that we have discussed, in maintaining a healthy balance between openness and flexibility, and clarity and structure, can be said to exist in any ordinary family or organization. However, they are especially critical in organizations that work with traumatized children because: (1) the anxieties involved in the task challenge everyone's capacity to maintain a healthy balance to the extreme; (2) the balance is in itself central to the therapeutic task. The children have come from environments where the balance has been severely distorted in one way or another. Sometimes their environments have been excessively permissive with no sense of order and appropriate boundaries, and at other times, excessively harsh, punitive, controlling and rigid. Therefore, the children have internalized an unhealthy and damaging model of how life is managed. One of their core needs is to internalize a different model where there is attention to individual needs within the context of a well-managed environment.

THE LIGHTHOUSE FOUNDATION AS AN OPEN SYSTEM

To put the task of leadership into context it is helpful to have a model of the organization as a living system and exactly what that entails. The biologist von Bertalanffy (1950a, 1950b) formulated the idea that organisms, human beings, organizations and societies are open systems. He applied an evolutionary model of the dynamic interactive relationship between an organism and its environment to organizations. Classical organizational models were primarily closed physical systems, mechanically self-sufficient, neither importing nor exporting. Under the open systems model an organization is in continual interaction with its task and the external environment. The organization has the ability to transform material or input, but is also subject to potential change through this process. Miller and Rice (1967) as well as other team members of The Tavistock Institute of Human Relations have further developed these ideas.

An organization is described as a system or a set of activities with a boundary and a purpose. The purpose of the organization or the activity it must perform to survive effectively is defined as its primary task (Miller and Rice 1967, p.25; Rice 1963, p.17). The primary task of Lighthouse is the recovery of traumatized children, and what this means is defined clearly so that there isn't ambiguity on this point. Traumatized children are the input taken into the organization, across its boundary. Following transformational therapeutic activity and processes within the organization, the input is converted to an output: 'recovered' children who leave the organization across its boundary. Using this simple example, it is apparent that the management of the boundary is critical to the organization's success and survival. If children are placed on a programme that is not suitable for them, the output may be too poor and referrals may decline rapidly. If children are allowed to leave before they have recovered, the organization will not be achieving its primary task, and if children are not allowed to leave when they are sufficiently recovered they may regress.

In an open system the boundary is permeable, represented by the dashed line (see Figure 7.1), so that there is a controlled flow of material, resources and information across the boundary.

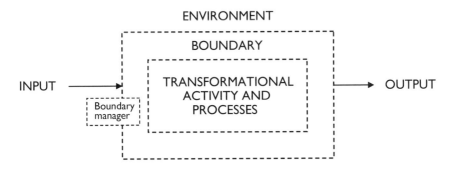

Figure 7.1 Open system process

The degree of permeability and control on the boundary will be determined by the nature of the primary task, but is also changed by external developments. For instance, the growth of IT has greatly increased the flow of information. The 'boundary manager' or system of boundary management is placed on the boundary of the organization. From this position, both the inside and outside are observed and the relationship between the two can be regulated appropriately. Lighthouse's relationship with government is an example of this. Over the years, Lighthouse has not been a programme funded by government as the government's approach has not been consistent with the way we work. Therefore, the boundary managers had resisted government funding. As the government's approach is now moving towards therapeutic care and trauma-informed practice that is consistent with our work, the boundary manager is now allowing the relationship with government to strengthen. As a result, the organization boundary has needed to become more open.

It is particularly critical in organizations that work with traumatized children that the boundary of the whole organization is effectively managed. If the boundary is too permeable too much information and activity will come into the organization, potentially leading children and workers to feel unprotected and overwhelmed. If the boundary is too rigid and impermeable the organization will tend to become closed and starved of valuable inputs from the outside world. Both of these dynamics reflect the nature of trauma and abuse environments and can become re-enacted within the organization. For example, in an abusive environment there may be a complete lack of appropriate protective boundaries. Alternatively, there may be very rigid boundaries to create an environment of secrecy where the outside world is kept out. The way the boundary of the organization is managed will set a template for the way internal boundaries are managed – between departments or 'sub-systems', and between people, including the direct work with children. The appropriate management of boundaries creates an environment which is potentially containing of the emotionality involved in the work with children. Boundary management is a central task of leadership, management and of therapeutic work in the management of personal/professional boundaries. Effective boundary management also has a positive effect on the development of identity – 'It gives a stronger sense of belonging to what is inside, of there being something comprehensible to identify with, of there being "my place", or "our place", where "I" belong and where "we" belong together' (Menzies Lyth 1985, p.245).

Miller (1989) has described the child in a setting like Lighthouse as being in the centre of an organization with a series of permeable boundaries, or containing membranes between him and the external world (see Figure 7.2).

For instance, 1 could be the child's primary carer, 2 the psychological wellness team, 3 the senior care team, and 4 the senior management team.

Children who have been severely traumatized in their early years are in many ways similar to infants and need their relationship with the outside world to be carefully managed. Too much outside world and they can feel engulfed and too little and they are the centre of the universe! They need buffering from the outside world and the outside world from them. If the child pushes his way through one membrane, there is another there to catch him, like a safety net. In the same way, the membranes protect the child from potential impingements coming from the outside world.

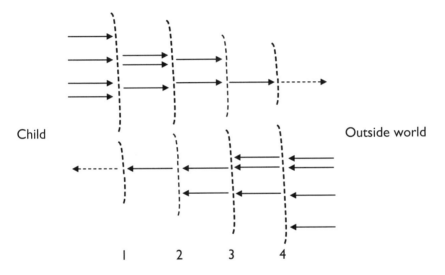

Figure 7.2 Containing membranes

A large organization will have a number of sub-systems within the whole system, such as clinical, human resources, financial and marketing departments. A key concept in open systems theory is how changes to one part of the system (sub-system) will also cause changes in all other parts of the system. In the same way, changes within the system as a whole will have an impact on the wider environment that the system sits within and vice versa. For changes in one area to be sustained there also needs to be supporting changes in other areas of the system. This means that it is necessary always to consider the system as a whole and where possible to anticipate potential 'side-effects' of any changes introduced. For example, changes that the human resources department make to the organization's recruitment process will have an impact on the other systems. Changes that are positive from one point of view may cause unforeseen negative consequences in other parts of the organization. Whilst this might seem obvious, one of the biggest obstacles to successful change implementation is often a lack of thinking through the 'knock-on' effects. Effective leadership will need to involve the organization as a whole in considering significant changes, but at the same time to guard against such unwieldy processes that positive change and adaptability become stifled.

LEADERSHIP

The organization's leader is ultimately responsible for the environment that we have described as being necessary for the treatment of traumatized children. The leader will have to contend with all of the difficulties we have described – the way trauma becomes re-enacted within the organization, the difficulty in maintaining appropriate boundaries and containing anxiety. Not only is the leader dealing with these internal issues, but also managing the boundary of the organization as a whole in relation to the outside world. Often the political, societal and economic climate that the work takes place in is ambivalent, if not directly hostile. This happens on different levels, which can be conscious or unconscious. The fact that so many children are abused, most commonly by their parents and others within their own families, is inherently challenging to the notion of family life as nurturing and protective. The denial within society can be blatantly seen by the way 'stranger danger' anxieties become so amplified, even though the possibility of being abused by a stranger is far less likely than being abused by a known person within the family.

Organizations that work with traumatized children are a painful reminder of this reality and can evoke defensive responses from those on the outside, such as politicians, social workers and the public at large. The reality of what has happened to the children is often denied. The organization is held responsible for managing their behaviour and is often expected to do this with inadequate resources. These organizations, like the children within them can be perceived as a 'nuisance', because: they remind us all that child abuse within families exists; they make us feel uncomfortable and to some extent guilty because society as a whole failed to protect these children; the children can actually cause difficulties for local communities and schools; and the services needed by these children are difficult to provide for in an economic climate where there are many competing needs. Farragher and Yanosy summarize some of the challenges involved:

> Residential centers provide 24-hour care, 365 days a year to traumatized children. These settings are very intense, highly volatile, often unpredictable

and exceedingly complex environments. Things can go very wrong, very fast. At the same time the high cost of residential care makes these centers a constant target for funding cuts and cost control efforts. Many are located in communities that are less than thrilled about having such troublesome neighbors. (Farragher and Yanosy 2005, p.99)

The leader of the organization is often between a rock and a hard place. Like Janus, the Roman God of gateways, sitting on the boundary of the organization with one eye looking out and one looking in – both views can seem equally challenging and hopeless. More importantly, the leader will experience powerful projections of these feelings from both inside and outside the organization. The environment both internally and externally is often unpredictable and uncertain. The leader needs to have considerable resilience and emotional intelligence to effectively manage the difficulties and emotions involved.

Having stated the difficult side of things, which is often the reality facing the leader – there are also positive dynamics that the effective leader will identify and use for the benefit of the children that we work with. For example, the guilt and disgust that might be felt about child neglect and abuse can mobilize reparative drives in individuals, groups, organizations and communities. Beneath the apparent ambivalence and hostility may also lie a wish to do something constructive and to influence systemic change. This is particularly evident in countries, such as the USA and Australia, where charitable involvement in care services both from individuals and organizations is a major part of the culture. Lighthouse is an example of the community working together for the wellbeing of children, having survived since 1991 from the goodness of philanthropy, the business community, community committees, volunteers and people who donate their money.

Within the organization there will also be much goodwill and commitment towards working with the children. At its best the care and commitment of workers can be inspirational. Similarly, the children can be inspiring in their own resilience and capacity to recover from such appalling experiences. Enabling the children to recover can be immensely satisfying. The leader of the organization is in both a potentially painful and privileged position. As van der Kolk and McFarlane (2007, p.573) have claimed, 'This struggle to transcend the effects of trauma is among the noblest aspects of human history.'

To manage the extreme emotions involved requires the leader to have mature, emotionally intelligent qualities that help maintain a realistic and balanced approach. For instance, a narcissistic leader may tend to feel like a saviour, personally responsible for the children's recovery. Equally, when things are difficult the leader may feel personally wounded and attacked. As we have discussed, these dynamics are potentially amplified in organizations that are prone towards 'magical' solutions and fight/flight tendencies. The leader can easily become an omnipotent saviour or the 'enemy' who is the cause of everything that is painful and difficult. These two extremes are particularly likely in organizations that are working with high levels of dependency and also hostility and aggression. The leader can come to represent the good 'maternal' provider who will nourish and take care of everyone, or the 'abuser' who is the cause of everyone's pain. This can happen in a way that mirrors the dynamics of a relationship with a traumatized child, or an infant. The 'maternal' caregiver is idealized as 'good' until she fails the child in some way and then she is suddenly all things 'bad'. She needs to be highly aware of these potential dynamics and her own vulnerability to the projections involved. She needs to be sensitive to the emotional climate of the organization but not so much so that she is easily overwhelmed. Therefore, the leader needs the right balance between being 'thick' or 'thin' skinned, or in other words emotionally defended and undefended (Khaleelee and Tomlinson 1997).

The emotional intelligence of the leader is now regarded to be the one of the primary requisites of leadership in general. This is even more so for a leader of an organization working with traumatized children, where the emotional intelligence of the whole organization is vital to the recovery process. Bennis and Goldsmith (1997, p.80) link the qualities of a leader to his or her development as a person, 'The process of becoming a leader is much the same as the process of becoming an integrated human being...leadership is a metaphor for centredness, congruity and balance in one's life.'

One of the key tasks of leadership is to create conditions that facilitate the growth of leadership throughout the whole organization. At all levels in the organization, appropriate delegation of authority and empowerment can lead to the development of responsibility and ownership. This is especially important for the children who may be perceived as and feel themselves to be victims. If the organizational culture is one where there is a high level of dependency on others to sort things out, whilst this might be done in a well-intentioned way the end result will be more dependency. One of the dangers of this for the children is that it can create a vulnerability to the kind of inappropriate dependent relationship with someone who is not so well intentioned and who can become abusive. The children need support to take charge of their own lives and hence become less vulnerable to abuse. For them to do this, those that work with them need to have an appropriate sense of responsibility and being in charge. Menzies Lyth explains that,

It is in general good management practice to delegate tasks and responsibilities to the lowest level at which they can be competently carried out and to the point at which decision-making is most effective. This is of particular importance in children's institutions, since such delegation downwards increases the opportunity for staff to behave in an effective and authoritative way, to demonstrate capacity for carrying responsibility for themselves and their tasks and to make realistic decisions, all of which are aspects of a good model. (Menzies Lyth 1985, p.239)

As we have said, the way the organization works as a whole will create a model that is internalized by the children. Obholzer (1994) gave a very clear example of this when he referred to an educational psychologist who was receiving numerous referrals because of bullying in a particular school. After a while she discovered that the headmaster was perceived by the staff to be a bully. This was being internalized by the children, who then acted in a manner that reflected the organizational culture. 'Once this came out into the open, and with the help of individual role-consultation to the headmaster as well as consultation to the staff group as a whole to discuss these issues, there was a dramatic reduction in the referrals for bullying' (p.137).

Possibly one of the most damaging environments for the children would be one where everyone says 'there's nothing I can do about it, it's not my responsibility'. This would only reinforce the children's feelings of helplessness. As with much of what we have discussed, it is a question of balance. Whilst children need to be enabled to develop responsibility, the abdication of responsibility by their carers is unhelpful and potentially damaging. Many of the children feel responsible for the things that have happened in their lives, including the abuse they have been subjected to. They need to experience adults taking responsibility for them in a way that is related to their emotional needs and stage of development. The leader of the organization, in the way she relates to others, takes and delegates responsibility, provides a role model for the nature of all relationships within the organization.

AUTHORITY

To manage the systems and their boundaries effectively, the organization beginning with its leader needs to know what her authority is and then exercise it appropriately in line with the therapeutic task. This has become increasingly complex, partly due to the way that the authority of the leader and organization is now more balanced against the authority of: staff through employment, occupational health and safety laws; children through children's rights; and external bodies such as regulatory bodies. For these reasons and others, the lines of command in today's organizations are not as clear cut as they have been. Therefore, the leader needs to know exactly what she has authority over and what she doesn't. Organizations are characterized by myriad changing relationships. The approach is no longer characterized by fighting your way forward but by strategic partnerships, joint ventures and relationship making. In this world, communication, trust, a strong sense of self and relationship skills are paramount (Cairnes 2006). Therefore, we consider processes that encourage and strengthen interpersonal relationships, like our 'I feel like saying', are sacrosanct.

With authority comes the requirement to take responsibility and to be held accountable. If authority is fudged, no one knows who is responsible for what and holding anyone accountable for anything is impossible. It is immediately clear how this issue is of direct relevance to the development of children, whose relationship with authority is often immature, negative and distorted by their experiences. The way the leader exercises her authority provides a role model for the whole organization and is central to the treatment task. Menzies Lyth argues that,

> It seems a fault in many children's institutions that they do not handle authority effectively. There may be too much permissiveness, people being allowed or encouraged to follow their own bent without sufficient accountability, guidance or discipline. If this does not work (and it frequently does not, leading to excessive acting out by both staff and children) it may be replaced in time by an excessively rigid and punitive regime. Both are detrimental to child development. The 'superego' of the institution needs to be authoritative and responsible, though not authoritarian; firm and kindly, but not sloppily permissive. (Menzies Lyth 1985, p.242)

MANAGING CHANGE

Managing change is one of the central tasks of leadership. During the last two decades, with the huge developments in technology, the pace of change has increased rapidly. The world we live in is changing quicker than ever before and organizations face a very competitive market, where nothing stands still for long. Organizations that work with traumatized children, where stability is so important, are faced with the challenge of managing necessary change and adaptation in a way that doesn't fundamentally rock the boat so much that anxieties become uncontained. Traumatized children are fearful of change, as it means the environment becomes unpredictable and potentially harmful. They are hypervigilant and constantly scanning the environment for signs of change, including the emotional states of the adults looking after them. Therefore, if a carer or team is aware of forthcoming changes that are causing some anxiety, the children will often pick this up unconsciously before they are told about it. The most difficult type of change for carers and children is sudden change that leaves little time for processing the implications. This can have a similar quality to it as some of the children's traumatic experiences, where they felt helpless and out of control. It is especially important for traumatized people to gain a sense of control and mastery over their lives. Therefore, even if the change is not their own choice, having some say and involvement in the process can help reduce the sense of helplessness.

Bloom (2005) has talked about the importance of involving as many members of the organization as possible in the process of management. Increasingly, children are consulted and involved in organizational processes. If this is managed appropriately it can have great benefits, for the children, their carers and the organization. This requires leaders to develop a flattened hierarchy within the organization and to devolve decision making as far as appropriate. Bloom claims that,

> Experience has taught that courageous leadership is always the key to system change and without it, substantial change is unlikely to occur. This change process is frightening for people in leadership positions and they rightfully perceive significant risk in opening themselves up to criticism, in levelling hierarchies and sharing legitimate power. The gains are substantial, but a leader only finds that out after learning how to tolerate the anxiety and uncertainty that inevitably accompanies real change. (Bloom 2005, p.69)

The process of change will inevitably lead to differences in opinion and potential conflict. However, the differences can often be vital to getting a full picture and improving the likelihood of successful implementation. By having an open dialogue there is the opportunity for details to be considered and potential problems to be identified. Also, the level of resistance can be gauged, giving an indication of further work that may be necessary.

Hoyle (2004) has discussed the danger of having a narrow view on people's responses to change. In her paper 'From Sycophant to Saboteur' she talks about the way organizations tend to encourage an overly positive response to change. This can lead to a polarization of attitudes where the staff are either completely for change (sycophants) or completely against change (saboteurs). Hoyle argues that we are all somewhere along a continuum in our attitude towards change. The majority of us are clustered around the middle ground, either being positive and challenging or negative and challenging. At the extreme ends are those who are generally against any kind of change and those that will go along with anything. Both these groups of people are unhelpful during a change process as they are lacking any kind of critical thinking capacity. Those around the middle, on the side that tends to be negative about change, will respond with comments like, 'I don't think that's a good idea, but maybe if we did this, it might work'. Those on the side that tends to be positive will respond with comments like, 'That's a good idea, but I think we need to think about such and such a bit more'. The key point is that the majority of people have something constructive to contribute whether they are generally positive or negative about change.

An organization with a 'top down' style of leadership, and especially when the leaders are anxious about pushing a change through, tend to hear any resistance and criticism as negative. The result of this is that those people who had something to say, even if they were slightly negative, feel silenced. They move further away from the middle and towards the group at the extreme that is very anti-change. Those who were generally positive but had something critical to say, perceive the risk of being judged as negative. They move along the continuum towards the sycophants. This dynamic is then likely to cause huge problems in the implementation stage of the change. The organization has been deprived of information that might have identified potential problems and allowed for a smoother implementation. Rather than having a majority of staff identified and invested in the change, there is now a significant group that have withdrawn. The group that are highly resistant to change have been strengthened in numbers. There are now more staff clustered at the extreme ends of the spectrum, rather than around the middle, which is a recipe for major conflict and potential sabotage.

Staff who work with traumatized children can be particularly wary of change, partly as their work is centred around making the environment predictable and stable for the children. It could be argued, that by being resistant and criticizing potential changes they are acting in what might feel to be in the best interests of the children. In addition, all change can be expected to raise anxiety on top of that already involved in the work. Therefore, it is essential that all staff are fully involved in the change process and have the opportunity to digest what is being proposed, to ask questions and to raise concerns. Inevitably, this can be very challenging for a leader and conflict will need to be worked through. It is more likely that the difficulties can be managed positively if the organization has developed a culture where conflict is seen as a potential learning opportunity and where there are processes in place for resolving conflict. As Bloom argues,

Democratic participation requires a level of civil discourse that is missing within many organization settings largely due to a lack of conflict resolution mechanisms within the organization. To be healthy, organizations must have the goals of conflict resolution and conflict transformation as organizational goals. This means learning to walk the talk, embedding conflict resolution strategies at every level, not turning them over to a separate department or individual who is the formal instrument of conflict resolution. An environment that encourages participatory democratic processes, complex problem solving, and routine conflict resolution, is an environment that encourages social learning. In an environment of social learning, every problem and conflict is seen as an opportunity for growth and learning on everyone's part (Jones 1968). In this way, error correction becomes a challenging group educational process instead of a way of punishing wayward individuals. This requires a growth in understanding of the power of the group process. (Bloom 2005, p.66)

The vehicle by which this is done at Lighthouse is the 'I feel like saying' process. This is a consistent approach that is used in all meetings within the organization from the board of directors to family meetings in the homes. The way change is managed in the organization has major implications for the recovery of the children. As well as the potential benefits of well-managed change in the general sense, it also provides a specific model of how change and conflict can be managed positively. It can give a sense of being a participant in change, rather than a passive bystander or even victim.

THE ORGANIZATION'S VISION

When you are inspired by some great purpose, some extraordinary project, all your thoughts break their bonds; your mind transcends limitations, your consciousness expands in every direction, and you find yourself in a new, great and wonderful world. Dormant forces, faculties and talents become alive, and you discover yourself to become a greater person by far than you ever dreamed yourself to be.

Patanjali 300–100 BC

The leaders in the organization will hold the organization's vision and articulate it inside and outside the organization. Without a strong vision it is unlikely that the work will be sustainable. In our organization we focus on developing leaders not only in the staff team but also in the children. We have a philosophy that any of our team members are ambassadors for the organization and advocates for the children. As such, they can be called on to represent the organization and talk as authorities on working with traumatized children.

Khaleelee (2004, p.271) argues that one of the central aspects of leadership is 'the capacity of the leader to keep steadfastly to his or her long term vision whilst containing the anxiety of followers during the implementation phases of that vision.' Similarly, Cameron and Maginn claim that,

> A crucial feature of all good leaders seems to be their ability to look beyond the near horizon, obtain a vision of 'what could be' and then share it with others in a way which inspires them to join in a professional journey towards the vision. On a more mundane level, leadership also demands tenacity to pursue a creative and exciting view of the future, despite the everyday distractions and obstacles. (Cameron and Maginn 2009, p.119)

A strong vision provides a sense of purpose and commitment for everyone, which inspires, motivates and makes sense of why we are all doing this work. For instance, the vision of the Lighthouse Foundation is 'Ending Youth Homelessness Together', and for the NSPCC in the UK it is to 'End Cruelty to Children in the UK'. At times when the realities of day-to-day work feel almost impossible, the vision can seem unrealistic. It is essential that the vision is something that everyone can relate to and believe in. Therefore, the leader needs to have the utmost belief and conviction in the vision. Many pioneers of organizations that work with traumatized children have had a huge passion and commitment to make a difference and with a strong vision of a better world. Without this level of commitment and belief, the organization will soon begin to doubt the vision and its capacity to overcome the challenges it faces.

Gardner emphasizes the importance of stories in the role of leadership, which he claims is

> a process that occurs within the minds of individuals who live in a culture – a process that entails the capacities to create stories, to understand and evaluate these stories, and to appreciate the struggles among stories. Ultimately, certain types of stories will typically become predominant – in particular, stories that provide an adequate and timely sense of identity for individuals. (Gardner 1995, p.22)

Whitwell (2010) describes how the story of the pioneering work and the organization's beginning often acts as a 'sustaining myth'. A sustaining myth is a story about the organization, often based around its pioneering beginnings, which the organization turns to when it is particularly challenged. The 'heroic' deeds referred to in the myth help give people a sense of strength and purpose to overcome obstacles. The story of Susan's pioneering work in starting Lighthouse Foundation is well known within our organization. Further stories of how the organization has grown and developed over the years, encapsulate the vision and also provide a reassuring sense of shared emotional connection and history (McMillan and Chavis 1986).

SENSE OF COMMUNITY

Sarason (1974) describes 'sense of community' as the feeling that one is part of a readily available supportive and dependable structure. Sense of community transcends individualism in that to maintain such an interdependent relationship one does for others what one expects from others.

A well-known African proverb says 'It takes a village to raise a child'. It also takes a village to welcome a child into its community circle. As we have discussed earlier, traumatized children and especially homeless children are often the forgotten children. Due to the abuse and neglect that they have experienced, the number of broken placements, the transient nature of their existence, they do not feel a sense of belonging to a community. We know that having a sense of belonging to a community is an essential element in human wellbeing. Studies have shown that sense of community and related factors can result in positive outcomes for individuals and groups. Factors such as being connected to the community, sense of belonging, group cohesion and social capital, play a major role in the overall wellbeing of individuals and groups. This includes physical and mental wellbeing (Pretty, Bishop and Fisher 2006).

Historically, promoting a sense of community, in the widest sense of the word, for the children in its care, has been a challenge for organizations that provide residential care. It is important that theoretical underpinnings and organizational systems support and enable meaningful community building for the children. By this we mean both with the internal and external communities. Programmes that have a focus on individual therapeutic approaches can forget the importance of community in the recovery process. The short-term nature of many treatment models has also impacted on the ability to build a sense of community. As discussed earlier, child abuse occurs within a family environment and also a wider community context. Prilleltensky and Nelson (2000) argue that, 'Child wellness is predicated on the satisfaction of material, physical, affective, and psychological needs. Wellness is an ecological concept; a child's well-being is determined by the level of parental, familial, communal, and social wellness.' Therefore, the therapeutic task must also address the need for a positive experience of community – one that is accepting and supportive and where the child can also make a meaningful contribution. This is vital in shifting the child's internal working model of the world and is essential in the recovery process. At some point in the future the child will also need to live independently as part of a community. The child's ability to transition into an autonomous adult, and be able to provide for himself and his family into the future will partly rely on his ability to be part of a community. The therapeutic process needs to take into account the many cultural 'sites' (Prilleltensky 2005) in which the original trauma occurred or was supported. These may include the family or home, extended family, and the wider community. In essence a therapeutic programme needs to provide a different experience of these sites, which promote a sense of safety, belonging and empowerment. This is what Prilleltensky refers to as 'sites of wellbeing' (2005, p.54).

SENSE OF FAMILY AND HOME

For many of the children we work with, the family home as ideally a 'site for wellbeing' (Prilleltensky 2005, p.54), has become quite the opposite. Therefore, it is essential that we provide a different experience of family and home. Many organizations do not like to refer to the children and carers living in their homes as a family, as it can be confusing for the children. This is understandable, especially when children do not stay in the homes for extended periods of time. By comparison, our approach actually emphasizes the idea of home and family. We believe this is an essential element of the recovery process. However, this can only be done with placement security and long-term consistent care, where there is the time and support to develop relationships to the point where the carers and other children who they live with become their immediate 'family'. We have seen children move through the programme and remain connected to the carers and other children that they lived with. In some cases, now as adults into their thirties, they consider each other and their previous carers as part of their family for life. As we have previously mentioned, Hannon *et al.* emphasize the importance of this from their own research:

> Several of the young people we spoke to who had experienced placements in residential care explained that they found the changes in staff destabilising and that it was more difficult to form attachments than in foster families. The young people who described positive experiences of residential care attributed this to the close relationships they had been able to form with staff: 'some of them treated me like their own' or with other children: 'My children's home was good and me and the kids there got really attached together and none of us wanted to separate anymore because we were all we knew and that's what we thought was family.' (Hannon *et al.* 2010, p.86)

At Lighthouse, the sense of extended family has been developed. Children are supported to develop relationships with carers and children in the other homes. Our homes are close geographically, through what we call a cluster model. At the moment each cluster has five homes. The clusters are supported by a senior carer and an extended care network of psychologists, community care workers and carers. The homes are encouraged to spend time together to promote a sense of wider family. Many of the children have relationships with other children in other homes, similar to that of cousins, as they have developed such a strong bond. Given the children's previous experiences, this helps to provide a positive model which can help prepare them for family life. The extended family provides another level to the circle of care, where the children develop strong relationships that expand their support network. The children spend time together celebrating birthdays, Christmases, achievements such as graduations and other events. This provides the opportunity to bond and also to develop a shared history for themselves.

CAROL'S STORY: AS A FAMILY

One of the most beneficial things about Lighthouse is the family environment. Two carers live with you at the house, you have 'brothers' and 'sisters' all with their own unique personalities, but you are all brought together by a common experience. I made many friends who I shared experiences with and I still keep in contact with some. We grew together, got into mischief together and cried together. We fought over who was going to do the dishes and what time we could come home. As teenagers we were exactly the same as any other, we lashed out, broke the rules but still needed love and support. But what really mattered was we actually felt a connection with the people that were looking after us, who we lived with. We actually loved them and cared for them and worried about them, like they worried for us. I often had sleepovers at other Lighthouses with the other children who were like 'cousins', we watched movies etc. I knew the other carers like aunties and uncles and they knew me, we had a bond, a strong bond that allowed us to be kids, heal and gain independence.

Jacinta explains below how her own family were supported and welcomed as part of the programme. It is clear that for Jacinta the concept of family used by Lighthouse didn't undermine or replace her own birth family and that she clearly recognized the differences between the 'Lighthouse family' and her birth family in a non-judgemental way.

JACINTA'S STORY: MY TWO FAMILIES

When I arrived at Lighthouse for the first time…I got sent from hospital. I had been in hospital on and off from the age of sixteen to twenty-two. So going to Lighthouse was like I was going to another hospital, but it ended up being really good because I had people to talk to. Also it was not judgemental like a hospital, which I got to realize over time, experiencing the Lighthouse model of care. What I remember most is the feelings I had…the long talks with Susan my primary carer, Julie my secondary carer (who eventually became primary carer) and Terence our psychologist. I remember knowing innately that my parents were welcome and were not excluded. That Lighthouse guys were not trying to replace my parents (who were unwell). It was like having support for both myself and my family, enabling us to build those relationships again in a healthy way. So we worked together (Lighthouse, my parents and me) and over time I had not just stabilized my accommodation, but more importantly had stability of relationships and medication. Over time my medication was reduced and although I still went into hospital when I became unwell, I was able to shorten the length of hospital stays. The most important thing for me was the emotional support. I know my parents wanted to give me this emotional support, but due to their own issues with mental health were unable to. They still do not have insight into their inability to provide this for me or their own mental illness does not enable them to do this.

In the following vignette by Jamie, he highlights how things may not always be so straightforward. This reminds us how sensitive we need to be to the child's experience and not to make assumptions.

JAMIE'S STORY: IN PLACE OF YOUR PARENTS

It was weird when the older carers played a parent role. I didn't like that the older carers were trying to play the role of the parent. I found that the younger carers were more open, and you could talk to them about things. They know what it's like now. It was weird living in Richmond. I don't know why, it was just weird. Until Krystal came in. She was a young happy person. It worked for me having a younger carer. I got along better with her. Krystal was more like a friend. If you needed help she would be there. A child needs to make its own path. Krystal was walking with me on that path. She was there to help me if something happened. In case I got in trouble. She was there as a guide. Everyone has their own two parents. I felt like the older carer was saying that I should let go of my parents. It wasn't anything she said, it was more what I felt. It was too smothering. My parents might have done wrong but nobody will ever let go of their parents. They are your flesh and blood. Having to let go of your family makes you feel bad. I like the carers that are not really carers. I like carers to be friends, not being there to replace.

One of the difficulties for children in residential care can be how they feel different to other children, especially if they attend a local school. For example, some children in care have explained their feeling of embarrassment when a different carer picks them up every day or writes a note for them. They feel like they stand out compared with children who they perceive to come from 'normal' families and have the same parents dealing with the school every day.

Carol explains how having just two main carers helped to make her experience feel more like family.

CAROL'S STORY: FEELS LIKE FAMILY

One of my fondest memories is of my year 12 graduation. I was chuffed because I had worked hard, and as a child I never believed that I could actually do it. We were allowed to invite two people to the event; all my friends had invited parents, siblings, grandparents, aunts and uncles. I chose to invite my two carers at the time, Vicki and Barry, who had become my surrogate parents. We sat at a table with my friends and their parents and family; it was like normal. One of the girls I was living with was doing her hairdressing degree and she did my hair and make-up and I had a nice dress. We walked in as a family. I spent the night dancing with family and friends. It was a fabulous night.

ORGANIZATION AS FAMILY

In a therapeutic community that also acts as if it were an extended family to the children, all operations and relationships within the organization need to be attuned to the therapeutic task. All members of the organization, from the board to the carers, need to role model a healthy sense of family. We refer to this as organizational parenting. All systems and relationships have a therapeutic purpose and promote a sense of family for the child. The children are supported to have appropriate relationships with all members of the organization; much like the village that takes in a child to raise, the organization becomes the village. Children in this environment develop a variety of relationships and a circle of care that helps them internalize a more positive view of family and community, as in Figure 7.3.

CASE EXAMPLE: JACKY

Jacky is a seventeen-year-old female who suffers from anxiety and has difficulty developing relationships with other people. Over the years she has developed a strong relationship with one of our administrative workers who is a member of the indirect care team. When Jacky is going through a tough time and needs close supervision as she may be a risk to herself, she comes into the Youth Resource and Administration Centre to give herself a bit of emotional space. One of the strategies she uses to manage her anxiety is to knit. When she comes into the centre, she sits on a bean bag next to the staff member as she does her administrative work. This experience is very soothing for Jacky as she feels safe with the staff member, who is not her carer but in some ways almost an extended family member who has been reliably there for her when she needs it. This process provides Jacky with a sense of family and community, which has been very important in her recovery process. The staff member is supported in the relationship by the care team, who ensure that she is safe at all times and that she is provided with the clinical advice necessary to ensure that the relationship is actually therapeutic for Jacky.

Figure 7.3 Therapeutic circle of care

LOCAL COMMUNITY

In modern times, the idea of 'community' has increasingly been expanded to include not just the place where one lives, but the web of relationships into which one is embedded. Work, school, voluntary associations, computer networks – all are communities, even though members live quite far apart.

Peck 1991, p.26

Ideally, children are raised by their family and extended family within the context of a supportive wider community. Many of the children that we work with have been alienated and disconnected from their local community. Many of their lives are transient, due to running away from unsafe relationships, or being moved around by the system from placement to placement. Therefore, the children feel no connection to a local community. Missing out on the support and potential opportunities that the local community can offer means that they feel no sense of belonging to a place they could call home. The first point in building a reconnection to the local community is ensuring that the personal wellness needs of the children are met, such as the need for a safe and nurturing environment and access to long-term accommodation. After a child has settled in and feels secure he can start to work on relational and community wellness, which involves building healthy relationships and networks in the local community. Programmes that are focused on supporting children's recovery from trauma must ensure that they provide a holistic approach. Such an approach must not only cater for the individual needs of the child, but also build a sense of belonging to the local community. The local community has a wealth of resources that are essential to the recovery process – access to specialist supports, education and training, employment, mentoring, recreation, groups and other resources. Our children are connected to a large extended 'family' of volunteers, organizational corporate partners, youth services and community committees.

COMMUNITY COMMITTEES AS A CONTAINING MEMBRANE

We referred earlier to the different membranes that provide a holding environment for our children. These membranes can be used to help manage the transition of children into the wider community. The community committee is an example of one of these membranes. In 1997, Lighthouse opened its second home in partnership with Cabrini Hospital, Melbourne. As part of this endeavour, we simultaneously developed a community committee to support the home. The idea behind this was based on the 'Clean up Australia' model that has now become an international model, demonstrating the community taking responsibility for the environment that they live in. Susan asked the question, 'Why is it that we can mobilize the community around the issue of the environment? But we can't mobilize the community to protect the most vulnerable children?' It became increasingly obvious that in preventing the further abuse, neglect and alienation of our children, we needed to engage the community as part of the solution. We value the statement made by NAPCAN

(National Association for the Protection of Children against Abuse and Neglect) that 'protecting children is everyone's responsibility'.

The community committee members are local people who live or work near the home. There is a thorough process for their selection and to ensure their suitability. They provide support in a number of areas – local knowledge, mentoring for the children, financial assistance, networking opportunities, legal matters, maintenance of the home, links to employment, education and training initiatives, and various other supports. The committee also provides practical support to the carers, so that they can be more effective in the therapeutic work that takes place in the home with the children. This is similar to the way parents may be supported by an extended network of family, friends, local and wider community. We are more confident as parents when we know we have people around to support and encourage us.

The children enjoy having committee members over for dinners and celebrations, as this creates a sense that they are part of a wider network of supportive adults. They are exposed to positive role modelling and get to hear about the lives of the committee members. Stories make up a tapestry of community and it is through sharing our stories that we can understand ourselves and others. The committee members also gain an insight into the experiences of the children. This can encourage the members to go back into the community to advocate for more community involvement and lobby for change. The children also feel a sense that they are listened to, that they matter and that the world actually cares for them. A huge shift can occur in the children's internal working model of the world to one that can be safe, caring and loving. When children feel heard and responded to, their concept of the world and their place in it is affirmed in a positive way. We see shifts from antisocial behaviour to more pro-social activities that are focused on giving to the community.

Each member of the committee will bring with them their own stories, experiences and special qualities. It is important that they are committed to the values of the organization and the wellbeing of all children, have an understanding of the model of care, and are generally active in the local community. Through their community activities, they become a voice for the children in our care. We have seen examples where members return to their workplaces or other community sites and raise awareness about child abuse, neglect and homelessness, and mobilize the local community to take action in numerous ways. For instance, members of the Cabrini Home Committee in Melbourne have provided friendship, employment opportunities, food for special occasions, maintenance to the home and support across the organization, such as teaching first aid to carers. Two young people are currently working at

Cabrini Hospital, with one of them having sustained employment for ten years. This young person now has a stable family and feels fully part of a supportive community. The Cabrini Hospital has taken the time to educate their own staff who are very supportive of the young person as well as our organization. It has also provided the Cabrini staff an additional sense of meaning as they feel that they are part of another important mission.

COLLECTIVE WELLNESS

When referring to community wellness and the importance of collective action, Prilleltensky (2007) uses the analogy of the private citizen of Venice. The citizen's only concern is for his own safety and his own dwellings and his ability to get about the city, while the entire republic is slowly being submerged. Prilleltensky (2007) states that 'individual citizens cannot afford to ignore their collective fate, because, in the end, they all drown together if nothing is done.' The same logic can be applied to the work with traumatized homeless children. We can do very important ameliorative work with them, however ultimately the depth and breadth of task requires a societal response. We explored in the Introduction the impact of child abuse, neglect and homelessness on society as a whole. As such, we require societal response to change the way we work with children and young people. We need a more preventative and early intervention focus, one that aims to break the cycle of intergenerational abuse, neglect and poverty.

The wellness of children relies on the wellbeing of the relationships they form, as well as the wellbeing of the wider community in which they live. Prilleltensky (2005) refers to wellness as 'a positive state of affairs in which the personal, relational, and collective needs and aspirations of individuals and communities are fulfilled.' (p.54) This definition challenges the narrow view that wellbeing is determined by individual physical and mental health. Although these are part of wellbeing, they are not the whole of it. It also places a focus on the importance of community, describing wellbeing as a satisfactory state of affairs for individuals and communities that is more than the absence of disease. This includes factors such as the psychosocial, economic, political and physical environment which influence wellbeing. The definition is also in line with the concept put forward by the World Health Organization, which identifies the importance of the values of self-determination, participation, community capacity-building, structural determinants and social justice (WHO 1986). Cowen (1996, p.46) states that, 'Optimal development of wellness... requires integrated sets of operations involving individuals, families, settings, community contexts, and macro-level societal structures and policies.'

CHAPTER 8

Therapeutic Group Processes

Therapeutic group processes have always been a core part of life in therapeutic communities. By their nature therapeutic communities involve living in groups, often smaller groups within a larger group. Therefore, children within these communities have the opportunity to relate to a small group, similar to a family unit, and also a larger group as in an extended family.

There are many opportunities in the daily life of such a setting for spontaneous therapeutic opportunities, for example a positive experience between a child and carer, between children and between a child and someone in the community as a whole. Where all staff in the community are attuned to the needs of children, difficulties that arise also provide the opportunity for something to be worked through. This might be a new and constructive experience for the child. Perry and Szalavitz emphasize the importance of the 'community' in enabling children to recover from trauma:

> What maltreated and traumatized children most need is a healthy community to buffer the pain, distress and loss caused by their earlier trauma. What works to heal them is anything that increases the number and quality of a child's relationships. (Perry and Szalavitz 2006, p.231)

> Brain development is use-dependent: you use it or you lose it. If we don't give children time to learn how to be with others, to connect, to deal with conflict and to negotiate complex social hierarchies, those areas of their brains will be underdeveloped. As Hrdy stated: 'One of the things we know about empathy is that the potential is expressed only under certain rearing conditions'. If you don't provide these conditions through a caring, vibrant social network, it won't fully emerge. (Perry and Szalavitz 2006, p.239, citing Hrdy 2000)

Many therapeutic community environments from the middle of the last century onwards resembled a small village, with children, care staff and their families living on site. As well as the care staff, other workers such as domestic assistants, maintenance workers and administrative staff would come in each day to carry out their work. Children had the opportunity to relate to a wide variety of people in formal and informal ways. Perry and Szalavitz point out the potential value of this:

> We learned that some of the most therapeutic experiences do not take place in 'therapy,' but in naturally occurring healthy relationships, whether between a professional like myself and a child, between an aunt and a scared little girl, or between a calm Texas Ranger and an excitable boy. (2006, p.79)

In our present time, many of the larger therapeutic communities have closed or reduced in scale. For a variety of reasons, such as the potential isolation from the outside world and the move towards smaller living groups, these types of communities have become less popular. However, it is still possible in an organization that has a number of small homes, perhaps spread over a geographical region or that has a number of foster homes, to create a sense of community. This can be done by establishing different networks within the community that bring people together, for example children's forums, staff support groups, community events, sports days and so on. In discussing Integrated Services Programme (ISP), a foster care organization, Hills states that,

> This model [does] not aim to set up a therapeutic community but rather create a therapeutic network operating for the child within a community-based, non-institutional setting. It [seeks] to maximise the possibilities for positive change by harnessing the transformative potential of both collaborative practice and the fostering relationship. (Hills 2005, p.120)

Diamond also refers to how the concept of the group has been developed at the Mulberry Bush, a therapeutic school for children:

> Within the new formulation, all the component parts of the school (group living, education, family team, art and psychotherapy, ancillary and maintenance staff) work interactively to create the totality of the 'organisation as therapist' rather than the dependency on the individualised relationship. In this way the therapeutic school can adopt the model of the therapeutic community for children. Consequently the school's theoretical basis and practice are increasingly systemic as well as psychodynamic. (Diamond 2003, p.5)

This links with what we have said in our chapter on the theoretical base. We need to have theories that can be applied to the individual work with children, group processes and the organization, but they need to be ideologically compatible.

Therapeutic communities have traditionally used formal group meetings as part of the therapeutic process. These processes are an opportunity for everyone involved to establish their sense of self by making their own unique contribution. They are a chance for everyone to reflect on what is happening for themselves, for others and the whole group. This enables the members of the group to learn about their own feelings, thoughts and relationships and to consider these alongside other people's experiences. This process of reflection has been referred to as a culture of enquiry. Keenan describes both the benefit and difficulty involved:

> As such, the concept of a culture of enquiry, where all are trying to be able to assess themselves and their reactions/responses is both a healthy learning environment and potentially a very anxious one. For adults to be able to effectively contain and help the children learn, they must feel contained themselves, through effective management and their own experiences of being contained. It is a fair judgement that this is a difficult task. (Keenan 2006, p.49)

A well run group provides a form of emotional containment where anxieties, conflicts and difficulties can be thought about and understood. Ruch (2010, p.37) argues that,

> A feature of reflective teams is their commitment to conveying their views in a tentative and open manner, refraining from adopting a position of expertise. From a social constructivist systemic perspective, all views carry equal weight and no one truth is sought after.

The group meeting provides the opportunity to observe the group dynamic and where it is helpful to intervene in a way that disrupts destructive dynamics that may be developing. For example, difficulties within the group may be projected onto one person who could then become a scapegoat for the group's difficulties. We would all be OK if it wasn't for so and so. One child insightfully described this dynamic: 'I've had enough of being the most difficult boy in the group. If I dump my problems onto Martin, then I'll be alright and Martin will have all the difficulties.' In working with the group dynamics, it is especially important for the adults to remember the point made by Bloom (2003, p.12) that 'all members of the community share many of the same psychological processes and no one is completely "well" or completely "sick"'. At a more basic level, the group enables communication to take place and for people to feel connected to each other. On this point, Diamond refers to the group analyst Foulkes in defining what he termed a 'group matrix':

> The hypothetical web of communications and relationships in a given group… It is the common shared ground which ultimately determines the meaning

and significance of all events and upon which all communications and interpretations, verbal and non-verbal, rest. This concept links with that of communication. (Diamond 2003, p.14)

We have developed a range of group meetings and forums that take place at all levels of the organization. Whether the specific meeting is a 'family meeting' within one of the homes or a larger community forum, we have a consistent approach to the process. As Bloom (2005, p.69) states, 'These meetings are structured, simple and designed to steadily and repetitively reinforce the norms of the community.'

'I FEEL LIKE SAYING' PROCESS

In therapeutic communities for children that have experienced long-term abuse and neglect, it is vital to provide an environment that fulfils our human need to strive for individual, relational and community wellness. We seek to provide spaces for all members of our therapeutic community to feel a sense of connectedness and belonging. Organizational processes and rituals are important in creating and maintaining a consistent culture, one that promotes overall psychological wellness of all members of the therapeutic community.

One of our unique processes that strongly reflects the culture of the organization is the 'I feel like saying' process. It is a process that is utilized at all levels of the organization from children, to staff, to the board of directors. It is understood that the process takes time that may not always be available and that at times not all staff feel comfortable with the format. This may be particularly evident in meetings that do not contain experienced care team members to initiate and role model the process. However, given the therapeutic nature of the work that all staff are involved in, they are expected to participate in this process. As a therapeutic community, community members must be committed to processes that are aimed at therapeutic progress for individuals, the community and the organization. We must also be committed to role modelling to children, that we are willing to walk in their shoes and that we don't expect them to do what we wouldn't have the 'courage' to do ourselves. As Lanyado argues,

> We are as resistant to the often painful process of personal growth as the next person and would much prefer to hide behind our defences. But we cannot possibly do our job well unless we constantly strive to respond to the children's needs. They force us to change as much as we try to get them to change. If the children do not experience us as adults honestly striving to accommodate to, and understand their needs – what kind of model change and

growth do they have to identify with? We have to be as open and receptive as possible – but in the process of doing this we often get wounded. Staff support and development is there to help us tolerate these wounds and learn from them – that is to increase our capacity to cope with anxiety. (Lanyado 1989, p.138)

We utilize an approach called the 'I feel like saying' process, which is separated into the three distinct stages we describe in the following section.

'I feel like saying'

The 'I feel like saying' stage is at the start of each meeting. It is an opportunity for participants to become present at the meeting and can also set the tone and context of the meeting. Some examples of things that could be said include:

- I feel like saying that I'm looking forward to this meeting.
- I feel like saying that I believe there are lots of issues that need to be addressed.
- I feel like saying that I am confident that everyone will treat each other with respect and be appropriate during any heated discussions.
- I feel like saying that I am feeling a little tired because I haven't been sleeping well because I am stressed, so don't be insulted if I am a little distracted.
- I feel like saying that I really enjoy the weather, it makes me feel great.
- I feel like saying that I don't really have anything to say today.
- I feel like saying that I am really sad that my carer is leaving me.

It is entirely up to the participant, how much or how little they share. The level of disclosure will depend on the purpose of the meeting, the relationships of those in the meeting and various other factors. As relationships develop the level of disclosures will change.

By demonstrating a sense of openness and vulnerability, others may be encouraged to be more open during their 'I feel like saying' and throughout the meeting. It is an opportunity for each person to reflect on what is being said, what resonates with their own experience and what is different. Tomlinson describes the value of this:

Giving an opportunity for each individual to express his own opinion or experience in a group meeting helps develop a sense of personal boundaries and identity. Statements like 'there seems to be such and such a feeling in the group, how do others feel?' promote a sense of curiosity and reflection, rather than the certainty coming from more definite and fixed statements. (Tomlinson 2004, p.97)

All who attend the meeting participate in the process and can choose to say as little or as much as they like. Another important note is that when someone is speaking there are no interruptions or questions, as the person holds the floor during their 'I feel like saying'. It is also helpful that we sit with the silence between participants, as it provides an opportunity for processing and reflection. This can be especially important in helping the children learn to sit with emotions, rather than getting their needs met immediately (the wish for immediate gratification is common for traumatized children) or running away (avoidance is also a common defence mechanism for traumatized children).

It is important that the facilitator of the meeting allows the process to continue until each participant has the opportunity to have their say. They should not interrupt, rush things or come to the rescue if things feel awkward, as this can reinforce maladaptive coping skills. If there is the need to move through the meeting quickly due to other commitments, the facilitator can inform the participants prior to the meeting, so that they can have this in mind when they go through the process.

'Things to share'

The second stage of the process is 'things to share'. This is an opportunity for participants to get to know one another by sharing their beliefs, values and experiences. It is a forum where participants can share the experiences they have had over the past week with their day-to-day activities and with each other. The aim is to create a safe space where participants are able to be open and vulnerable without fear of being judged or ridiculed. The main guideline is that participants 'own' their experiences and the group acknowledges that what a member shares is 'true for them'.

The importance of this is eloquently captured by Chesterman (2011):

Two encounters had a profound effect on me. The first was going into psychotherapy. For what, I believed, to be the first time, I experienced a conversation where the other person listened attentively as I told my story uninterrupted, my 'truth' about the experiences in my life and the sense I had made of them. Where there was not going to be any fight about the meanings that I had constructed and the conclusions I had come to about the 'truth' of it all. (p.1)

This approach helps to develop a non-judgemental and open culture, which can be helpful in developing a deeper understanding of what is happening. As Ruch argues, in referring to a systemic approach,

> Multiple perspectives and an inclusive 'both/and', as opposed to a polarised 'either/or', stance are embraced. In the same way that containment creates a safe space to explore the issues being faced, a curious stance allows for inclusive, non-threatening thinking that is respectful of each individual perspective and does not seek to attribute blame but to gain a fuller understanding of the problem. (Ruch 2010, p.44)

During the sharing time, members may ask each other questions to elaborate on points or themes that have been raised. Sharing time can often become a forum for airing grievances and challenges with one another and this is encouraged. Being open about relationships in the 'sharing' time can provide participants with the opportunity to proactively address issues in a safe space. Members can learn that their behaviour affects other members and that a number of people care about them and how they do things. In essence, we reinforce to children that the person is separate from the behaviour. Your behaviour can be inappropriate but that does not make you a bad person. It can feel overwhelming to have to change your 'self' rather than your behaviour. It is a parallel process for staff in that they can be honest about their actions and also feel that they are not being judged, and that the team is there to support them. It provides a reflective space to look at oneself and also to receive feedback from others who care.

An important part of the sharing process is making connections and links between the various issues that have been raised, or in some cases not raised. For instance, there may be a theme of loss that has been mentioned by different individuals. Sometimes this may be related to a wider theme that is happening in one part of or the whole organization. On other occasions it may become apparent that an important aspect of the group's or organization's life is being avoided or denied. Making links and connections and bringing themes into consciousness enables the group and everyone within it to gain a deeper understanding of what is happening. It also encourages everyone to consider their individual experiences in the context of the group and how the two are interrelated.

In some meetings the things to share can be more operational in nature and may have a formal agenda that is followed. For instance, in the senior care service team meeting the focus is on operational issues that are part of an agenda. However, there is also the opportunity for more emotional processing if need be. In the senior management team meeting, there is a formal agenda that is followed and is very much operational in nature. Though, once again there can be the opportunity for emotional processing if required, as this can help with developing team cohesion. Cairnes explains the importance of making space for feelings to be acknowledged and worked on:

> We have replaced the reality of life and humanity with testable, scientific mental maps – theories of how realities should be. The problem is that emotions and feelings cannot be so easily dismissed. They can be forced into silence, hidden for fear of ridicule, and punishment, and denied, but they don't go away. They merely go underground, from whence they pop up continuously, out of our continuous control and dressed in a manner acceptable to our market place – that is, intellectualized and presented as rigid mental maps. (Cairnes 2006, p.57)

We have a philosophy that the success of the programme relies on relationships. Therefore, there needs to be space in meetings to ensure that relationships are strong, as any splits in the team provide an unstable environment.

'Acknowledgements'

The third stage of the process is 'acknowledgements'. In the same spirit of 'I feel like saying', the acknowledgement process is an opportunity for participants to role model sincere acknowledgements about the other participants, members of the community or anyone that has had a positive impact. As with the 'I feel like saying', the person making an acknowledgement holds the floor and there are no interruptions by other participants. It is expected that all participants must make an acknowledgement. It is also important that the facilitator allows the process to continue until each participant has had the opportunity to have their say.

The following section explains some of theoretical underpinnings of the process.

SHARED HISTORY: CULTURE PASSED ON THROUGH STORIES

Psychological 'sense of community' literature talks about the importance of shared emotional symbols and shared history in the development of a connected community or organization (McMillan and Chavis 1986). Leaders create culture, but culture creates the next generation of leaders. One of the concerns for us is how we create a sustainable culture that will allow the organization to grow and thrive, long after our founder and present directors have moved on. The rigorous processes we have established have helped to develop a generation of future leaders who live daily the core values and business principles. This then contributes to creating and preserving the organization's culture. These values, traditions, learnings, experiences, mistakes, successes are shared through the stories told in processes such as 'I feel like saying'. Susan has role modelled how the history of the organization is passed on through stories. During the 'I feel like saying' and other processes, Susan will share stories from her experience as a carer. Through these stories participants gain an understanding of the organization's way of working with children. They also gain some valuable knowledge of how to manage certain situations therapeutically. The process allows for more experienced carers and other team members to pass on their knowledge to others in the team.

Story telling is an integral part of organizational culture. In tribal cultures the elders and shamans tell stories and pass on their knowledge to new generations. Stories get repeated and retold and they form the fabric of a culture. Telling stories is especially important for traumatized children. Through the verbal articulation of their experience, possibly for the first time they have a voice. After living in environments of abuse and neglect, many children have been 'voiceless', with their own wishes, needs and interests being completely neglected and overridden. It is vital to encourage the children and all members of the therapeutic community to have a voice and to be part of the passing on of the culture. The risk of failing to share stories and to listen is to lose one's history, one's historical context, one's founding values. Without the continuity brought by custom, any group of people will begin to lose a sense of their collective identity and forget who they are.

STRONG CULTURE

There is a wealth of literature on organizations that highlights the importance of having a strong culture. Strong culture is said to exist when staff respond to situations because of their alignment to organizational values. In these environments, strong cultures help organizations operate like well-oiled machines (Janis 1982). An important element of strong culture is consistency. As such, traditions, rituals, systems and processes are necessary for organizations to maintain a strong culture that can survive the test of time. In our organization, the 'I feel like saying' process is one of the rituals that is consistent across the organization. One of its aims is about ensuring the maintenance and development of our culture. It helps to ensure that all members of the community are living the values of the organization. Conversely, when an organization has a weak culture with little alignment to organizational values, often control is exercised through rigid bureaucratic systems. These organizations often have high levels of turnover and interpersonal conflict between staff (Janis 1982). We have talked throughout the book about the importance of consistency in the care of the children, as it provides predictability, which in turn helps provide a sense of safety. Processes throughout the organization also need to offer consistency and predictability.

CHILD SAFETY

From a child safety perspective, it is essential that all members of the community are aware of, and support the values of the organization. An organization that is fractured, and where negative behaviours and serious relationship conflict exists, could potentially place the children at risk. We discussed in Chapter 7 that we need to be careful not to re-enact the environment in which the trauma occurred for the children. An organization that promotes awareness through trauma-informed processes across all departments becomes less vulnerable to trauma re-enactment. The organization needs to be consistent and emotionally intelligent and the children need to experience the adults role modelling this. Bloom (2005, p.67) defines a trauma-informed organization as one 'that heals from its own past history of chronic stress and trauma and rejects the notion of inevitable crisis is an organization that is able to contain the emotional turmoil so characteristic of working with traumatized individuals without becoming "trauma-organized" itself.' In Australia, the Quality Improvement Council (2004) and the Australian Council for Children and Youth Organisations (2008) highlight the importance of consistent culture. The accreditation processes of these organizations focus on the consistency of processes and systems throughout the organization, and the awareness and participation of all members.

REFLECTIVE PRACTICE

We have considered the importance of thinking and reflective practice as essential elements in the work with traumatized children, as well as for the personal and professional development of staff. A reflective environment is one that is continually challenging itself, learning from experience and developing better ways of doing things. Ward (1998, p.218) describes reflective practice as, 'the individual process of thinking things over, turning them over in your mind to re-evaluate them and perhaps to make new connections.' The 'I feel like saying' process provides an opportunity for self-reflection. It is also an opportunity for peer support and feedback to ensure the therapeutic work with the children is at the forefront. The process provides participants with the opportunity to share their experiences, learnings, doubts, mistakes and successes, and to influence decision making. Each person also contributes to the learning of others and can be an agent of change. This learning from experience allows the organization to mature, to work more effectively and be more informed. A danger involved in the work is getting overwhelmed with feelings, becoming too busy and reactive. Therefore it is necessary for organizations to have processes that create a space for 'thinking', which includes thinking about feelings and what they might mean.

We have talked about the importance of all community members having the opportunity to be part of the decision-making process. This often improves decision making as it is better informed; it leads to better implementation as there is a greater sense of ownership and when people feel heard there is more commitment and less resentment. Where decisions are made in an atmosphere of resentment the children will pick up on it and it is easy for splits to develop. For example, staff and children may collude in blaming the decision makers and disowning responsibility. In many organizations there is a top-down approach to decision making. Rarely are the views of all taken into consideration and in many cases staff are discouraged to challenge or share their own opinions. Our process allows everyone to share their experiences and views. Some of the greatest innovations at Lighthouse have come from sharing in the 'I feel like saying' meetings, where managers have really listened to the emotional and practical experiences of the team, and learnt from this wealth of knowledge.

CASE EXAMPLE: JENNY

Jenny, a sixteen-year-old girl, began her process in a meeting by saying 'I feel like saying that this is a waste of time and nobody listens to me anyway'. The carer allowed Jenny to express this, and did not respond during the 'I feel like saying', as this is the guideline for the process. When the meeting reached 'things to share', the carer expressed that she was 'concerned that Jenny did not feel heard'. The carer also went on to ask, 'What is it that you are trying to say that people are not hearing?' Jenny spoke about feeling that she did not like it when they would receive visitors to the home with little notice. Although she had not verbally said anything, she expected carers to be attuned to her needs (which is common when trauma occurs at a pre-verbal stage).

Jenny had a history of her mother bringing strangers to her home when she was a child, and these strangers would abuse her mother as well as Jenny, with much of the abuse occurring in infancy. Although it was clear to the care team that the adequate security measures such as social and psychological screenings, supervision and other screening procedures were in place for people entering the home, the experience for Jenny was that these were just strangers. In addition, nobody had thought to explain to Jenny that there was such an intensive process to ensure the safety of the children. The team decided that we needed to provide more information to the children about how we protect the homes, but also ensure that we looked more carefully at the individual needs of each child, as well as the dynamic in the home before we allow visitors into the home.

EMOTIONAL INTELLIGENCE

Salovey and Mayer (1990) define emotional intelligence as the ability of an individual to monitor one's own and others' emotions; to discriminate among the positive and negative effects of emotion; and to use emotional information to guide one's thinking and actions. One of the aims of the 'I feel like saying' process is to develop emotional intelligence. Much recent research in organizational psychology has highlighted the importance of emotional intelligence in the productiveness of organizations. Emotionally intelligent organizations are likely to have higher productivity rates than those that who have lower levels of emotional intelligence (Chernis 2009). Our emotional intelligence determines our potential for learning the practical skills that are based on its five elements – self-awareness, motivation, self-regulation, empathy and adeptness in relationships. Organizational processes that focus on developing the emotional intelligence of team members create a foundation for a highly functioning organization.

EMOTIONAL WELLNESS

As an organization we are committed to the psychological wellness (Prilleltensky and Nelson 2000) of all community members. The 'I feel like saying' process provides the opportunity for community members to give emotional support to each other in what can be a very challenging work environment. On a daily basis at all levels of the organization we make decisions that can have an effect on the future of our children. The responsibility of this has an emotional impact. As a therapeutic community we rely on everyone feeling a sense of belonging and that they are being cared for. The process allows us to be attuned to the emotional state of our colleagues and children, and to provide support when required.

TRANSPARENCY AND OPENNESS

It is essential that the organization has a culture that values the importance of relationships. Carers are encouraged to build meaningful relationships with the children in their care and this should be the case in all relationships within the organization. If staff treat each other in an impersonal way this can reflect a lack of concern, which is not supportive of the therapeutic task. We can't expect children to develop healthy relationships if this is not role modelled by those responsible for their care. The result of a breakdown in staff relationships or the carers not feeling supported by management can be that carers are not so forthright in disclosing what is going on for them. This can soon lead to a split between management and direct care staff. One of the risks when the organization becomes less transparent is that management becomes less aware of what is going on at a home level and how carers are coping. In an open and transparent organization, individuals are more likely to be accountable to each other. They know that being open and transparent is likely to result in support rather than persecution. The 'I feel like saying' process provides an opportunity for senior staff to form more meaningful relationships with staff and, therefore, the ability to make more informed and supportive decisions.

FAMILY MEETINGS

The 'family' meeting is a process that is commonly used across therapeutic communities, and may have different names – group home meetings, house meetings, children's meetings and so on. The purpose and structure may be different depending on the organization and the therapeutic task. At Lighthouse, the meetings within the homes that involve the carers and the children are referred to as family meetings. It is common to be asked why call it a family meeting? The meeting is attended by those who live in the home, what we would refer to as the family. The model of care is aimed at recreating a family environment, hence the use of the term family.

The family meeting is a process aimed at enabling and encouraging children to become more confident in expressing themselves, listening to and respecting the rights of others. It is a process that assists children in developing solution-orientated approaches, including conflict resolution and creative problem-solving skills, rather than remain in the role of a victim with a sense of powerlessness. It is also an opportunity for carers and other team members to provide positive role modelling in the form of effective emotional regulation and pro-social behaviours to the children.

When children have input into how their life is managed they feel that they have a sense of control over their environment, and as such their positive self-esteem develops. When they feel that their opinion is as important as anyone else's it enables them to also value others' opinions and points of view. The same can be said for team members and other stakeholders in an organization. We seek to develop a parallel process for team members and key stakeholders, similar to that of the children. The psychological wellness of all members needs to be cared for. Everyone needs to feel that their views are respected, and that they will be supported. It is essential that all adults are able to role model to children that they are also willing to grow and develop as human beings, and to manage the uncomfortable emotions and experiences that may be involved in this.

The meetings provide a space, which enables children to develop confidence in expressing themselves and to listen to each other in a respectful way. They encourage children to become solution-oriented individuals who are empowered to manage their own environment. The meeting is an opportunity for children to have input into the running of their home and also to have a say in what happens in the organization. Issues raised by the children are shared by their carers in the carers' meeting, where a member of the senior care team is also present. When children have this kind of input they are more likely to take on responsibility for themselves and the consequence of their input. The group/peer environment greatly facilitates the likelihood that children will keep any agreements that they make in front of the group and hold other children accountable to agreements that they make.

We aim for family meetings to be a 'safe space' where children can share their points of view without fear of being ridiculed or judged. Children observe that their opinion is as important as everyone else's and thus learn to attribute the same value to the opinions and views of others. No one is protected by 'status', such as being the eldest in the group and each child's point of view is as valid as any other. Very often children are listened to and taken seriously for the first time in their lives. The meetings provide an opportunity for children to develop empathy and for them to experience being empathized with, by asking questions such as 'I wonder how that makes so and so feel?' This kind of exploration is very important for children who have little capacity to empathize. As Cameron and Maginn (2009, p.42) explain, 'Empathy is the ability to see another person's perspective – it is a defining ingredient in being able to sustain a close relationship. Empathy is the single greatest inhibitor of the propensity to violence.' They go on to point out how the child's development of empathy will be shaped by how they see others responding to distress. The adults provide a crucial role model in demonstrating this.

The meetings provide house members with an opportunity to share their experiences with one another. Through sharing day-to-day events, challenges and solutions, children can quickly learn that other people's histories do not prevent them from getting on with their lives. This can often motivate them to proactively manage their own lives.

We recognize that peer pressure can be either negative or positive. Negative peer pressure is often conforming in order to be accepted by others.

Positive peer pressure, on the other hand, is more about being accountable to commitments made to others. Family meetings can be a forum for positive peer pressure. Children make commitments to the group and are held accountable to those commitments.

Whitwell (2009) emphasizes the way in which children as well as adults contribute to the wellness of the group:

> Within a group living household the health of the household has to outweigh the illness for it to be a positive living experience. The majority of the health (wellness) will come from the staff team but some needs to come from within the group of children. When a group becomes established some of the children whose development is well under way become culture carriers, i.e. positive role models for the newer children. (p.4)

Through open and non-judgemental communication, children learn how to effectively communicate their point of view and negotiate outcomes for themselves. They learn the ability to express contentious issues openly and honestly and that 'being right' is not what matters. Effective communication skills are role modelled and, through experience, children learn to utilize these skills in other areas of their lives.

The structure of the family meeting is the same as for all group processes. It includes the 'I feel like saying' process, which was originally developed for family meetings, and was later introduced to all organizational group processes.

Scheduling

Family meetings are a regular event and not just held when there is a problem. They are held in each home on a weekly basis. Ensuring the meetings are regular reduces tension in the home by often keeping issues contained until they can be addressed at the meeting. Therefore, it is helpful for the timing of the meeting to be reliable and to occur at the same time of the week. This also helps the weekly routine to feel consistent. It is also important that carers have the opportunity to debrief following their family meeting experience and the challenges that they may have faced. This should be done in clinical supervision and peer supervision processes.

Duration

We don't put a clear time boundary on the length of the meeting and we allow as much time as necessary to address fully the issues of the group. Sometimes this can be for a couple of hours, and when there are important matters to discuss the children tend to value this rather than resist it. Knowing that the meeting is not expected to finish quickly creates more opportunities for children to safely voice their opinions without fear that they will extend the length of the meeting by doing so. For instance, a child may feel pressured not to speak if she is holding up other children from their free time. If children refrain from sharing in the hope of decreasing the length of the meeting, carers will challenge this and ensure that meetings are given the appropriate time to fully address important issues. Carers may wish to bring up a topic that they know children will feel strongly about or engage in an activity that requires everyone's contribution.

Environment

Family meetings are held at the home usually in a circle in the family room or other relaxed setting. Meetings are free from distractions such as televisions, radios and food. Occasionally, the meetings may be held in a quiet outdoor space. It is important that the environment does not impact on the children's ability to concentrate on the group process.

Effective communication

The family meeting is an opportunity for role modelling effective communication skills. Carers demonstrate effective communication strategies to the children such as reflective listening, active listening, positive language, unconditional positive regard and non-judgemental language.

It is important to tackle issues like bullying or pairing during the meetings, and ensure that everyone acknowledges each other's points of view as 'valid'. The following guidelines are important:

- Everyone has the opportunity to contribute their point of view.
- Members do not interrupt each other.
- Only one person speaks at a time.

- Each member is paying attention to the speaker.

- Communication and language are respectful.

- 'I' statements rather than 'you' statements are used.

- There is a brief time lapse between speakers to give time to digest the last person's communication.

Encourage openness and honesty

Children are encouraged to 'speak their truth', which can require a high level of openness and honesty that some children may not be accustomed to. Honesty can often mean sharing feelings of inadequacy and vulnerability. Children should not be ridiculed, attacked or negatively judged for sharing such feelings. Carers encourage and acknowledge children's attempts to be honest with themselves and others. In the children's pasts, being honest has often resulted in conflict or punishment. Thus, some children may refrain from being open about what is true for them out of fear. Children are regularly reminded that committing to communicate openly and honestly means that potential problem areas are faced head on in a manner that encourages resolution. The acknowledgement process in the meeting is an opportunity to provide positive feedback to children about their courage in being open and honest, and provides a different experience to the past.

Promoting democracy

Family meetings provide a useful system for working towards meeting everyone's needs in a democratic way. When children see things happen as a result of decisions made jointly, their self-esteem improves, as it provides them with a sense of influence (McMillan and Chavis 1986). The meetings utilize the process of compulsory voting to make decisions that affect everyone in the home. The use of compulsory voting provides an opportunity to identify children – who may otherwise have remained silent – who disagree with a particular decision. Doing so opens up the opportunity for creative solutions and focused discussion on how everyone in the home can get their needs or desires met around decisions that affect everyone. Ideally decisions will only be made when there is a unanimous vote. Attempting to reach this outcome is an effective strategy for teaching conflict resolution, negotiation and solutions-focused skills.

As Whitwell (2009) explained:

Something important happens within the whole group (children and grown-ups) when discussion takes place, disagreements take place, before arriving at a consensus. This might be over what colour the crockery should be, what to do in leisure time, or the ground rules of living together. (p.8)

The process involved is often as important, if not more, than the decision that is made.

Everyone contributes

Family meetings are a forum for every member of the home to contribute their views. Carers encourage the more reserved children to voice their opinion as often as possible and 'check in' from time to time to ensure that every child feels that they have been heard.

At times a child may be asked to leave the meeting because she is being disruptive. In these circumstances the child is told that her behaviour is inappropriate, however she needs to come back to the meeting when she can manage her behaviour appropriately. It is important that the child sees the consequence is for her behaviour and that she is still valued as a person and required for the meeting. At other times, a child may voluntarily leave the meeting as she is struggling with the emotional process and feels she needs a little space to manage her feelings. Similarly, the child is asked to return to the meeting when she can, as she is a valued member of the group. Carers use their discretion as to whether the meeting can take a break until all members can be present again.

Breaks

Everyone in the meeting needs to be able to give each other their full attention, so if children are becoming restless and distracted a short break may be required. Carers are mindful about the content of the meetings when breaks are requested. They determine whether a break will unhelpfully disrupt the process of the meeting, especially if a child is sharing something important. It is also common for children to seek an escape or 'flight' when working through is occurring. This is monitored to ensure that the process is continued if there is going to be a potential breakthrough.

Role of the carers

In order to empower the children, carers contribute to the running of the meeting as little as possible. To support children's development, carers allow them to figure out solutions to problems on their own in their own style. Carers avoid correcting children too often and if input is required, it is given as a suggestion as opposed to a direction. However, in some circumstances a carer may be required to step in, take control and set reasonable limits, particularly when children are being bullied or treated unfairly. In most other circumstances carers support the running of the meeting through the occasional prompting and advising of the meeting's chairperson, which is one of the children. Carers role model the meeting guidelines and effective communication strategies through their own contributions and advice to the chairperson. The involvement of the carer will also depend on the developmental needs of the children and how much the children are able to manage.

Role of the chairperson

We use a weekly rotational process, where all children have an opportunity to chair the meeting, and the role of the carer will be less intensive depending on the developmental stage of the child who is chairing. The carer also provides the chairperson the opportunity to debrief following the family meeting. The role of the chairperson is to facilitate the meeting ensuring that the culture of the meeting is followed and agenda items are addressed. The chairperson manages the time boundaries of the meeting and ensures that accurate minutes are taken. One of the carers sits next to the chairperson and provides feedback and prompts as required. However, in supporting the child the carer gives the chairperson every opportunity to figure out the role on their own. This helps children to develop leadership qualities that can be useful in the future for their careers or life generally. It also prepares children to develop the skills they require to be leaders in our community. We have had children move on to take on leadership roles in the organization, such as a position on the board of directors, as youth representative on committees, or work as carers.

Celebration

Following the family meeting with a relaxing and enjoyable experience can be a good way of acknowledging the hard work that has been done and creating a sense of togetherness. Susan talks about the benefits of finishing family meetings with acknowledgements, as well as a treat. She traditionally provided ice creams following meetings. It is important that the home has a tradition about what occurs after family meetings, and that there is a positive ending to what can be a challenging process. The children's courage in participating, the hard work they have done in developing their emotional intelligence, and their ongoing commitment to the family unit should be acknowledged and celebrated.

COMBINED FAMILY MEETINGS

This involves more than one home coming together for a meeting. The meetings provide an opportunity for children in the different homes to connect with other children and learn from each other's effective family meeting processes. As we have said, in a model that is focused on developing a sense of family and community, the children and carers in the other homes are like an extended family. The use of combined family meetings provides the opportunity to experience how other homes function. It also extends the network of family and friends. Scheduling some time for recreational activity helps children from different homes to make connections with each other, which can help the group process to feel more relaxed and open.

WHOLE FAMILY MEETINGS

Periodically, usually every six months, we hold a family meeting with all the homes. The purpose of these meetings is to bring everyone together and provide important information about child safety, to remind children of their rights and give an appropriate opportunity to air grievances, report concerns and contribute ideas for development. Senior staff, carers and all children attend the meeting. This provides an opportunity to gain insight into what is happening in the homes and helps children and adults to connect and build bridges across the whole organization.

YOUTH FORUMS

This is a consultative session where children are informed about what is happening in the organization. The children are also consulted on the future directions of the organization and are provided with an opportunity to raise any ideas or concerns they have about this. The forums usually have a theme, for instance, a 'vision day' or the development of a new programme such as the ACT (Adult Community Transition) programme, which was developed with the feedback from children (see Chapter 9).

CLINICAL SUPERVISION (RELATIONSHIP BETWEEN CARERS)

The relationship between the carers and the children who live in the home together is the most pivotal in the organization. This relationship is the guiding light in caring for and also mentoring the children to develop their own healthy relationships into the future. It provides children who have experienced traumatic home environments, which included inappropriate or neglectful parenting, a different experience to this, which they can internalize as being the norm.

As an organization we need to be attuned to the needs and concerns of the carers. We need to act quickly when we see that the relationship between the carers is at risk of adversely affecting the children in the homes. The relationship between carers is much like that of a regular family – there can be harmonious times and there can be conflicts. Traumatized children are especially attuned to the relationship between their parents, and can easily pick up any fractures in the relationship. Difficulties in the relationship between the parents may have resulted in the child's abuse, neglect or even abandonment. Therefore, these children have often learnt to 'read' the relationship between their parents as a way of protecting themselves. The children's heightened state of alert and constant fearfulness, as well as challenging behaviour, can create a tense atmosphere, which puts a strain on the relationship between carers. As discussed earlier, children may attempt to split the carers into 'good' and 'bad', in the same way an infant splits good and bad aspects of the mother. This can be seen as a primitive survival mechanism, by trying to preserve the good and get rid of the bad. When this split is being projected onto two carers the danger is that it becomes enacted by the carers as they take on the roles assigned to them.

Without appropriate clinical supervision this dynamic is easy to collude with. Our carers receive individual clinical supervision to understand their own psychodynamic process and also supervision which is focused on the relationship between the carers. This focuses on how the carers are working together with the children, exploring the dynamics of their relationship and any issues that may be arising, like splitting. The supervision relationship has an aspect to it that is similar to couple counselling between parents. It is about strengthening the relationship so that the carers can provide the most appropriate level of care to the children as a team.

Our approach to clinical supervision is a psychodynamic model. The focus is on supporting the carers to gain insight into the unconscious processes that impact on their reactions to the work with the children and team members.

In particular there is a focus on understanding their work with children and their defence mechanisms, as well as the processes of transference and countertransference. Defence mechanisms form a kind of psychological protection against threat or stress. This protection is necessary in order to cope with or endure difficult situations without becoming overwhelmed, and of which we are, for the most part, completely unaware. According to psychoanalytic theory, we need defence mechanisms in order to maintain stability when in a state of anxiety, so as not to become overwhelmed (Freud, A. 1986; Freud, S. 1926). Because of constitutional factors and formative experiences, we all differ in our ability to tolerate and manage stress (Khaleelee 2007). Under great stress or in a critical situation, defence mechanisms function as the 'shock absorber' of the mind. However, too great an amount of defence, or a defence setup of a certain kind, may be a serious disadvantage. It will prevent us from getting a correct perception of reality and thereby guide us to the wrong decisions, possibly with catastrophic results (Khaleelee 2007).

The defence mechanisms of traumatized children, due to the extreme situations which they have been subjected to, are often so extensive that they have a major distorting effect on the child's ability to perceive reality and relate to others. In turn, because of the emotional challenges that working with such children pose to us, our own defence mechanisms are likely to be activated. Working on these issues in supervision is critical, so that we are able to maintain helpful responses to the children rather than ones that become increasingly defensive and reactive.

CLINICAL PEER SUPERVISION (CARERS' MEETING)

When group dynamics are managed effectively, and the emotional aspects of the supervision process are attended to, the group supervision setting can provide invaluable resources that are not available in the context of individual supervision.

Andersson 2008, p.36

The carers' meeting provides a holding environment for the carers to be supported in thinking about and processing the work that they do with children. Carers come together on a weekly basis for half a day, with the intention of providing each other with emotional and practical support and to participate in training. This is an opportunity for carers to:

- share their insights with each other
- look at other ways of managing the challenges of the work
- share resources

- develop strong relationships with each other

- build a sense of community with carers in other homes

- celebrate achievements and acknowledge each other's work

- gain more insight into their own processes.

As Andersson (2008, p.38) said, 'when supervision takes place in a group setting, a greater range of feedback, support, challenges and viewpoints on clinical issues can be obtained.'

At Lighthouse this process is facilitated by a psychologist. As well as being attuned to the carers the psychologist will also have a strong understanding of group and family dynamics, which is especially important in facilitating such a process. Because of the strong relationship with the children and the personal nature of the work, inevitably the carers become emotionally invested in their work. It is particularly important in the group process that the facilitator understands the emotional investment involved. The facilitator needs to be attuned to how personal it can feel to be challenged on issues such as one's parenting role.

We have mentioned the saying 'that it takes a village to raise a child' and that ideally parents have the support of an extended family in raising a child. The statement that 'two (or more) heads are needed for one' is also relevant when talking about the carers' meeting. The meeting provides the carers with many heads to think about the work with the children. Not only do carers provide each other with insights, advice and emotional supports, the group also acts as what Altfeld (1999) describes as a group container for various affects and defence mechanisms that emerge in the therapeutic work. The capacity of a group to act as a container is potentially much larger than what can occur in individual supervision.

MEDIATION PROCESSES

Traumatized children need to be provided with a holding environment to have their primary needs met, and to develop long-term healthy relationships. We believe that all interactions within a therapeutic community are an opportunity for healing, and that all interactions should have a therapeutic purpose. As such, when community members experience conflict we provide a safe space for conflict to be resolved, and for the role modelling of positive relationships. If a conflict arises between members of the therapeutic community, whether between a child and carer or between workers in different roles, they are always encouraged to resolve the issue directly with each other. If they are unable or lack confidence to do this, we utilize a mediation process which seeks to strengthen the relationship. This plays an important role in healing relationships in the therapeutic community.

It is particularly important for children who have had a number of abusive and broken relationships throughout their lives to experience the reparation process and learn that although relationships can become very strained, they can also be healed. If handled positively the strain in the relationship can often become a point of growth. It is also empowering for children to have the opportunity to have their voices heard. A skilful facilitator ensures that all parties come out of the process feeling heard. We have many layers of mediation process from the family meetings that can mediate between children in the home; the carers' meeting that allows for mediation between members of the care team; and the 'I feel like saying' process that is in all meetings and provides opportunities to address relationship difficulties. We also have more formal mediation processes which are facilitated by in-house psychologists or the senior care team, when a more specialist approach is required.

CHAPTER 9

Moving On

Transitions, Aftercare and Outreach

Moving on can be a time to celebrate achievements and progress made. It is also a time of change and loss and therefore a time of ambivalence. It is an emotional time for the child and all involved in caring for the child. We see the child developing into an autonomous person, but we experience the reality that the child is now ready to separate from us. It is this mix of happiness and loss that makes it one of the most emotional stages of the work.

In this chapter we shall be drawing significantly on the recent research carried out by Hannon *et al.* of Demos (a UK independent think tank and research institute) in collaboration with Barnardo's and supported by Loughborough University. Their research has analyzed the short- and long-term outcomes for children living in residential care in the UK. They examine the factors that correlate positively and negatively with achieving positive outcomes. They found that the way a child's transition from care is planned is one of the major determinants of the outcomes achieved. We believe that their findings would apply to all children making the transition from care, wherever they may be.

> There are four factors that can significantly improve a young person's experience of leaving care and give young people a chance of better adult outcomes: the age at which young people leave care; the speed of their transition; their access to preparation before leaving care and support after leaving care; and maintaining stability and secure attachments after leaving care. (Hannon *et al.* 2010, p.15)

Humans can be considered to be much like herd animals; we are social beings that have a need to belong to a group. When our children transition into interdependence in the community there is often a coming and going over the years as they develop a sense of autonomy. They return to the secure base of their parents and family, as they explore and experiment with the outside world. As Winnicott (1990, p.84) explains, 'Independence is never absolute. The healthy individual does not become isolated, but becomes related to the environment in such a way that the individual and the environment can be said to be interdependent.' Some children will take longer than others to separate from their family of origin.

In children with trauma histories the process, although similar, can be more anxiety provoking for the child and much more complex. Not only do they lack the internal resources, but also external resources, as they may have limited relational and community supports. The response of a loving family during periods of transition is to envelope their child with a knowledge that they are there for him for life. Parents do the dance of encouraging exploration, letting him know that he can and will achieve autonomy but also picking him up if he falls. It is about the child learning through practice, and being able to fall and be picked up again. We have noticed over the past twenty years that children will make a couple of attempts of testing the water, before they move to independent living successfully for the long term. It is vital that the child has a secure base to return to from time to time. The internalization of this secure base is really the recipe for success. Hence, the work that is done in the home provides the child with a secure internal working model of the world. This provides him with the confidence to develop into an autonomous person, which is so vital for a successful transition to independent living.

TRANSITION AS SEPARATION EXPERIENCE

The separation experience can be a period of excitement but also of great sadness for the carers and children. As a therapeutic parent, the carer is encouraged and supported to develop a close bond with the child. This is a vital process in the journey to recovery for the child. The relationship with the young person is similar to that of a parent and their own child. When our children transition into adulthood, we are excited for them, and we may reminisce on the many wonderful and challenging moments, and we may also enter a grieving process. It is no different for the carer, who invests so much energy into the care of the children. The separation process is further compounded by the fact that with the transition of one child, comes the arrival of another. The carer is grieving, but also having to divert attention to ensure a positive beginning for the child arriving. It is important that carers are supported through their clinical supervision to process the emotionality of the work. The carer's emotional state will impact on the transition for the child, either positively or negatively.

CASE EXAMPLE: JANICE (CARER) AND CRAIG (CHILD)

Janice, a middle-aged carer, was asked by Steven, the psychologist facilitating the carers' meeting (peer supervision), how Craig was progressing in his therapeutic journey. As Janice spoke it became increasingly clear that Craig was ready for a transition into more independent living. He had held a steady job for twelve months, he had saved up money, his relationship with his girlfriend and her family was stable, and he was spending less time in the home. Steven facilitated a process with the group to explore Craig's readiness for transition and the group came to the conclusion that it was clear Craig was ready.

During the group process it came to the surface that what was holding back the transition was actually the carer's own grieving process, as the potential transition of Craig brought feelings to the surface that she experienced when her own biological son moved out of home. The process was a very helpful way to gain insight into the transference relationship with the child, and how the carer's own unresolved grief was holding back the child's development. At the end of the group process, a plan was developed to begin a planned transition for Craig and to ensure that Janice was also supported to separate from Craig.

Waddell explains how the carer being able to let go and work through feelings of loss, like those experienced by Janice, is crucial in enabling the child to separate:

> It is the mother who has been through the pain of mutual relinquishment who will be able, in turn, to enable her child to develop a sense of inner independence, not the one who offers herself as an object-to-be-clung-to, unable to modulate the force of her infant's separation anxiety – the one who fearfully slips out without saying goodbye: 'It will be less upsetting if I just disappear.' It is the mother's feelings that are here being attributed to the child, and it is she who has the difficulty in tolerating mental pain. (Waddell 1989)

The separation experience is challenging for the children in our care, as it can be for any child transitioning into more independent forms of living. As we have discussed, traumatized children who have experienced many broken placements in their lives, have been abandoned by their own families and abused by people that should have cared for them, can find it extremely difficult to build a healthy attachment. The separation process can be especially challenging, as it can bring on once again the feelings of grief and loss associated with their trauma. We need to understand that attachment trauma for these children is very much associated with grief and loss, and the process of transition can be interpreted as another loss in their lives. As Hannon *et al.* argue, we cannot underestimate the extent of change which many children leaving state care are faced with,

> The process of moving from 'looked after' to 'care leaver' status might be compared to being released from prison in the suddenness with which a person's life changes, and certainly reminds the young person (if they had ever forgotten) that they are very much part of a 'system'. The speed with which a young care leaver finds themselves 'independent' has been reported to be traumatic for many, as they are ill prepared practically and emotionally for what this transition entails. (Hannon *et al.* 2010, p.138)

The care team has to be attuned to the emotional needs of the child. A trauma-informed approach helps to understand the impact of the child's grief and loss, and hence will involve a long-term, gentle and therapeutic approach to the transition of the child. The child needs to be supported by the whole circle of care, whether in the home, by the clinicians and anybody else responsible for his care. In particular he needs support to make sense of the feelings associated with the separation, to process how he is feeling, to normalize the experience, and to ensure a healthy separation. The role of the therapist can be particularly important, as it opens up the opportunity to really explore issues around loss, and the chance to internalize a different relational experience associated with separation that is less traumatic.

LIFE MEMBERSHIP

Lighthouse Foundation provides life membership to all the children who live in our homes. In a regular family when a child moves out of home, his parents and siblings will continue to be in his life forever. This concept of family for life has been incorporated into our Therapeutic Family Model of Care. The support that is provided to young people transitioning from the homes is varied and is based on their individual needs. The nature of it will depend on issues such as the child's resilience, mental health, general health, developmental needs, support networks in the community, relationship with family of origin, and other factors that can impact on the child's ability to manage independent living. For instance, when a child has just moved out the support may be more intensive, such as case management and regular counselling. Alternatively, the child may return to the home for respite stays as he continues to build his capacity to manage in the community. For those who have been in the community long term, they may be coming home for a lunch or dinner, or to celebrate birthdays and personal achievements, or for Christmas celebrations. Hannon *et al.* confirm the importance of this concept:

> Charities such as Barnardo's and Rainer carrying out research into the experiences and outcomes of children leaving care have suggested that care leavers – in line with the experience of children leaving their birth families – should be able to return to a supported environment after they have left care if they feel they cannot cope. Rainer's support for this proposal stems from a survey it carried out with care leavers in 2006 as part of their project What Makes The Difference?, which found that 88 per cent of leavers felt they should have had the option to return to supported accommodation if a move to independent living was not successful. (Hannon *et al.* 2010, p.101)

TRANSITIONAL PLANNING AND TRANSITIONAL OBJECTS

Transitional planning is an important element of preparing children for independent living in the community. When moving from an intensive therapeutic programme that supports children in all domains of their life, it can be challenging for the child to move into more independent forms of living. A programme with a focus on children building primary attachments with a carer needs to have structured transitional processes to help prevent another unhealthy separation with feelings of abandonment. Positive transitions are an important part of the child's development from being totally dependent on a primary attachment, to developing into an autonomous self. If the separation is a healthy one, the child develops faith in relationships, trust that relationships can change over time and separation does not need to be a traumatic experience.

Winnicott (1953) wrote about the importance of what he terms transitional objects in the development of a child. During infancy when a child separates from his mother, he may use a transitional object such as a blanket or a teddy bear. These objects signify the beginning of the separation process from being totally dependent and part of the mother, to developing a relationship with the outside world. Winnicott explains the significance of the transitional object in the separation process:

> When we witness an infant's employment of a transitional object, the first not-me possession, we are witnessing both the child's first use of a symbol and the first experience of play... The use of an object symbolises the union of two now separate things, baby and mother, *at the point in time and space of the initiation of their state of separateness.* (Winnicott 1971, p.96)

The same process, is followed when working with traumatized children from an attachment model. Once the primary attachment is developed between the child and carer, we need to provide the opportunity for a child to find and use a transitional object. And when a child is moving on, it is also important to provide a transitional relationship that can act as a bridge between the relationship with his carer and the community he is moving into. This role may also assist the child to further expand his networks in the community to support the transition.

The period of transition needs to be matched to the recovery process of the child. We have talked about the importance of long-term, consistent and repetitive work with traumatized children throughout the book. One of the positive aspects of the relationship that develops is that it can allow the care team to plan carefully the transition with attunement to the child's needs. Many of the children that we work with will be in the programme for two or more years and the transitional process will also take considerable time. We ensure that we begin the transition process six to twelve months prior to the child moving to independent living. This provides plenty of time to prepare the child for the transition. Hannon *et al.* emphasize the importance of giving the child time:

> If we are to promote resilience in looked-after children and young people, there needs to be more recognition of the nature and *timing* of young people's transitions from care, including the psychological space needed to cope with the significant changes taking place in their lives. (Hannon *et al.* 2010, p.15)

It is vital that all care team members are working towards the same therapeutic goals for the child. It is common during transition for a child to regress. Everyone in the therapeutic team needs to be aware of the normality of this and to be consistent in their approach.

TRANSITION CELEBRATIONS

It is important that the children have the opportunity to celebrate their transition with their extended 'family' in the home and organization. The celebration provides the children with a sense of achievement for the work they have done during their therapeutic journey. It also provides them with a sense of love and belonging as the family gathers together to wish them well on the next stage of their journey. It provides a physical demonstration that they are part of a family and community that will still be there if they need support in the future. It can also act as an inspiration for other children who are still early in their journey, to experience what the future may look like.

STEPPING STONES: TRANSITIONAL PROGRAMMES

One of the biggest challenges for children that are transitioning from an intensive therapeutic care programme is providing a continuum of care that prepares them for more independent forms of living. A major gap in the out of home care system in Australia and in other countries has been that such children often have limited options to support their transition into autonomous adulthood.

At Lighthouse we have developed a programme called the Adult Community Transition (ACT) Programme. The ACT Programme provides homes for the young people, which they move into as a transitional stage before moving into independent living. The ACT Programme was created in response to the needs of children to assist their move from dependency to interdependency. It was designed with the input of the children and is dedicated to encouraging children to become active members of society. It assists them in developing the skills and confidence to make the transition. Whilst living within the Therapeutic Family Model of Care the children are provided with a long-term, consistent, safe, supportive and understanding environment, where they can confront and deal with past trauma and maladaptive and destructive patterns of relating. They learn how to form and sustain positive and reciprocal relationships with others. The transitional model goes one step further by allowing those learnings to be put into practice in a more independent, less structured environment, empowering children to: learn from their choices; gain a sense of ownership over their future interests and goals; and practice their living skills in a more independent environment, whilst still receiving support. Hannon *et al.* explain the value of this transitional stage:

> Anthropological research also suggests that young people tend to deal with change by using a transition phase – known as the 'liminal state' or opportunity to 'space out'. This liminal state provides a time for freedom, exploration, reflection, risk taking and identity search, which is critical to the promotion of resilience in adulthood. This time exposes young people to challenging situations that provide opportunities to develop problem-solving abilities and emotional coping skills. For a majority of young people today, this is gained through the experience of further and higher education, but could also be achieved through graduated responsibilities being taken on in line with graduated independence. Stein *et al.* [Stein 2005] conclude that in promoting resilience, there needs to be more recognition of the nature and timing of young people's transitions from care, including the psychological space needed to cope with changes over time, and the significance of the middle-stage 'liminal stage' of transition. (Hannon *et al.* 2010, p.101)

During the transitional stage a child's anxieties about being on his own and abandoned can be triggered. A child may feel overwhelmed and present with a crisis of some kind. The response to these crises needs to strike a balance between providing practical support, but also enabling the child to gain insight into his feelings and actions, and to find his own solutions.

We have up to five young people living in each ACT home, which includes a senior resident (lead tenant) who acts as a positive role model for the young people. The senior resident is supported by the Community Care and Psychological Wellness teams to support the young people in the home. They ensure that the young people maintain a day programme that involves education and/or training, and are developing the skills to manage more independent forms of living in the future. The young people in the home also receive case management support from the Community Care Team and counselling from the Psychological Wellness Team. The programme provides the senior residents with the opportunity to develop their own youth work skills and opens the doors to a career in the youth sector. The senior residents enter the LIGHT (Lighthouse Internship and Graduate Holistic Training) programme, which provides them with the opportunity to gain their youth work qualifications through Royal Melbourne Institute of Technology. This approach correlates positively with what Hannon *et al.* have found to be important in enabling a positive transition:

> A number of studies have associated positive outcomes for care leavers with: receiving adequate planning and preparation before leaving care, so they had developed strong life and social skills; being engaged in education, employment or training; having a positive sense of their own wellbeing; having a network of informal support, including family and friends; having access to 'good' housing on leaving care: those who failed to secure good housing arrangements early on tended to fare worse over the follow-up period; having good-quality support in accommodation after leaving care. (Hannon *et al.* 2010, p.15)

ASSESSING READINESS FOR TRANSITION

Treatment is described in psychodynamic literature as a process of working through. Working through refers to the 'systematic interpretation, observation, confrontation, and clarification of repetitive patterns in the patient's life' (Gabbard 2004, p.186). The therapeutic process for the child is one of gaining insight into relational patterns and internalizing a more positive working model of the world. In assessing readiness for transition, we use the yardstick that is used in long-term psychodynamic therapy. A child is perceived to be ready for transition when he has internalized the psychotherapeutic process (Gabbard 2004). That is, he has gained insight, and is now able to autonomously apply what he has learnt about himself and the relational world in practice. In a therapeutic care programme, the child internalizes things such as what it is like to be loved and thought about, what a parent should be like, what a home is like, what a healthy relationship looks like and so on. Skills development is also an important yardstick.

We separate learnings into the categories of individual, relational and community wellness (Prilleltensky and Nelson 2000). For instance, for individual wellness we look at things like physical health and developmental milestones. When it comes to relational wellness, we look at areas including capacity for attachment, healthy relationships and networks of friends. And when we look at community wellness we consider things like access to safe accommodation, community networks, employment and education. It is vital that the child has developed mastery across these three major domains to ensure that the transition is successful. Hannon *et al.* found that a child's readiness to leave care correlates strongly with the age of the child:

> Looked-after children who leave care early, for example at 16, tend to do less well than those who leave care later. Evidence suggests they have a higher instance of substance abuse, homelessness, unemployment and poor educational outcomes. Young people doing well with their careers tended to have left care later. (Hannon *et al.* 2010, p.15)

CARER RELATIONSHIP BEYOND TRANSITION

The role of the carer beyond transition can be a crucial support for the child. It is well documented that often when children leave care they are not provided adequate support and to a large extent they have to fend for themselves. There can be various reasons for this, some of them regarding the regulations around children in care and some more to do with concerns about being unhelpful in the process of separation for the child. However, with appropriate boundaries in place an ongoing relationship between the child and previous carers can be immensely valuable for the child. A connection for the child with his carers and the home can provide a secure base for the child to transition into an autonomous adult. However, it is especially important that boundaries are clear and that the ongoing relationship is supervised to ensure that it is healthy and safe for everyone involved. The continued relationship between a child and carer can help to give the child a sense that the relationship was real and that the carer's commitment was really there. This is in much the same way that parents show ongoing care and concern for their children as they grow up. It also provides the child with a sense of belonging to the home that he lived in and the organization as part of his community.

As we discussed, the children at Lighthouse are members for life and are welcome to return to their homes as one would in a family. We understand that for many of the children that we work with, we are the only family that they have and losing this could be damaging to their long-term wellbeing. Hannon *et al.* (2010, p.214) emphasize the importance of maintaining the child's attachments that he has formed during and after transition and 'that transition is gradual and responsive to a young person's needs, emulating more closely the natural experiences of young people leaving their birth families.'

Jamie describes his experiences of separation and moving on: how there is both the need for a sense of independence and also support to fall back on.

JAMIE'S STORY: FACING FEARS; TRANSITIONING

After about a year at Lighthouse, it was hard to make that decision to leave, but if I didn't make the movement of leaving I wouldn't be where I am today. I have succeeded. I have a family, houses that I own and everything I want. I had to face my fear of failing. I had to do it myself. But Lighthouse was still there, but they weren't. I was making my journey but they were there if I fell. I didn't want them to be there for me, I thought I might fall on my arse, but I didn't. But Lighthouse was there in case. It gave me a sense of security. I sometimes still visit Lighthouse. Just to say hello.

AFTERCARE PROGRAMME

One of the downfalls of residential care programmes can be the lack of aftercare planning and support. Many children transition into living arrangements that they are not developmentally ready for. This can be particularly challenging if the children have not had enough preparation with learning life skills and how to make choices. They may struggle to live independently and to make the most basic life choices. We discussed earlier the importance of transitional planning, but what happens once a child leaves an intensive support programme and the reality hits that he is now in some ways on his own? Aftercare is vital for the successful transition of children into more independent forms of living. Our Aftercare Programme provides children with the much needed support in their transition out of the more intensive live-in care programme. The programme provides the children with intensive case management in at least the first six months post-transition. Counselling is also provided by a psychologist from the Psychological Wellness Team, to support them emotionally with the challenges of living independently. Hannon *et al.* support the importance of this:

> Given the prevalence of mental health problems among children in care, it would seem obvious that in addition to emotional preparation before leaving, targeted emotional and mental health support for young people after leaving would also be a priority. A rapid break with carers, change of home and living alone may well trigger or exacerbate underlying mental health problems. (Hannon *et al.* 2010, p.103)

Jacinta's story shows the importance of an aftercare programme with ongoing support and the opportunity to return to supported accommodation, should the transition be difficult.

JACINTA'S STORY: TRANSITION INTO INDEPENDENT LIVING

When I first moved to Lighthouse, it was straight from hospital. I moved in but I did not have the insight or wellness at the time to appreciate what was on offer, or to realize the value of this opportunity. The first time was about having a period of settling in my life and building relationships, but subsequently I moved out after two years. I was not at the stage where I appreciated the opportunity and did not value change. I wanted to move out so I could continue my behaviours without interference and reflection. I was still seeing Julie, the Lighthouse psychologist.

After about seven months, I realized my living conditions/situation were out of control. I needed to change and was very unhappy with my situation. I knew I needed to get out of my bad situation but I did not know how to do it by myself. It was Julie who suggested and supported me to move back into Lighthouse for a little while – to remove myself from danger. I was also ready this time for change but first I needed the support of Lighthouse outreach to remove myself from my situation. You can't change if you are surrounded by negativity or patterns you are trying to break in yourself.

OUTREACH

To provide the concept of life management effectively it is necessary to have an outreach programme. By this we mean the engagement with children who are no longer living in our homes, but are still part of the Lighthouse family. The support may vary from access to education and training, to sending a birthday greeting, to more intensive case management. The programme is flexible in nature and responds to the needs of the children living in the community. The focus of the programme is very much on supporting the child's reintegration into the wider community. As such it works closely with other service providers and community partners to ensure that outreach children are supported in their independent living arrangements.

Carol's story highlights the vulnerability of the young person making a transition and how vital it is that she is ready and has the necessary support, as we have described in this chapter.

CAROL'S STORY: TRANSITION INTO INDEPENDENT LIVING

I formed many different relationships at Lighthouse. These relationships then helped me gain independence. I remember when I first moved into government care I had to catch a bus to school. I had never caught a bus before in my life. I had no idea how to catch a bus and I was scared of the unknown, so I walked; I walked the hour to school every day. No one even thought twice, I mean who can't catch a bus? It's such a simple thing to do. So when I moved into Lighthouse I still had this fear. It was time to conquer the bus. Before my first day of school one of the carers showed me, we caught the bus together and took the same route that I would when school started. Once we did it together, I had lost that fear, I was confident. I remember that first feeling of independence, knowing the bus route and doing it on my own, a very simple thing, but an important step to independence.

The most powerful aspect of Lighthouse is their belief that you can be someone. That you will grow into an independent, strong human being. They believed in me and that I would actually move past the shit and live a healthy and happy life. All kids and children need to know is that someone actually believes in them. What a powerful thought. They actually believe that any child has the strength in him/her to succeed in life. This belief eventually turned into a belief in myself. You never really leave Lighthouse. There were many times while living there that I wanted to leave, unfortunately at that time I didn't have the skills to move into independent living and I became frustrated and annoyed at my carers and myself. We had to discuss the issues and they would help me to gain the skills needed to move into independent living.

I was fortunate enough to go on an overseas trip with the university I was at, just as I was ready to leave Lighthouse. I had the money, my bags packed and people who loved me at the airport to say goodbye. It was sad, I'm not going to lie, but I knew I had learnt and grown enough to be able to move out and look after myself. I knew I would see these people again, I knew I could come over for dinner, stay the night, hang out whenever I needed or wanted. If I was having a bad day I would hang out at the office or go for coffee and talk shit over. It hasn't all been easy but with a great support network of friends and Lighthouse's family for life gift, I have had the support I needed to stay independent.

CHILDREN RETURNING TO WORK WITH THE ORGANIZATION

As we have mentioned, older young people are provided with the opportunity to gain their youth work qualifications and hence gain employment in the youth sector. One of the tasks for the organization is providing opportunities for young people to develop the skills to gain employment. Where young people have the appropriate skills and commitment there can also be a great benefit in them coming back to work for the organization. The LIGHT programme has been a great success, as 20 per cent of the current carers have actually been Lighthouse residents. We hope that this number will grow over the years as we move even closer to being a youth-run organization. We believe that with young people returning, who have experienced our programme and who have personally experienced homelessness, we can provide a better-informed programme for children. We now see young adults into their thirties coming back to work with the organization. This provides hope for children who are in the programme, that if others can do it, then they can also, and that their 'experiential expertise' (Martin 2009; p.18) is valued. It also provides the children with a sense of the organization's history – that it has been around for a while and will continue to be.

CHAPTER 10

Outcomes-Based Practice

CAROL'S STORY: DREAMS CAN COME TRUE

I was on the beach with my family, this was a regular outing. There was my dad, mum, and my older brother, who would put me on his shoulders and carry me to the water from the car. It was our special thing, which we did every time we went to the beach.

My older sister was so pretty; she had beautiful blonde hair bleached from the sun, and smooth skin. When the family went to get ice cream after a day at the beach she and I would always share ours, we'd pick the flavours together, it was our special thing. Next was my little sister, we were especially close and shared all our toys and dolls. She was into dolls more than me but we would spend the day playing with her Barbies in the water and changing their clothes. My younger brother was still little and would feel left out, so we would incorporate a game with his cars and car mat and my sister's dolls, or we would play dress-ups. I liked that best. I was the middle child and, you know what, I didn't care one bit, I had the perfect family.

This day on the beach was the same as every other day on the beach and I liked it that way. I would build sandcastles with my brothers and dad. They would be really big and come up to my shoulders and when they were finished Dad would pick me up and sit me on top of the castle and for that second before the castle came falling down I'd be so tall, like I was on top of the world.

My big brother would run over and start tickling me and I'd scream with laughter until I said 'Stop! Stop!' and he'd pick me up, carry me to the water and threaten to throw me in. We kids would chase each other in and out of the water and when I was it, I would always go for my little brother because I knew he was littler than me and I knew I would always get him.

I guess you're thinking what a wonderful family this was, and it was. This family never existed in my real life. It could only exist in my dreams. When my head hit the pillow my reality died and my imaginary family came to my rescue and took me away from the pain that haunted me in my waking hours.

This is where dreams really do come true. After living part of my life through the care system I've found a real home and family, and although I did not know it yet, the next few years were going to change me and here I was going to grow into a woman – an independent, strong and loving woman. I was stuck between the life I knew and the life I had no idea about. I moved into Lighthouse, an old house in the heart of town. From my very first experience Lighthouse was warm and caring. Despite having that feeling, it took me a while to settle in, seeing everyone so independent, even the kids who were younger than me. I cannot begin to express what Lighthouse has done for me, for lifting me up out of the gutter and giving me warmth, comfort and not just a home but a family full of love. Love that I struggled to understand but love that is forever with me. I've found my home, the one that was in my dreams, the dream that kept me alive for so many years, the dream that has finally come true. I am safe, I am happy, I am loved, I belong and most importantly I am hugged.

Since leaving Lighthouse, I have completed a Bachelor in Social Science Youth Work. I have worked with different youth organizations, some with migrant and refugee children and of course children who are or have been in the government care system. I have then moved on to do a teaching degree. I have been a secondary teacher for nearly four years now. I love it, I love the challenge and excitement in it; I love that I learn from my students every day.

I have a passion for travel and have travelled through parts of Asia and Europe and am planning to travel more in the near future, maybe even work overseas for a bit. Sometimes I get asked about the scars on my arms; everyone has scars from their past, some of mine just happen to be showing on the outside. Sometimes when I do look back on my life I think about how it shapes us into who we are today. Our beliefs, our hopes and our dreams, all come from experiences past. I have a lot to thank Lighthouse for (and I really mean it). One of the most, in fact the most important part, is that they teach you how to look after yourself, to believe in yourself, and to love yourself.

Carol is clearly making a positive and insightful statement about her life, which suggests a positive outcome for her. However, it is when this is supported by other evidence about her life that we can confidently claim that the programme has contributed to positive outcomes being achieved. The brief story presented can lead to several assumptions: that the programme has been effective in providing Carol with a sense of belonging and family; that she has been able to develop cognitive resources such as the use of imagination to lift herself out of the traumatic situation she was living in; that she has developed reflective capacities over time that may not have been possible when she was in a traumatic state, as creative functions may have been impaired or blocked; that she has hope for the future, which is a major contributor to resilience and positive outcomes. Her story is one way of assessing the outcomes of the programme for Carol. However, what is clear from research in the field is that outcome assessment needs to be systematic and reliable, if it is to provide a picture of the overall effectiveness of the programme. In the case of Carol, we can see that she believes that the outcomes for her have been positive, but we also need other measures to determine the effectiveness of the programme across a number of domains for all children.

OUTCOMES-BASED APPROACHES

Outcomes are the changes, benefits, learning or other effects that happen as a result of our work. They can be wanted or unwanted, expected or unexpected. Information should be collected in a way that tells you about intended and unintended outcomes. In our work with traumatized children we aim to achieve outcomes that can be identified by the children as positive. Willis (2001, p.139) reminds us of the statement that the UK Department of Health initiatives of the 1990s were founded upon: 'Social care services are likely to be most effective when they are orientated towards outcomes: concerned with, designed, provided and evaluated in terms of the results experienced by the people for whom they are intended' (Social Services Inspectorate 1993, p.9). Stewart (1998, p.44) supports this point of view: 'Services are only of value if they are of value to those for whom they are provided.'

In recent years there has been a significant move towards what can be defined as outcomes-based approaches. Terms like evidence-based practice and results-based accountability have become increasingly familiar. Making the connection between systematic practice and an outcomes-based approach, Thompson (2008, p.3) summarizes three key aspects of this approach:

- What are you going to achieve?
- How are you going to achieve it?
- How will you know when it is achieved?

Friedman (2005) outlines a clear way of evaluating our work using the grid in Figure 10.1.

How much we delivered is easy to quantify; how well is also not too difficult. For instance, we delivered ten therapy sessions, following all of the professional standards. The next two quadrants can be more challenging to evaluate – how many people benefited from our service and what was the quality of their benefit? In an outcomes model we are primarily concerned with these last two quadrants, whereas in a process model we may be more focused on the first two.

	Quantity	Quality
Input Effort	How much service did we deliver?	How well did we deliver it?
Output Effect	How much change/effect did we produce?	What quality of change/effect did we produce?

Figure 10.1 Programme performance measures (Friedman 2005)

An outcomes-based approach is a conceptual approach to planning services and assessing their performance that focuses attention on the results – or outcomes – that the services are intended to achieve. It is also seen as much more than a tool for planning effective services. It can become a way of securing strategic and cultural change: moving organizations away from a focus on 'efficiency' and 'process' as the arbiters of value in their services, and towards making better outcomes the primary purpose of their organization and its employees. This does not mean that high quality processes are not important and in many cases the vehicle through which outcomes are achieved, but we need to remember that processes are a means to an end rather than end in themselves. It is essential that we always keep in mind that all of our work – training, supervision, assessment, consultancy and quality assurance is only of any use if it contributes to the delivery of the desired outcomes for children. As Thompson (2008, p.4) states,

> What is required is not a simplistic approach that sets process against outcome, but rather a more holistic approach that incorporates both the process involved and the outcomes that process is geared towards achieving. That is, it is a matter of 'both…and', not 'either…or'.

Further distinguishing features of the approach are: the use of simple and clear language; the collection and use of relevant data; and the involvement of stakeholders, including children and the wider community in achieving better outcomes. All of this is designed to 'shift the focus from activities to results, from how a programme operates to the good it accomplishes' (Plantz, Greenway and Hendricks 1999).

THE NEED FOR EVIDENCE

Despite this shift towards outcomes-based practice in the UK, USA and Australia, the vast majority of research studies on looked-after children have been carried out for the purposes of generating knowledge – having been initiated either by policy makers or academics rather than organizations who provide the service. Currently there is little evidence as to what actually works in enabling positive outcomes for looked-after children. Wise claims that,

> Despite the increasing demand for a means of assessing the outcomes of looking after children away from home, child care services in Australia and elsewhere have rarely gathered information to find out how the experience of being looked after affects children's subsequent health and wellbeing... Many child care agencies gather information only haphazardly about both the characteristics and the progress of children for whom they accept and share responsibilities rather than measuring aspects of their service related to the quality of care and the effect on short-term, medium-term and long-term outcomes of interest. (Wise 1999)

Ten years later Wise and Egger (2010) found that not much had changed:

> Since 1996–97, the Australian Institute of Health and Welfare (AIHW) has published national data on children in care and protection orders from administrative datasets in the Child Welfare Series (AIHW 2002). However, these data are very limited and tend to focus on inputs and key descriptors and do not contain information about child outcomes... These types of data do not permit *assessment* of the effectiveness of intervention, nor do they permit the identification of significant factors that may have contributed to a particular outcome that can then be used to inform practice and policy. (Wise and Egger 2010, p.19)

Explaining why there has been a greater focus on outcomes in recent years, Thompson (2008, p.2) argues that, 'An emphasis on outcomes linked to the notion of value for money is clearly part of this development: how can we justify expenditure without clarity about whether we have achieved our aims – that is, produced the desired outcomes?' Therefore we need to evidence how approaches focused on improving a child's state of mental health and overall wellbeing can actually make a difference in these areas in the short and long term. To achieve this we need validation in the following three areas:

- How well does our approach enable children to achieve the desired outcomes?

- What is the method of measurement and how reliable is this?

- How do short-term outcomes correlate with long-term outcomes for these children?

In a paper titled, 'Avoiding the Fate of the Dodo Bird: The Challenge of Evidence-Based Practice', referring to Parry and Richardson (1996, p.43), Winter (2006) claims that the same challenge faces all treatment interventions:

> It is unacceptable…to continue to provide therapies which decline to subject themselves to research evaluation. Practitioners and researchers alike must accept the challenge of evidence-based practice, one result of which is that treatments which are shown to be ineffective are discontinued. (p.42)

One argument against empirical evidence-based studies is that it will lead to an overly prescriptive approach. However, Winter argues that,

> If the results of an outcome study will only be considered if the therapy studied is manualized, then we should manualize, being mindful that a treatment manual need not be written in the prescriptive style of *The Complete Psychotherapy Treatment Planner* [Jongsma and Peterson 2003] but rather in terms of more superordinate principles guiding the therapist's choice of alternative courses of action. (Winter 2006, p.43)

They continue to argue that refusing to accept the need for evidence will lead to some effective therapies becoming obsolete in favour of those that do have evidence to support their outcomes. They conclude that the Dodo bird will be our favoured model of therapy. As a result our potential clients will be denied an approach that is able to combine humanity with effectiveness.

However, we do need to be cautious about some of the difficulties in measuring such complex matters as changes in a child's mental health, how this is linked to a specific intervention and how it enables the child to achieve long-term wellbeing in adulthood. As Wise argues,

> The absence of a means of routinely collecting the information necessary to make such assessments and the complexity involved in differentiating the effects of interventions on children's outcomes from other effects are problems likely to have inhibited attempts to measure the effects of services on child outcomes. (Wise 1999)

We should also keep in mind what Thompson (2010) states about truth with a small rather than capital T. Whilst accepting the argument that practice based on demonstrable effectiveness is both desirable and a right for children and their families, Clough, Bullock and Ward (2006, p.4) also emphasize the difficulties involved and the need to keep research in perspective: 'In any review of research evidence, therefore, there is a further critical point to be made about knowledge in context: findings are not absolute truths but are products of their time, conditioned by knowledge in other areas.'

MEASURING OUTCOMES

Before we can begin to measure outcomes, they must be clearly defined and relevant to the children. There must be a clear understanding of what needs to be done to support children to achieve the desired outcomes. There needs to be a plan based on this understanding and there needs to be a reliable way of measuring progress towards the outcomes. As Thompson (2010, p.7) points out, 'If we are to have an outcome-based approach, then this places considerable emphasis on high-quality assessment.'

The UK Ofsted report makes the following points about assessment in its summary of its national inspections:

> Good assessment, which also addresses a child's emotional and physical needs, is critical to achieving the right package of support. Inspections of children's homes, fostering services and joint area reviews have found too much inconsistency in the quality of assessments of the needs of looked after children. Assessments that describe the history and experiences of the child can fall short on analysis of the impact of key events such as loss, trauma and separation on the child's well-being, capacity for forming trusting relationships or on their perception of the world around them. In outstanding authorities (organisations), assessments are comprehensive in content and analysis and provide a proper foundation for planning the individual care of the child... Comprehensive assessments, clear arrangements for how support can be accessed, strong communications between mental health professionals and care staff, and consultation with young people about their treatment are some of the factors that underpin the most successful provision of mental health services for looked after children. (Ofsted 2009, p.89)

A well designed assessment tool and process is a useful way of measuring progress. The tool and process can also be designed to maximize other potential benefits. Tomlinson and Philpot (2008, p.46) describe how an assessment process can help a team working with traumatized children to:

- think about children together providing the child with the experience of being thought about in a positive and caring way

- understand children better – which enables us to respond more effectively

- integrate our work between the different professional disciplines – so that everyone is working together, consistently and in a focused way to achieve the same aim. Models similar to this have been referred to elsewhere by Cant (2002) as 'Joined up Psychotherapy' or by Woods (2003) as 'Multi-Systemic Therapy'. It is not a question of which therapeutic approach is the best, but of how the different professional disciplines can combine to achieve the most positive outcomes for the child

- develop a shared language and approach – very valuable when working in multi-disciplinary teams

- evaluate our approaches – what works and what does not

- clarify what we need to put in place to achieve these outcomes.

Ward makes two important points on the subject of assessment:

1. You can have assessment without treatment but you certainly can't have treatment without assessment.

2. What matters most…is that the whole team is engaged both in the process of assessment and in the process of treatment.

(Ward 2004, p.9)

An assessment process needs to embrace these potential benefits, but also be a reliable indicator of progress and practical to administer. Prior and Glaser (2006, p.88) refer to 'clinical usefulness', which they explain as, 'a summary of how useful the assessment might be in a clinical setting, based on what has been said about its established reliability and validity, and an assessment of the ease with which it can be administered.' They go on to say that this assessment of usefulness takes account of the time and resources needed to train and administer the assessment and what comes out of it. In the draft consultation on the framework for assessment, the Department of Health, Home Office and Department for Education and Employment (UK) (1999, p.66) argue that 'good tools cannot substitute for good practice, but good practice and good tools together can achieve excellence.' What is needed, then, is an intelligent approach, which embraces both knowledge and the ability to use it to best effect.

Assessments need to measure and evidence where a person is in their progress towards desired outcomes. The assessment process needs to be thorough; 'People who are tempted to 'skimp' on assessment and try to move swiftly on to service provision or other forms of help are taking a very significant risk. If we are not clear about the situations we are engaging with, the goals we are aiming for and what needs to be done to achieve them, then we risk becoming involved in complex situations without being adequately equipped to deal with them' (Thompson 2010, p.7).

Assessment can be both quantitative and qualitative. Where subjective evaluation is made, for instance, by responding to a question about a child's emotional development, a simple scoring system can help to make the assessment more reliable. The meaning behind these scores can be further elaborated to provide more detailed guidance on what would equate to each of these levels of functioning (see Tomlinson and Philpot 2007, p.122).

1 = severe concerns; poor functioning in this area

2 = substantial concerns; some signs of progress but a range of aspects to address

3 = moderate concerns; one or two aspects to address

4 = positive functioning in this area, possibly some minor concerns.

CHALLENGES IN MEASURING OUTCOMES

As our children return home for celebrations or just to visit, we hear about where they are today and the difference the therapeutic interventions have made in their lives. One of the questions for us in this line of work has been: How do we demonstrate to funding bodies and other stakeholders that the programme works and what the outcomes are? This is a challenge, as it is very difficult to measure success. For one child just being alive is a success, whereas for another it can be that she has completed her studies in university. Both can be positive outcomes worthy of celebration. We need to keep this in mind when measuring success so that we keep a perspective on what success might mean for different children.

Traditionally, psychodynamic approaches in particular have often been criticized for their resistance to the concept of measurement and for failing to promote a culture of systematic evaluation. One of the concerns expressed by some psychotherapists has been that the process of measurement actually distorts the transference relationship in a detrimental way.

In addition, the outcome of such therapies is relatively difficult to measure. However, if such services are to continue to operate and receive funding in the modern culture, which emphasizes accountability and transparency, they will have to develop such systems of evaluation to justify their practice (Adelman, Ward and Davison 2003)

Leiper explains how the process of evaluation can raise anxieties leading to defensiveness:

the element of appraisal increases this sense of threat. Any system of evaluation can all too easily come to feel like an accusation of inadequacy...the current fashion for quality assurance can be viewed with some suspicion as an inappropriate attempt to objectify difficult choices about values and priorities, and to dispense with inevitable conflicts and uncertainties by hiding behind the appearance of scientific method. (Leiper 1994, p.201)

Therefore, senior staff may view evaluation with suspicion, as a process that is politically necessary but of dubious clinical value, and also a burden on already overstretched staff.

Whilst we might live in an era where there is an increasing trend towards measurement, it is also clear that some things are far easier to measure than others. Measuring psychic change or emotional development is complex. If it can be measured, working out exactly what the change is attributed to is equally if not more difficult. van der Kolk, McFarlane and van der Hart, referring to a research study on the outcomes of a therapy programme for traumatized soldiers, highlight the difficulty involved in evaluation:

> At the end of the study, both therapists and participants were generally positive about its effectiveness and outcomes. However, contrary to these subjective outcomes impressions, careful psychometric assessment demonstrated both short-term and long-term negative effects. Compared with a control group, treated veterans developed *more* symptoms and disabilities in several areas of functioning. (van der Kolk *et al.* 2007, p.418)

To complicate things further in the case of therapeutic work with children, the outcomes may not become clear until adulthood by which time numerous other variables have entered the equation. Turner *et al.* emphasize the importance of attempting to measure outcomes despite the difficulties involved:

> The expectation in medicine is that any new pharmacological treatment should be examined in placebo-controlled trials before the agent can be marketed. The same criterion cannot necessarily be applied to psychosocial interventions, in which the nature of the relationship and the establishment of therapeutic rapport are vital but often elusive therapeutic elements. Yet measuring treatment outcomes is critical. (Turner *et al.* 2007, p.541)

Measuring outcomes also requires a degree of user involvement and there will be resource implications to this. In a study on routine outcome measurement (ROM) in UK child and adolescent mental health services, Johnston and Gowers (2005) found that less than 30 per cent of services carry out ROM and cite resource issues as the main obstacle. The difficulty in measuring outcomes can contribute to the lack of focus on outcomes. For example, in work with children there may be a considerable gap between service delivery and the appropriate time to measure the outcomes. Willis (2001 p.146) argues that, 'The problem with not trying to measure outcomes is that we are left with defining and measuring what is more readily measurable, the quality of the inputs, processes and outputs.' Inputs are all the resources an organization uses to deliver various outputs and be human, material or financial, or can be expressed as time. Outputs are all the products and services delivered – training courses, staff support sessions and direct work such as a therapy session. Processes are the specific way that something is done, for example, how an output like a staff support session takes place. He continues that,

> the danger is that managers and practitioners will spend considerable resources in measuring and seeking to improve the quality of inputs, processes or outputs that are either unimportant or possibly counterproductive to the realization of outcomes, culminating in an over-emphasis on procedural adherence at the expense of benefits for the users. (Willis 2001, p.146)

Willis (2001, p.153) defines three broad outcomes categories – safety, happiness, and development. He suggests that the intended outcomes should be measured using SMART outcome indicators.

Specific – People (children, parents, commissioners, practitioners, managers, etc.) know what it means in practice.

Measurable – People know if it has been achieved, but how do we measure outcomes and how reliable is this?

What is the evidence of how progress in the short term translates in the long term? Rose (1997), in his book on the outcomes of therapeutic work with troubled adolescents, describes how perceived progress within the therapeutic environment may not be sustained once the child has moved on from that environment. The reasons for this may be varied. Rose suggests that the emotional 'holding' provided by a therapeutic community can be so intensive that it may provide a falsely positive picture of the child. On the other hand, as we have discussed, the aftercare support may be so poor that it impacts in a very negative way on the child and undermines the progress that has been made.

Achievable – Is everything in place to ensure that the outcomes are achievable? In the USA social care organizations are evaluated under four areas – programme, governance, finance and administration. Having an effective programme is only one part of being an effective service. The organization also needs to demonstrate effectiveness in the other three areas if it is to receive funding.

Relevant – How do we know the outcomes matter to children and young people?

If the outcomes are clearly linked to the fundamental human needs of safety, happiness and development, there can be little doubt as to whether the outcomes matter. We know that achievement of these outcomes should bode well for a child's future. However, the child may neither fully understand the significance of the outcomes, nor be willing to acknowledge whether the outcomes matter to her.

Time limited – How often will we measure progress and how will we know these time periods are reliable?

As already discussed, it is also not clear whether short-term measurements are a reliable indicator of long-term outcomes.

The aim is to produce outcomes that are desired, achievable and measurable – DAM outcomes! (Institute of Public Care 2006). When measuring outcomes it is important that we measure equality outcomes. In other words, we need to measure whether the outcomes are achieved equally by different groups receiving the same service, for example, different gender and ethnic groups.

Some critics of outcomes-based approaches claim that a focus on outcomes detracts from the importance of high-quality processes. Thompson argues that a healthy balance is required:

> I regard prioritising process over outcomes as in itself an oversimplification of a very complex situation. A focus on process that takes little or no account of outcomes can be a major waste of time and resources. What point is there in having a good process if there are no clear outcomes to justify that process and the resources invested in it? Similarly, a narrow focus on outcomes that does not take account of the importance of processes would be a very one-sided and unhelpful approach. (Thompson 2010, p.4)

POTENTIAL BENEFITS AND VALUE OF DEVELOPING AN OUTCOMES-BASED APPROACH

The primary benefit that underpins all further benefits will be improved outcomes for children. A focus on outcomes should mean a better service for children. It is possible to deliver the volume of service required in the manner agreed and at the right time to high-quality standards, but still not achieve the desired outcomes.

Further benefits of an outcomes-based approach include:

- The development of a coherent model, which will unify the organization's practice and further distinguish its model.

- Improvements in the organization's understanding of an outcomes-based approach and alignment between the organization's activity and outcomes. Information on outcomes can help to make work more effective by identifying what works well and what could be improved.

- It helps to ensure that limited resources are used most efficiently to meet needs. A clear focus on outcomes can inform the organization's strategic decision making on how to use its resources, where to make investments and where to make cutbacks. How does every aspect of the organization's activity best support positive outcomes?

- A shared understanding of the organization's outcomes can greatly improve the team's sense of purpose. It is also highly motivating for employees and children to see clear evidence of the outcomes of their work. Overall outcomes can link into personal targets and appraisal systems, e.g. what are you doing to achieve the outcomes the organization is required to meet?

- A coherent model will support long-term sustainability of the organization as it will become embedded, providing continuity and consistency through any period of organizational change.

- A large organization is in an excellent position to evidence the outcomes of its work as large amounts of data will be available for analysis. A consistent approach with a large group of children is ideal for academic research.

- A well-designed outcomes approach can provide opportunities for children's involvement in their own development as well as the wider organization.

- The process of assessment and planning will strengthen the professional networks by everyone being involved in the same processes and speaking the same language.

- Improvements in relationships with referrers/funders by providing clearer information on outcomes. For both funder and provider it encourages a knowledge-driven approach to practice. Both sides need to know and understand the rationale behind each outcome and to identify methods of practice that can achieve demonstrable results.

- Once established, the process of assessment, outcome evaluation and planning will lead to clear identification of the best and most effective practice, and hence contribute to the culture of continuous improvement and the development of a learning organization.

The cyclical evaluation approach, similar to that of Wadsworth (2011), has been useful in evaluating our programmes. The process involves a cycle (shown in Figure 10.2) that includes evaluation of processes and outcomes, reflection/thinking, planning, action, and back again to evaluation. The evaluation process is continuous and ongoing.

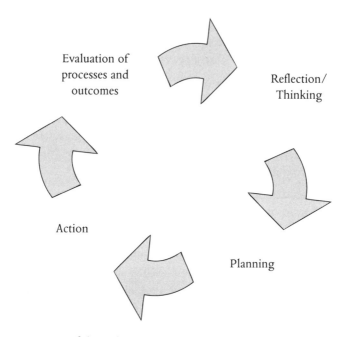

Figure 10.2 Diagram of the cycle

An outcomes-based approach encourages us all to focus on the difference that we make and not just the inputs or processes over which we have control. It is right that we should be judged by tangible improvements in the things that matter. Successfully achieving and sustaining outcomes goes hand in hand with embedding a culture of continuous improvement. One of the challenges to organizations, therapists and others who work with traumatized children is to find ways of measuring longitudinal outcomes. Over the last few years, we have developed a data management system so that we can now track the recovery process for each child from intake to outreach. We do this across all domains including individual, relational and community wellness. The On For Life database, which we have developed, now provides us with the opportunities to have qualitative as well as quantitative measures to track the therapeutic process for children. It is vital that those who carry out effective, high-quality work with traumatized children find ways to demonstrate their outcomes and learn from their findings.

Susan's Story

My Transition from Caring Mother to Developing a Therapeutic Care Programme

Over the last thirty-five years of my life I have been passionately focused on advocating for change in Australia in the way that we care for our most traumatized and troubled homeless children. Although we know that attachment disruptions and trauma characterize children in care, we continue to provide a system of care that sustains, and so many would say worsens the trauma for these children, rather than treating or healing the damage caused to the children. I have found it difficult over the years to remain silent while our children are provided often inadequate care that does not provide the opportunities to be nurtured and develop into healthy young people.

My life changed direction thirty-five years ago. I was a young woman in my twenties from Melbourne, Australia, volunteering in an orphanage in Sri Lanka, when a baby I had held during the afternoon died later that evening. This one single occurrence changed my life. Having gazed into the eyes of this little boy, I thought to myself: 'you could be my child and if you were my child, there would be no doubt that I would do anything in my power to make sure you survived and thrived and you knew you were loved intensely'. And after another two hours, having continued to gaze into this little boy's eyes, I knew that this was 'my child'. I had not given birth to him but I was responsible for him as a human being. But due to my lack of skill and knowledge at the time, I did not know how to respond to the situation I found myself in. To this day I remember with deep sadness and regret not doing anything except hold him in those short few hours he was to have left – I hope he felt comforted and loved – if but for those few short hours.

On my return to Australia, this experience had a profound effect, and from that point I knew that I had to do something to make a change to the way we care for children. I also knew that I lacked any qualifications or knowledge to know how to move forward. So I began a life journey to discover who I was as a mother and a human being. What did I stand for? And how could I contribute to our community and our world? I wanted to make it a better place for all children who were not as fortunate as my children and those children who were not lucky enough to be born into loving families. I began by ensuring that I could be the best possible mother to my own children. I then started fostering children in my own home and thus developed the foundations for what is now known as the Lighthouse Therapeutic Family Model of Care (TFMC) – a model of therapeutic residential care for homeless young people, based on attachment and psychodynamic theories of psychosocial development.

I discovered that what I was doing naturally as a mother with my own children was what I wanted to emulate for my foster children, which worked really well for my children. What I also learnt as I developed my own parenting skills was that this approach had a theoretical foundation, which was attachment-based parenting. I also discovered that what I was doing was very different to the way the care system was responding to our vulnerable and traumatized children in 'out of home' care, and to our homeless young people.

Intrinsically, I knew that my children didn't care where we lived or what we had, what was important to us was that we belonged to each other, we were a family and we cared about each other's welfare. We showed through our eyes and our being how thrilled we were to see each other in the mornings and again the delight when we came together at the end of the day – after we had been apart during the day doing our own thing. I often ask myself, isn't this what we all want? To love and be loved.

We felt a sense of belonging in the knowledge that we had each other to lean on in the good and not so good times, and that we hugged and kissed and held each other and were familiar to each other. We had the bond of growing together, building our family stories, and the collecting of those stories as we went along over the years. We were safe in the knowledge that we had a life membership to this family. Both at home with my family and also with our Lighthouse family, we place great importance on the value of telling stories. A book that I read about the importance of keeping culture alive in a corporate environment, which was written by Kevin and Jackie Freiberg (1998), highlights the importance of gathering stories of the organization's rituals and our celebrations, our graduations, our achievements and our challenges. The same can be said of Lighthouse, as we have found over the years – all of this gives a sense of order and connection to our lives. Our lives are unique and our uniqueness is what gives us value and meaning and telling our stories is what makes us similar, what connects us all, what helps us transcend the potential isolation of separateness.

A deep trust of life emerges when you listen to and share your stories. Great organizations are ones where the stories of our people matter and where relationships are important and bound by a deep sense of loyalty to each other. Rather than a fair day's work for a fair day's pay, we share common sets of values, norms, and guiding philosophies. We have a common purpose and deep-rooted beliefs, and we are willing to forgo self-interest for the common good – a family of employees who are connected by a web of common beliefs, shared commitments and collective memories.

As I said, knowing what I now know, I could not live in a world where there are children languishing who do not have at least one person in their lives to care about their welfare and to love them. There is a quote by Joseph Chilton Pearce, 'It all begins with children feeling unconditionally wanted, accepted and loved'. Joe, as he likes to be called, goes on to say, 'but if the children are lacking that initial experience of being unconditionally loved by at least one person, and if they do not feel safe and secure in their learning environment, then nothing is going to happen very positively. This cannot be overstated (Mercogliano and Debus 1999, p.2). Ideally, children have a couple and an extended family caring for them. So I feel a huge responsibility to make sure that every child who is in 'out of home' care has the opportunity to have the choice of experiencing a sense of family and a home – for as long as it takes. It is my absolute. It is my drive. Surely our world wants this for every child? We cannot let one more child die on our watch… Surely we can be a truly civil society – where every child matters like our own?

In 1991, I was lucky to be offered an opportunity to do a personal development programme called 'Money and You', where I honed in on what it was I wanted to achieve as a human citizen who had a concern for traumatized and abandoned children. During the training I was first introduced to a group process, which was referred to as 'What I Feel Like Saying' (WIFLS). WIFLS was the inspiration for a group process that we developed to fit the therapeutic milieu at Lighthouse called 'I Feel Like Saying'.

It was at the training that I met a group of business people headed up by a man committed to making a difference, Harry Baruhas. This group, who was also on a journey to understand how they could make a difference in their communities, were captivated by what I was doing with children and offered their support. With the support from this business community, the Lighthouse Foundation was officially formed, to eventually fulfil my vision to provide traumatized homeless children the opportunity to develop a sense of belonging and attachment and have the opportunity to live in a therapeutic family model of care. And I hope in my lifetime to see the implementation of a more humane system of care of children.

As I look back over the years I realize that much of my life's work has been to understand how trauma affects children and to develop innovative ways to support the recovery process. I have had the incredible privilege to witness the courage of children who have experienced the most traumatic experiences and have been willing to trust us with their care – from the victims of cult abuse, to children who have been prostituted by their own parents, to neglected orphans from third world countries. I have worked with children who were locked in cupboards or left locked in a room with very young siblings day after day whilst their parents left them to go to work, children tied under the family home as punishment for nothing more than being hungry and asking for food, and children who have been brought up in families where drug addiction, mental illness, prostitution, incest and torture have been part of daily life.

In 1999, I had the good fortune to be introduced to Dr Sarah Crome, a psychologist with an academic and public service background, which included a private psychotherapy practice. She was invited to sit on the board of directors but was so captivated by the uniqueness of our model of care that I had developed, that she started to work as the Lighthouse community's psychologist and later became the Clinical Care Manager. Through a process of observation, social mapping and documentation, she formalized the structure of the Lighthouse model of care. This included the realization that all the organizational operations are governed by the principles of attachment and psychodynamic theories through the focus on relationships. The model of care was conceptualized as an *interdependent* system, rather than disparate units of residential operations for traumatized and socially isolated children. This led to the development of the Lighthouse community into a clinically systematized and recognized model of rehabilitation for children suffering from significant mental health concerns and social dislocation.

Sarah dedicated eight years of her life to systematically documenting and articulating the model of care through policies and processes. This was developed from an array of theoretical sources predominantly from the school of psychoanalysis, in particular attachment and object relations theories. Sarah welcomed Greg Lolas into the organization; a volunteer she spotted as someone with great aptitude and commitment. Sarah took Greg under her wing teaching him the ins and outs of the model of care. Greg tells the story of the day Sarah asked him if he 'gets the work Lighthouse does'. Greg initially answered 'We look after children', to which Sarah replied. 'No, I mean what do *you* get from the work?' It was then that Greg began to understand what Lighthouse was really about. It was not just about looking after children; rather it was about relationships with children that leave a lasting positive impact on children and staff alike. By being in a relationship that was focused on supporting children to improve the quality of their lives, Greg realized he was improving the quality of his own. That is what *he* got. Greg quickly understood that the model of care was not transactional; it was transformative.

Greg commenced working for Lighthouse in 2001. Under the guidance of Sarah, Greg spent the next four years transitioning through each key role within the Care Department. His understanding of the model of care was reflected in the manner in which he performed each role. He coined the phrase, 'The Lighthouse Experience', describing it as the experience of feeling privileged and honoured to have the opportunity to work with the children. Greg believed that rather than doing something for a child and expecting thanks we should be thanking the child for allowing us to do something for them.

Greg helped bring the focus of 'the relationship' to the forefront of the work that Lighthouse does. He demonstrated that overtly discussing relationship dynamics with children highlighted their maladaptive beliefs about themselves and others. These beliefs could then be challenged by providing children with a different relationship experience to what they were used to; a different experience to what they expected. It is this *in-vivo* experience that brought about lasting therapeutic change for the children. Greg demonstrated that it is the quality of relationship that predicted success.

As Greg transitioned through each of his roles at Lighthouse, he passed on his Lighthouse experience to each of his successors. In this way, he systematically ensured that the interpersonal and experiential component the model of care was expressed in every function of the Care Department, thereby creating a consistent culture of caring, centred on building meaningful relationships. In 2005 Sarah left Lighthouse to begin her own journey into motherhood and passed the torch to Greg as the new Clinical Care Manager. In his new position, he continued the work of Sarah by advocating that caring for children required a systematic response from the whole organization. Greg continued in the role of Clinical Care Manager for the next three years. His work expanded the groundwork Sarah had laid by further articulating and documenting a model of care that was centred on creating a therapeutic community that leaves a lasting, positive impact on the lives of children.

Greg left Lighthouse in 2008 to pursue further studies in psychology. Greg knew the importance of finding a successor who could carry the torch and continue the Lighthouse way of working with children. He searched extensively for someone not only with the relevant skills and experience, but someone who embodied the values of Lighthouse; someone who was a perfect cultural fit. After six months he found Rudy Gonzalez.

Rudy had been previously working with the most marginalized adults in a prison setting, as well as working with complex needs families. So he was capable in dealing with the most traumatized and vulnerable members of the community. He had a deep understanding of attachment and object relations theories. He continually demonstrated his love of this theoretical work and practised it not only in his work life but also in his home life with his family – what a gift this would provide to our Lighthouse community. He was also trained in community psychology, and had experience working in therapeutic communities which was vital for the work that is done at Lighthouse.

Since Rudy joined Lighthouse, he has fulfilled my vision of changing the way that children are cared for in out of home care and in the homelessness sector. In this period, Lighthouse has become a nationally accredited provider of homelessness services for young people. We have developed stronger relationships with government and other organizations that are contributing to a change in the way that systems support traumatized children. We have moved towards playing a more active role in training and supporting other organizations to develop systems that are trauma informed and focus on the best interests of the child. We have documented the Therapeutic Family Model of Care, and have been working on this book which will make a major contribution to the body of knowledge in child, youth and family work. He has demonstrated his commitment to ensuring that the Therapeutic Family Model of Care can be available to more children across Australia.

Over the last twenty years I believe that Sarah took the model from infancy to primary stage, Greg through the teenage years and Rudy has brought it to adulthood. I will always be grateful for the years of dedication by these three extraordinary people, who have brought their brilliance to developing a model which can significantly contribute to providing young people a better future.

The Lighthouse Therapeutic Family Model of Care

The Therapeutic Family Model of Care (TFMC) is a model of therapeutic residential care developed by the Lighthouse Foundation. It is for homeless young people aged fifteen to twenty-two years of age who come predominately from a background of long-term neglect and abuse. There is empirical evidence from a range of disciplines, which demonstrates that if traumatized children are offered a safe and consistent physical living environment, with positive parental role models, as well as clinical and support services, they can (re)build their sense of self, learn new ways of trusting and relating to others, and develop pro-social behaviours.

The TFMC presupposes that new and constructive behaviours can be learned by children from carers, who act as therapeutic parents (Pughe and Philpot 2007) and relate to children in a consistent, positive and trusting way. The family-like setting, the developing relationship with the carers and the support of other specialists allows a child to confront and work through the impact of childhood trauma; to address their self destructive behaviours; and to learn new ways of successfully and confidently engaging with others.

THEORETICAL UNDERPINNINGS OF THE PROGRAMME

Attachment Theory describes the biological and psychological need to bond with and relate to primary caregivers as fundamental to the survival of human beings. The ability to trust and to relate to others is established in infancy to early childhood through the quality of the infant/primary caregiver relationship, which influences and shapes development and behaviour in later life. The TFMC provides the opportunity for traumatized children who have experienced broken attachments to develop a primary attachment with a primary carer, which is vital for the development of healthy relationships in their lives. The development of a healthy attachment to a primary caregiver assists the child to build the confidence to develop relationships with others.

Object relations theory suggests that a prime motivational drive in every individual is to form relationships with others. The style of relationship that develops in early childhood becomes part of an internal blueprint or a learned way of relating to others. This is replicated when we establish and maintain future relationships. Young people who have experienced trauma in infancy and early childhood may have difficulty in forming and maintaining constructive and healthy relationships with others. The more traumatic their early experience the more self-destructive some of their interpersonal relationships can be.

Psychological wellness is a psychoecological concept that highlights the importance of promoting favourable conditions that nurture the personal (individual), relational, collective (community) wellbeing of individuals. Overall psychological wellness can only be achieved through the combined presence of personal, relational and collective wellbeing. The TFMC supports the young people to develop wellness in all these areas, by providing holistic therapeutic care. As Prilleltensky (2006) said, 'There cannot be well-being but in the combined presence of personal, relational, and collective well-being'. The way these three areas overlap to create wellness is captured in Figure A2.1.

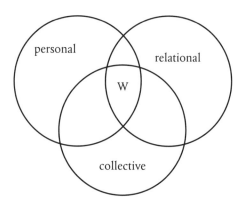

Figure A2.1 The synergy of wellbeing (Prilleltensky 2006)

The following section discusses the key features of the TFMC.

Live-in Care Programme (Youth)

The Live-in Care Programme (Youth) is the core programme in the TFMC. It is based on a primary and a secondary carer living in the home with young people (with respite carers covering annual and other leave). It provides therapeutic care to four young people with complex needs, twenty-four hours a day, seven days a week in a 'family' home setting. The carers act as therapeutic parents to the young people, role modelling healthy relationships.

Live-in Care Programme (Young Mothers and Babies)

The Live-in Care Programme (Young Mothers and Babies) contains the same elements of the core Live-in Care Programme (Youth), with the added distinction that it is focused on providing therapeutic care to young mothers and their babies. The young mothers who access the programme predominantly come from a background of long-term neglect and abuse. They are at risk of homelessness and may have a history of complex issues – mental illness, substance abuse, self-harming, suicide risk, poor education, limited life and social skills and difficulties with maintaining and building healthy relationships. As such, without intensive care and support, they may pose a risk to themselves and to their babies at the most critical time in the infant's development.

The programme has an early intervention focus, and supports young mothers and their babies during the transition into motherhood. This is a time of massive change for young women, and for those who are homeless the levels of risk are greater. By providing a safe and caring environment, and strong community supports, the mothers and their infants have the opportunity to build a secure and healthy attachment.

Psychological Wellness programme

The TFMC relies on the support of a team of psychologists to provide psychotherapeutic and psychoeducational support to the children. The Psychological Wellness Programme's major focus is on providing this crucial support to young people, as well as providing training and support to carers to facilitate their therapeutic work with the young people. The team is also responsible for overseeing the psychological wellbeing of Lighthouse community members, and as such plays an active role in monitoring the wellbeing of community members, and develops programmes to promote a healthy community.

The Adult Community Transition (ACT) Programme

The ACT Programme provides a safe environment for young people who are 'almost ready' for independent living. Up to five young people reside in a home, with one of them holding the senior resident (lead tenant) role. The programme provides the young people with a stepping stone from the intensive support in the Live-in Care Programme to more independent forms of living in the community.

Aftercare and Outreach Programme

The programme is provided by the Community Care Team. Young people who have transitioned from the Live-in Care or ACT Programmes are supported in transition into more independent forms of living. The Community Care Team provides the practical and emotional and moral support necessary for these young people to make their transition into independent living successful. Sustainability is achieved by the ongoing outreach offered by Lighthouse for the young people according to their needs.

The Home

The children and young people live in suburban homes in Victoria, Australia. The typical home can accommodate for up to four children and provides twenty-four hour, seven days a week physical and emotional support. On average, each young person stays in our homes for between eighteen and twenty-four months. Each home is managed by a primary carer and is supported by a secondary carer.

Carers

The two carers share the home with the children. They are available twenty-four hours a day to support the children in the home in all aspects of their life, much like a parent. The carers act as parenting role models for the children and provide the children with the experience of being parented, and being loved.

Individual Development Plans

Lighthouse recognizes the importance of individually tailored responses to the needs of all young people participating in the TFMC. A mutual agreement of care between the young person and Lighthouse is facilitated through an Individual Development Plan (IDP). A young person's IDP sets out and documents all relevant information on the young person, including their personal short- and long-term goals, life skills, emotional, psychological and physical wellbeing. Ongoing assessment in these, as well as other areas of a young person's life, forms an important part of the IDP process.

The purpose of the IDP is to document the young person's goals, achievements and activities that aim to support and facilitate their ongoing development and growth. The development of IDP is fundamentally driven by the young person and identifies the key pathways from which ongoing personal development and support will occur. Comprehensive assessment and the development of the IDP are seen as important processes toward identifying the most appropriate range of support programmes and activities that may be available for the young person to access. IDPs are therefore monitored regularly and reviewed at a six-month interval or as each case requires. The IDP provides a care plan in the following domains: education and employment; relationship building; emotional, psychological, physical, cultural and spiritual wellbeing; support networks; living skills, finances, recreation and fun; and transitional planning.

Community Care Team

The Community Care Programme manages the Lighthouse intake services, aftercare and outreach services, as well as monitoring the young people's Individual Development Plans. The Community Care workers are the first point of contact for young people referred to Lighthouse. They are responsible for assessing the eligibility of a young person to enter the Live-in Programme, as well as their compatibility with the programme and the dynamics in the homes. The Community Care Team also manages young people who are on the waiting list to enter a Lighthouse home, as well as providing outreach support to young people who have moved on from the Live-in Programme.

Senior Care Team

The Senior Care Team is made up of the Director of Care Services who manages the overall TFMC; the founder who acts as a cultural consultant and guide to the team; the Clinical Care Manager who is responsible for clinical governance of the TFMC and managing the Psychological Wellness Programme; and the Residential Care Manager who manages the carers and Community Care Teams.

Community Committees

All the homes have a Community Committee that usually comprises around ten members of the local community who volunteer their time to support the home. The committee plays an active role in helping the children and young people feel connected to their local community. The committee has partly a fundraising role for the home, as well as providing specific supports that are required for the home. The committee becomes part of the extended family for the children and is their link to the wider community.

Life membership

All the children and young people who live in our homes are considered life members and part of the Lighthouse family. In a regular family when a child moves out of home, parents and siblings will continue to be in the child's life forever. This concept of family for life has been incorporated into our TFMC. The support that is provided to young people who transition from the homes is varied and is based on the individual needs of the young person. The support offered to the young person will depend on issues like his or her resilience, mental health, general health, developmental needs, support networks in the community, relationship with family of origin, and other factors that can impact on the young person's ability to manage independent living.

About the Authors

SUSAN BARTON

Susan Barton is the founder of Lighthouse Foundation. She is the mother of six children, two of whom are adopted, and has eleven grandchildren. She has been a foster carer and also worked as a primary carer at Lighthouse Foundation. She is a nationally recognized expert and spokesperson on issues such as parenting, family systems, trauma-informed practice, youth homelessness, child and adolescent mental health and children's rights.

Susan has received a number of awards for her work with homeless children in Australia. Susan was awarded a centenary medal in 2001 for her work with homeless youth, to mark her achievement for contribution to Australian society at the commencement of the twenty-first century. In 2002 she was further recognized as a Member of the Order of Australia (AM) for services to youth. Other awards have included: the Prime Minister's State and Territories business award for community organizations; Australian Humanitarian Award for her work in education; Ambassador for Oxford Houses; Victoria Day Association Award for Community and Public Service; Melbourne Rotarian and Rotary International Paul Harris Fellow; recognized in *Who's Who of Australian Women*; and Melburnian of the Year 2009–2010.

Susan has formal qualifications in youth work and psychotherapy, parenting, leadership, business, neuro-linguistic programming, and numerous personal development programmes. She is co-author of the book entitled *Building Your Teenager's Self-Esteem* (2001). She provides training as part of the Lighthouse Foundation Seminar Series to Lighthouse staff and other professionals who work with children and young people. Susan is also a board member of Mecwa*care*. Mecwa*care* is a leading non-profit organization with a reputation for excellence. It has provided care to the community for fifty years, offering residential aged care, respite care, in-home support, and disability and nursing services, providing optimal choice for people of all ages, irrespective of financial, religious, cultural or lifestyle background.

RUDY GONZALEZ

Rudy is the Director of Care Services at Lighthouse Foundation. He began his studies in community development at Victoria University and went on to complete his Bachelor of Art Honours in Social and Cultural Studies, and later studied in the field of psychology where he completed a Masters in Applied Psychology (Community Psychology). In his studies, his major areas of specialization were psychodynamic approaches, community psychology and the psychology of identity, oppression and otherness. He is a registered psychologist and a member of the Australia Psychological Society. Rudy's professional career has spanned from work as: a community development worker with Culturally and Linguistically Diverse (CALD) communities; a family counsellor and case manager working with low socio-economic and complex needs families; a psychologist in a therapeutic community for violent offenders; and working as a psychologist and managing a programme for traumatized children in out of home care and homeless children. Rudy is also a lecturer of psychology at Victoria University in the areas of: counselling and psychotherapy; ethics; psychological wellness; value-based practice; culturally inclusive practice; history and theories of psychology; practicum and community psychology approaches. Rudy works as a consultant and trainer to professionals and organizations who work with children, adolescents and families who have experienced trauma, as part of the Lighthouse Professional Development Series Team and in his private practice.

PATRICK TOMLINSON

Patrick is a consultant and interim director for organizations working with children and young people (www.patricktomlinson.com). He has over twenty-five years' experience in work with traumatized children, as a practitioner, service manager, director and consultant. He began his career at the Cotswold Community (Wiltshire, UK), a therapeutic community for emotionally damaged boys. He spent fourteen years there, the last six as Assistant Principal. Following a two-year period working with Young Options as Head of Therapy and Regional Director, he joined SACCS (Shropshire, UK) as a Director in 2002. SACCS provides an integrated treatment programme for traumatized children, in residential and foster care. Working with Mary Walsh, he was central to the development of the SACCS Recovery Programme. He remained with SACCS until 2008. His qualifications include an MA in Therapeutic Child Care and Postgraduate Certificate in Strategic Social Care Leadership. He is the author of numerous papers and two books – *Therapeutic Approaches in Work with Traumatized Children and Young People* (2004) and with Terry Philpot, *A Child's Journey to Recovery: Assessment and Planning with Traumatized Children* (2008). He was also the series editor for the SACCS five-book series – Delivering Recovery for Traumatized Children.

References

Adelman, S., Ward, A. and Davison, S. (2003) 'Setting up clinical audit in a psychodynamic psychotherapy service: A pilot study.' Available at http://pb.rcpsych.org/cgi/content/full/27/10/371, accessed 6 May 2011.

Albee, G.W. (1996) 'Revolutions and counterrevolutions in prevention.' *American Psychologist 51*, 11, 1130–1133.

Altfeld, D.A. (1999) 'An experiential group model for psychotherapy supervision.' *International Journal of Group Psychotherapy 49*, 2, 237–254.

American Psychiatric Association (APA) (2000) *Diagnostic and Statistical Manual of Mental Disorders (DSM IV-TR), Fourth Edition.* Washington, DC: APA.

Andersson, L. (2008) 'Psychodynamic supervision in a group setting: Benefits and limitations.' *Psychotherapy in Australia 14*, 2, 36–41.

Australian Council for Children and Youth Organisations (ACCYO) (2008) *Safeguarding Children Program.* East Melbourne: ACCYO.

Australian Institute of Health and Welfare (2002) 'Child protection Australia 2000–01.' *Child Welfare Series No. 19, Cat. No. CWS 16.* Canberra: Australian Institute of Health and Welfare.

Balbernie, R. (1971) 'The impossible task.' Unpublished paper.

Balbernie, R. and Miller, E.J. (1984) 'The Cotswold Community: Management implications of the therapeutic task.' Unpublished paper – property of the Cotswold Community.

Barton, S. and Ingram, K. (2001) *Build Your Teenager's Self-Esteem: And Enjoy Being a Parent Again.* Melbourne: Anne O'Donovan Pty. Ltd.

Baumrind, D. (1991) 'The influence of parenting style on adolescent competence and substance use.' *Journal of Early Adolescence 11*, 1, 56–95.

Becker-Weidman, A. and Shell, D. (2005) *Creating Capacity for Attachment.* Oklahoma City, OK: Wood and Barnes.

Belsky, J. (1993) 'Etiology of child maltreatment: A developmental-ecological analysis.' *Psychological Bulletin 114*, 3, 413–434.

Bennington-Davis, M. and Murphy, T. (2005) 'Restraint and Seclusion: The Model for Limiting Their Use in Healthcare.' In L. Davidson (2010) *More FAQs for recovery oriented practice. Recover to Practice: Weekly Highlight, October 1 2010, Issue 21.* US Department of Health and Human Services. Available at www2.dsgonline.com/rtp/WH%202010/Weekly%20Highlight%20 October%201.pdf, accessed 6 May 2011.

Bennis, W. and Goldsmith, J. (1997) *Learning to Lead.* London: Nicholas Brealey Publishing.

Bentovim, A. (1992) *Trauma Organized Systems.* London: Karnac Books.

Bertalanffy, L. von (1950a) 'An outline of general system theory.' *British Journal of the Philosophy of Science 1*, 2, 134–165.

Bertalanffy, L. von (1950b) 'The theory of open systems in physics and biology.' *Science 111*, 2872, 23–29.

Best, D. (2009) 'Staff: Taking care of ourselves and each other.' Paper presented at Making All the Difference: A Therapeutic Community Approach to Residential and Community Care conference, 9 March, Carlow College, Carlow, Eire.

Bettelheim, B. (1950) *Love is not Enough: The Treatment of Emotionally Disturbed Children.* Glencoe, IL: Free Press.

Bettelheim, B. (1974) *A Home for the Heart.* London: Thames and Hudson.

Bion, W.R. (1962) *Learning from Experience.* London: Heinemann.

Black, C. (1989) *It's Never too Late to Have a Happy Childhood: Inspirations for Adult Children.* New York: Ballantine Books.

Bloom, S.L. (2003) Creating *Sanctuary: Healing from Systematic Abuses of Power.* Available at www.sanctuaryweb.com/PDFs_new/Bloom%20Creating%20Sanctuary%20Healing%20From%20Systemic.pdf, accessed on 12 June 2011.

Bloom, S. (2005) 'The Sanctuary model of organizational change for children's residential treatment.' *Therapeutic Communities 26*, 1, 61–78.

Boese, M. (2010) *From Participation to Leadership: Evaluation of the Leadership Service Program.* Victoria: Brotherhood of St Laurence.

Boston, M. and Szur, R. (eds) (1983) *Psychotherapy with Severely Deprived Children.* London: Maresfield Library.

Bowlby, J. (1969) *Attachment.* London: Hogarth Press.

Bowlby, J. (1979) *The Making and Breaking of Affectional Bonds.* London: Routledge.

Bridgeland, M. (1971) *Pioneer Work with Maladjusted Children.* Available at http://archive.pettrust.org.uk/survey-dockardrysdale1.htm, accessed 6 May 2011.

Brown, J. (1956) *Routines, Limits and Anchor Points: Handbook re. Management of the Child in the Therapeutic Family Throughout the Day.* Browndale, ON: John Brown.

Burt, H. and Halfpenny, N. (2008) 'The place for specialised residential care.' *Children Australia 33*, 2, 50–52.

Cairnes, M. (2006) *Approaching the Corporate Heart: Breaking through the New Horizons of Personal and Professional Success.* North Sydney: Simon and Schuster.

Cameron, R.J. and Maginn, C. (2008) 'The authentic warmth dimension of professional childcare.' *British Journal of Social Work 38*, 6, 1151–1172.

Cameron, R.J. and Maginn, C. (2009) *Achieving Positive Outcomes for Children in Care.* London: Sage Publications.

Canham, H. (1998) 'Growing up in residential care.' *Journal of Social Work Practice 12*, 1, 65–75.

Cant, D. (2002) 'Joined up psychotherapy: The place of individual psychotherapy in residential therapeutic provision for children.' *Journal of Child Psychotherapy 28*, 3, 267–281.

Chernis, C. (2009) *The Business Case for Emotional Intelligence.* New Brunswick, NJ: Rutgers University.

Chesterman, N. (2011) *Keeping the Faith.* Available at www.ispchildcare.org.uk/pdfs/keeping%20the%20faith.pdf, accessed 20 March 2011.

Chu, J.A. (1998) *Rebuilding Shattered Lives: The Responsible Treatment of Complex Post-Traumatic and Dissociative Disorders.* New York: John Wiley and Sons.

Clifford-Poston, A. (2001) *The Secrets of Successful Parenting: Understand What Your Child's Behaviour is Really Telling You.* Oxford: How To Books.

Clough, R., Bullock, R. and Ward, A. (2006) *What Works in Residential Child Care: A Review of Research Evidence and the Practical Considerations.* London: National Children's Bureau.

Cook, A., Blaustein, M., Spinazzola, J. and van der Kolk, B. (eds) (2003) *Complex Trauma in Children and Adolescents: White Paper from the National Child Traumatic Stress Network Complex Trauma Task Force.* Los Angeles, CA: National Child Traumatic Stress Network.

Cowen, E.L. (1985) 'Person-centered approaches to primary prevention: Situation-focused and competence enhancement.' *American Journal of Community Psychology 13*, 1, 31–48.

Cowen, E.L. (1996) 'The ontogenesis of primary prevention: Lengthy strides and stubbed toes.' *American Journal of Community Psychology 24*, 2, 235–249.

Department of Health (DoH), Home Office and Department for Education and Employment (DfEE) (1999) *Working Together to Safeguard Children*. London: The Stationery Office.

Diamond, J. (2003) 'How does your garden grow?' Paper presented at the Association of Therapeutic Communities conference, Windsor, Berkshire.

Dockar-Drysdale, B. (1953) 'Some Aspects of Damage and Restitution.' In B. Dockar-Drysdale, *Therapy and Consultation in Child Care* (1993). London: Free Association Books.

Dockar-Drysdale, B. (1958) 'The Residential Treatment of 'Frozen' Children.' In B. Dockar-Drysdale (1993) *Therapy and Consultation in Child Care*. London: Free Association Books.

Dockar-Drysdale, B. (1961) 'The Problem of Making Adaptation to the Needs of the Individual Child in the Group.' In B. Dockar-Drysdale (1990) *The Provision of Primary Experience*. London: Free Association Books.

Dockar-Drysdale, B. (1963) 'The Possibility of Regression in a Structured Environment.' In B. Dockar-Drysdale (1968) *Therapy in Child Care*. London: Longman.

Dockar-Drysdale, B. (1969) 'Meeting Children's Emotional Needs.' In B. Dockar-Drysdale (1993) *Therapy and Consultation in Child Care*. London: Free Association Books.

Dockar-Drysdale, B. (1988) 'The Difference Between Child Care and Therapeutic Management.' In B. Dockar-Drysdale (1990) *The Provision of Primary Experience*. London: Free Association Books.

Dockar-Drysdale, B. (1990a) *The Provision of Primary Experience: Winnicottian Work with Children and Adolescents*. London: Free Association Books.

Dockar-Drysdale, B. (1990b) 'The Management of Violence.' In B. Dockar-Drysdale (1990) *The Provision of Primary Experience*. London: Free Association Books.

Dockar-Drysdale, B. (1990c) 'Collusive Anxiety in the Residential Treatment of Disturbed Adolescents.' In B. Dockar-Drysdale (1990) *The Provision of Primary Experience*. London: Free Association Books.

Dockar-Drysdale, B. (1993) *Therapy and Consultation in Child Care*. London: Free Association Books.

Dowdy, E., Furlong, M., Eklund, K., Saeki, E. and Ritchey, K. (2010) *Screening for Mental Health and Wellness: Current School-based Practices and Emerging Possibilities*. Santa Barbara, CA: University of California Santa Barbara Graduate School of Education, Department of Counseling, Clinical and School Psychology. Available at http://web.me.com/michaelfurlong/HKIED/Welcome_files/4Dowdy_Furlong_submitted.pdf, accessed 6 May 2011.

Fahlberg, V. (ed.) (1990) *Residential Treatment*. Indianapolis, IN: Perspective Press.

Farragher, B. and Yanosy, S. (2005) 'Creating a trauma-sensitive culture in residential treatment.' *Therapeutic Communities 26*, 1, 93–109.

Fletcher, A. (2008) *Ladder of Young People's Participation*. The Free Child Project. Available at http://freechild.org/ladder.htm, accessed 6 May 2011.

Fox, D. and Prilleltensky, I. (eds) (1997) *Critical Psychology: An Introduction*. London: Sage Publications.

Freiberg, K. and Freiberg, J. (1998) *Nuts! Southwest Airlines' Crazy Recipe for Business and Personal Success*. New York: Broadway Books.

Freud, A. (1986) *The Ego and Mechanisms of Defence*. London: Hogarth Press.

Freud, S. (1912) 'The Dynamics of Transference.' In J. Strachey (ed.) (1978) *The Standard Edition of the Complete Psychological Works of Sigmund Freud, Vol. XII*. London: Hogarth Press.

Freud, S. (1914) 'Remembering, Repeating and Working-Through: Further Recommendations on the Technique of Psychoanalysis II.' In J. Strachey (ed.) (1978) *The Standard Edition of the Complete Psychological Works of Sigmund Freud, Vol. XII.* London: Hogarth Press.

Freud, S. (1926) 'Inhibitions, Symptoms and Anxiety.' In J. Strachey (ed.) (1978) *The Standard Edition of the Complete Psychological Works of Sigmund Freud, Vol. XX.* London: Hogarth Press.

Freud, S. (1950) 'Fragment of an Analysis of a Case of Hysteria.' In J. Strachey (ed.) (1978) *The Standard Edition of the Complete Psychological Works of Sigmund Freud, Vol. VII.* London: Hogarth Press.

Friedman, M. (2005) *Trying Hard is Not Good Enough: How to Produce Measurable Improvements for Customers and Communities.* Bloomington, IN: Trafford Publishing.

Fuller, A. (1998) *From Survival to Thriving: Promoting Mental Health in Young People.* Camberwell: Australian Council for Educational Research.

Garbarino, J. (1990) *Lost Boys: Why our Sons Turn Violent and How we can Save Them.* New York: Free Press.

Gabbard, G.O. (2004) *Long Term Psychodynamic Psychotherapy: A Basic Text.* Washington, DC: American Psychiatric Publishing.

Gabbard, G.O. (2010) *Long Term Psychodynamic Psychotherapy.* Arlington, VA: American Psychiatric Publishing.

Gardner, H. (1995) *Leading Minds.* New York: Basic Books.

Gerhardt, S. (2004) *Why Love Matters: How Affection Shapes a Baby's Brain.* Hove: Brunner-Routledge.

Gordon, R. (2010) 'The passage of trauma through life.' *Aware Newsletter 24,* 6–9. Melbourne: Australian Centre for the Study of Sexual Assault.

Green, V. (ed.) (2003) *Emotional Development in Psychoanalysis, Attachment Theory and Neuroscience: Creating Connections.* Hove and New York: Brunner-Routledge.

Hamil, J. (2004) 'The symbolic significance of food in the treatment, care and recovery of emotionally damaged children.' Unpublished paper.

Hannon, C., Wood, C. and Bazalgette, L. (2010) *In Loco Parentis: 'To Deliver the Best for Looked After Children, the State must be a Confident Parent…'* London: Demos.

Hart, R. (1992) *Children's Participation from Tokenism to Citizenship.* Available at www.unicef-irc.org/ publications/pdf/childrens_participation.pdf, accessed 6 May 2011.

Harvey, J. (2006) *Valuing and Educating Young People: Stern Love the Lyward Way.* London and Philadelphia: Jessica Kingsley Publishers.

Heeswyk, P. van (1997) *Analysing Adolescence.* London: Sheldon Press.

Heeswyk, P. van (2004) 'Foreword.' In P. Tomlinson, *Therapeutic Approaches in Work with Traumatized Children and Young People: Theory and Practice.* London and Philadelphia: Jessica Kingsley Publishers.

Hills, J. (2005) 'Holding the looked after child through reflecting dialogue.' *Context 78,* April, 18–23.

Holmes, E. (1983) 'I'm Bad, No Good, Can't Think.' In M. Boston and R. Szur (eds) *Psychotherapy with Severely Deprived Children.* London: Maresfield Library.

Hoyle, L. (2004) 'From Sycophant to Saboteur: Responses to Organizational Change.' In C. Huffington, D. Armstrong, W. Halton, L. Hoyle and J. Pooley (eds) *Working Below the Surface: The Emotional Life of Contemporary Organisations.* London: Karnac Books.

Hrdy, S. (2000) *Mother Nature: Maternal Instincts and How They Shape the Human Species.* New York: Ballantine Books.

Institute of Public Care (2006) *An Approach to Outcome Based Commissioning and Contracting. Certificate in Commissioning and Purchasing for Public Care.* Oxford: Institute of Public Care.

International Society for the Study of Disassociation Task Force on Children and Adolescence (ISSD) (2000) 'Guidelines for the evaluation and treatment of dissociative symptoms of children and adolescents.' *Journal of Trauma and Dissociation 3*, 109–134.

Jacobs, D.W. (1995) *Winnicott.* London: Sage Publications.

Janet, P. (1904) 'L'amnésie et la dissociation des souvenirs par l'émotion.' ['Amnesia and the dissociation of memories by emotions.'] *Journal de Psychologie 1*, 417–453.

Janis, I.L. (1982) *Groupthink.* New York: Houghton Mifflin.

Janzing, C. (1991) 'One foot in hell: On self-destructive staff dynamics.' *International Journal of Therapeutic Communities 12*, 1, 5–12.

Johnston, C. and Gowers, S. (2005) 'Routine outcome measurement: A survey of UK child and adolescent mental health services.' *Child and Adolescent Mental Health 10*, 3, 133–139.

Jones, M. (1968) *Beyond the Therapeutic Community: Social Learning and Social Psychiatry.* New Haven, CT: Yale University Press.

Jongsma, A.E., Jr., and Peterson, L.M. (2003) *The Complete Adult Psychotherapy Treatment Planner, Third Edition.* New York: John Wiley and Sons.

Kahan, B. (1995) 'The importance of child care training.' Paper presented at Association of Residential Child Care (ARCC) conference, 12 July 1995.

Keenan, K.A. (2006) 'Food Glorious Food: An Exploration of the Issues of Anxiety and its Containment for Children and Adults Surrounding Food and Mealtimes in a Residential Therapeutic Setting.' MA Dissertation, Planned Environment Therapy Trust. Available at http://archive.pettrust.org.uk/library/keenan2006.pdf, accessed 4 April 2011.

Khaleelee, O. (2004) 'Not leading followers, not following leaders: The contemporary erosion of the traditional social contract.' *Organisational and Social Dynamics 4*, 1, 268–284.

Khaleelee, O. (2007) 'The use of the defence mechanism test to aid understanding of the personality of senior executives and the implications for their careers.' Paper prepared for Current Developments in the Use of Projective Techniques Across the Life Span conference, London, 15 June 2007.

Khaleelee, O. and Tomlinson, P. (1997) 'Intrapsychic factors in staff selection at the Cotswold Community.' *Therapeutic Communities 18*, 4, 255–269.

Klein, M. (1946) 'Notes on some schizoid mechanisms.' *International Journal of Psycho-Analysis 27*, 99–110.

Lamont, A. (2010) *Effects of Child Abuse and Neglect for Children and Adolescents.* Melbourne: National Protection Clearinghouse.

Lanyado, M. (1988) 'Working with anxiety in a primary residential special school.' *Maladjustment and Therapeutic Education 6*, 1, 36–48.

Lanyado, M. (1989) 'United we stand.' *Maladjustment and Therapeutic Education 7*, 3, 136–146.

Leiper, R. (1994) 'Evaluation: Organisations Learning from Experience.' In A. Obholzer and V. Zagier-Roberts (eds) (1994) *The Unconscious at Work: Individual and Organisational Stress in the Human Services.* London: Routledge.

Levy, T.M. and Orlans, M. (1998) *Attachment, Trauma and Healing: Understanding and Treating Attachment Disorder in Children and Families.* Washington, DC: CWLA Press.

Lindy, J.D. (2007) 'Psychoanalytic Psychotherapy of Post Traumatic Stress Disorder: The Nature of the Therapeutic Relationship.' In B.A. van der Kolk, A.C. McFarlane and L. Weisaeth (eds) *Traumatic Stress: The Effects of Overwhelming Experience on Mind, Body and Society.* New York: Guilford Press.

Loewenthal, D. and Winter, D. (2006) *What Is Psychotherapeutic Research?* London: Karnac Books.

Maher, M. (2003) 'Therapeutic Childcare and the Local Authority.' In A. Ward, K. Kasinski, J. Pooley and A. Worthington (eds) *Therapeutic Communities for Children and Young People.* London and Philadelphia: Jessica Kingsley Publishers.

Main, T. (au.) and Johns, J. (ed.) (1989) *The Ailment and Other Psychoanalytic Essays.* London: Free Association Books.

Martin, N. (2009) *From Discrimination to Social Inclusion.* Brisbane: Queensland Alliance.

Mattinson, J. (1970) *The Reflection Process in Casework Supervision.* London: Tavistock Institute of Marital Studies.

Mawson, A. (2008) *The Social Entrepreneur: Making Communities Work.* London: Atlantic Books.

McCluskey, U. and Duerden, S. (1993) 'Pre-verbal communication: The role of establishing rhythms of communication between self and other.' *Journal of Social Work Practice 7,* 1, 17–27.

McKnight, J. (1995) *The Careless Society: Community and its Counterfeits.* New York: Basic Books.

McMahon, L. (1995) 'Developing skills in therapeutic communication in daily living with emotionally disturbed children and young people.' Available at www.johnwhitwell. co.uk/index.php/developing-skills-in-therapeutic-communication-in-daily-living-linnet-mcmahon, accessed 6 May 2011.

McMahon, M. (2003) 'Applying the Therapeutic Community Model in Other Settings.' In A. Ward, K. Kasinski, J. Pooley and A. Worthington (eds) *Therapeutic Communities for Children and Young People.* London and Philadelphia: Jessica Kingsley Publishers.

McMillan, D.W. and Chavis, D.M. (1986) 'Sense of community: A definition and theory.' *Journal of Community Psychology 14,* 1, 6–23.

Menzies Lyth, I. (1959, 1961, 1970) 'The Functioning of Social Systems as a Defence Against Anxiety.' In I. Menzies Lyth (1988) *Containing Anxiety in Institutions: Selected Essays, Vol. 1.* London: Free Association Books.

Menzies Lyth, I. (1979) 'Staff Support Systems: Task and Anti-Task in Adolescent Institutions.' In I. Menzies Lyth (1988) *Containing Anxiety in Institutions: Selected Essays, Vol. 1.* London: Free Association Books.

Menzies Lyth, I. (1985) 'The Development of the Self in Children in Institutions.' In I. Menzies Lyth (1988) *Containing Anxiety in Institutions: Selected Essays, Vol. 1.* London: Free Association Books.

Menzies Lyth, I. (1990) 'Foreword.' In B. Dockar-Drysdale (1990) *The Provision of Primary Experience: Winnicottian Work with Children and Adolescents.* London: Free Association Books.

Menzies Lyth, I. (1998) 'Foreword.' In R. Davies (1998) *Stress in Social Work.* London and Philadelphia: Jessica Kingsley Publishers.

Mercogliano, C. and Debus, K. (1999) 'An interview with Joseph Chilton Pearce.' Available at www.lorien.nsw.edu.au/joomla/images/ReferenceMaterial/an%20interview%20with%20 joseph%20chilton%20pearce.pdf, accessed 4 April 2011.

Miller, E.J. (1986) *The Cotswold Community: A Working Note.* London: The Tavistock Institute.

Miller, E.J. (1993) *The Healthy Organisation: Creating a Holding Environment: Conditions for Psychological Security.* London: The Tavistock Institute.

Miller, E.J. (1989) 'Towards an organizational model for residential treatment of adolescents.' Unpublished paper.

Miller, E.J. and Rice, A.K. (1967) *Systems of Organization: The Control of Task and Sentient Boundaries.* London: Tavistock Publications.

Mollon, P. (1996) *Multiple Selves, Multiple Voices: Working with Trauma, Violation and Dissociation.* Chichester: John Wiley and Sons.

Obholzer, A. (1994) 'The Troublesome Individual and the Troubled Institution.' In A. Obholzer and V. Zagier Roberts (eds) *The Unconscious at Work: Individual and Organizational Stress in the Human Services.* London: Routledge.

Ofsted (2009) *The Annual Report of Her Majesty's Chief Inspector of Education, Children's Services and Skills 2008/09.* London: The Stationery Office.

Oxford Pocket Dictionary (1992) New York: Oxford University Press.

Panksapp, J. (1999) 'Emotions as viewed by psychoanalysis and neuroscience: An exercise in consilience.' *Neuro-Psychoanalysis 1,* 1, 15–39.

Parry, G. and Richardson, A. (1996) *NHS Psychotherapy Services in England: Review of Strategic Policy.* London: NHS Executive.

Peck, M.S. (1991) 'The joy of community.' Available at www.context.org/ICLIB/IC29/Peck.htm, accessed 4 July 2011.

Perry, B.D. (1997) 'Incubated in Terror: Neuro-developmental Factors in the "Cycle of Violence."' In J.D. Osofstey (ed.) *Children in a Violent Society.* New York: Guilford Press.

Perry, B.D. (2004) 'Maltreatment and the Developing Child: How Early Childhood Experience Shapes Child and Culture.' Margaret McCain lecture, London Convention Centre, 23 September 2004.

Perry, B.D. (2005) *Maltreatment and the Developing Child: How Early Childhood Experience Shapes Child and Culture.* Margaret McCain lecture on September 23, 2004, Centre for Children and Families in the Justice System. Available at www.lfcc.on.ca/mccain/perry.pdf, accessed on 1 June 2011.

Perry, B.D. (2006) 'Applying Principles of Neurodevelopment to Clinical Work with Maltreated and Traumatized Children: The Neurosequential Model of Therapeutics.' In N. Boyd (ed.) *Traumatized Youth in Child Welfare.* New York: Guilford Press.

Perry, B.D. and Hambrick, E.P. (2008) 'The neurosequential model of therapeutics.' *Reclaiming Children and Youth 17,* 3, 38–43.

Perry, B.D., Pollard, R., Blakey, T.L. and Baker, W.L. (1995) 'Childhood trauma, the neurobiology of adaptation and "use-dependent" development of the brain: How "states" become "traits".' *Infant Mental Health Journal 16,* 4, 271–291.

Perry, B.D. and Szalavitz, M. (2006) *The Boy who was Raised as a Dog: And Other Stories from a Child Psychiatrist's Notebook.* New York, NY: Basic Books.

Perry, B.D. and Szalavitz, M. (2010) *Born for Love: Why Empathy is Essential and Endangered.* New York: HarperCollins.

Phillips, A. (1988) *Winnicott.* London: Frontier Press.

Phillips, A. (2009) 'In praise of difficult children.' *London Review of Books 31,* 3, 16.

Piper, H. and Smith, H. (2003) '"Touch" in educational and child care settings: Dilemmas and responses.' *British Educational Research Journal 29,* 6, 879–894.

Plantz, M., Greenway, M. and Hendricks, M. (1999) *Outcome Measurement: Showing Results in the Non-profit Sector.* Available at www.nationalserviceresources.org/filemanager/download/ProgramMgmt/Outcome_Measurement_Showing_Results_Nonprofit_Sector.prf, accessed 6 May 2011.

Pretty, G., Bishop, B. and Fisher, A. (2006) *Psychological Sense of Community and its Relevance to Wellbeing and Everyday Life in Australia.* Melbourne: Australian Psychological Society.

Prilleltensky, I. (1989) 'Psychology and the status quo.' *American Psychologist 44,* 5, 795–802.

Prilleltensky, I. (1994) *The Morals and Politics of Psychology: Psychological Discourse and the Status Quo.* Albany, NY: State University of New York Press.

Prilleltensky, I. (1997) 'Values, assumptions, and practices: Assessing the moral implications of psychological discourse and action.' *American Psychologist 52,* 5, 517–535.

Prilleltensky, I. (2005) 'Promoting wellbeing: Time for a paradigm shift.' *Scandinavian Journal of Public Health 33*, 66, 53–60.

Prilleltensky, I. (2006) 'Psychopolitical validity: Working with power to promote justice and well-being.' Paper presented at the First International Conference of Community Psychology, San Juan, Puerto Rico, 10 June 2006.

Prilleltensky, I. (2007) 'Happy but dead: From paradox to paradigm in the quest for justice and well-being.' Keynote address to the meetings of International Society for Theory and Psychology, Toronto, Canada, 21 June 2007.

Prilleltensky, I. and Fox, D. (2007) 'Promoting well-being and preventing child maltreatment.' Presentation to Prevent Child Abuse, University of Miami, March 1 2007.

Prilleltensky, I. and Nelson, G. (2000) 'Promoting child and family wellness: Priorities for psychological and social interventions.' *Journal of Community and Applied Social Psychology 10*, 2, 85–105.

Prilleltensky, I., Peirson, L. and Nelson, G. (2001) 'Mapping the Terrain: Framework for Promoting Family Wellness and Preventing Child Maltreatment' In I. Prilleltensky, G. Nelson and L. Peirson (eds) (2001) *Promoting Family Wellness and Preventing Child Maltreatment: Fundamentals for Thinking and Action.* London: University of Toronto Press.

Prior, V. and Glaser, D. (2006) *Understanding Attachment and Attachment Disorders.* London and Philadelphia: Jessica Kingsley Publishers.

Pughe, B. and Philpot, T. (2007) *Living Alongside a Child's Recovery: Therapeutic Parenting with Traumatized Children.* London and Philadelphia: Jessica Kingsley Publishers.

Putnam, F.W. (2004) 'Foreword.' In P.T. Stien and J. Kendall, *Psychological Trauma and the Developing Brain: Neurologically Based Interventions for Troubled Children.* New York: The Haworth Maltreatment and Trauma Press.

Quality Improvement Council (QIC) (2004) *Health and Community Services Standards.* Melbourne: QIC.

Raman, S., Inder, B. and Forbes, C. (2005) *Investing for Success: The Economics of Supporting Young People Leaving Care.* Melbourne: Centre for Excellence in Child and Family Welfare.

Read, J., Fink, P.J., Rudegeair, T., Felitti, V. and Whitfield, C. (2008) 'Child maltreatment and psychosis: A return to a genuinely integrated bio-psycho-social model.' *Clinical Schizophrenia and Related Psychoses 2*, 3, 235–254.

Rice, A.K. (1963) *The Enterprise and its Environment.* London: Tavistock Publications.

Rose, M. (1990) *Healing Hurt Minds: The Peper Harow Experience.* London and New York: Tavistock/Routledge.

Rose, M. (1997) *Transforming Hate to Love: An Outcome Study of the Peper Harow Treatment Process for Adolescents.* London and New York: Routledge.

Rose, R. and Philpot, T. (2005) *The Child's Own Story: Life Story Work with Traumatized Children.* London and Philadelphia: Jessica Kingsley Publishers.

Ruch, G. (2010) 'Theoretical Frameworks Informing Relationship-Based Practice.' In G. Ruch, D. Turney and A. Ward (eds) *Relationship-Based Social Work: Getting to the Heart of Practice.* London and Philadelphia: Jessica Kingsley Publishers.

SACCS (2010) *The SACCS Recovery Programme.* Available at http://saccs.co.uk, accessed 6 May 2011.

Salovey, P. and Mayer, J.D. (1990) 'Emotional intelligence.' *Imagination, Cognition and Personality 9*, 185–211.

Salzberger-Wittenberg, I. (1988) *Psycho-Analytic Insight and Relationships: A Kleinian Approach.* London and New York: Routledge.

Sarason, S.B. (1974) *The Psychological Sense of Community: Prospects for a Community Psychology.* San Francisco: Jossey-Bass.

Schmidt Neven, R. (1997) *Emotional Milestones from Birth to Adulthood: A Psychodynamic Approach.* London and Pennsylvania: Jessica Kingsley Publishers.

Schofield, G. and Beek, M. (2005) 'Risk and resilience in long-term foster care.' *British Journal of Social Work 35,* 8, 1283–1301.

Seligman, M. (2002) *Authentic Happiness: Using the New Positive Psychology to Realise your Potential for Lasting Fulfilment.* London: Nicholas Brealey.

Shapiro, E.R. and Carr, W. (1991) *Lost in Familiar Places: Creating New Connections Between the Individual and Society.* New Haven, CT and London: Yale University Press.

Sharpe, C. (2008) 'Residential care can do with all the help it can get.' *Irish Journal of Applied Social Studies 8,* 1, 30–50.

Smith, M. (2009) *Rethinking Residential Child Care: Positive Perspectives.* Portland, OR: The Policy Press.

Social Services Inspectorate (SSI) (1993) *Inspecting for Quality: Guidance on Standards for Short-Term Breaks.* London: HMSO.

Stapley, L. (1996) *Personality of the Organisation.* London and New York: Free Association Books.

Stein, M. (2005) *Resilience and Young People Leaving Care: Overcoming the Odds.* York: Joseph Rowntree Foundation.

Stern, D. (1985) *The Interpersonal World of the Infant: A View From Psychoanalysis and Developmental Psychology.* New York: Basic Books.

Stewart J. (1998) *Understanding the Management of Local Government.* London: Longman.

Stien, P.T. and Kendall, J. (2004) *Psychological Trauma and the Developing Brain: Neurologically Based Interventions for Troubled Children.* New York, London, Oxford: The Haworth Maltreatment and Trauma Press.

Stokoe, P. (2003) 'Group Thinking.' In A. Ward, K. Kasinski and A. Worthington (eds) *Therapeutic Communities for Children and Young People.* London and New York: Jessica Kingsley Publishers.

Thomas, G. (2000) *Parent Effectiveness Training: The Proven Program for Raising Responsible Children.* New York: Three Rivers Press.

Thompson, N. (2000) *Theory and Practice in Human Services.* Buckingham and Philadelphia: Open University Press.

Thompson, N. (2008) 'Focusing on outcomes: Developing systematic practice.' *Practice 20,* 1, 5–16.

Thompson, N. (2010) *Theorizing Social Work Practice.* Basingstoke: Palgrave Macmillan.

Tomlinson, P. (2004) *Therapeutic Approaches in Work with Traumatized Children and Young People: Theory and Practice.* London and Philadelphia: Jessica Kingsley Publishers.

Tomlinson, P. (2005) 'The capacity to think: Why it is important and what makes it difficult in work with traumatized children.' *Therapeutic Communities 26,* 1, 41–53.

Tomlinson, P. (2008) 'The experience of breakdown and the breakdown that can't be experienced.' *Journal of Social Work Practice 22,* 1, 15–25.

Tomlinson, P. and Philpot, T. (2008) *A Child's Journey to Recovery: Assessment and Planning with Traumatized Children.* London and Philadelphia: Jessica Kingsley Publishers.

Trevithick, P. (1995) 'Cycling over Everest: Groupwork with depressed women.' *Groupwork 8,* 1, 5–33.

Trickett, P.K., Allen, L., Schellenbach, C.J. and Zigler, E. (1998) 'Integrating and Advancing the Knowledge Base About Violence Against Children: Implications for Intervention and Prevention.' In P.K. Trickett and C.J. Schellenbach (eds) *Violence Against Children in the Family and the Community.* Washington, DC: American Psychological Association.

Trickett, P. and Putnam, F. (1993) 'Impact of Child sexual abuse on females: Toward a developmental, psychobiological integration.' *Psychological Science 4*, 2, 81–87.

Trist, E.L., Higgins, G.W., Murray, H. and Pollock, A.B. (1963) *Organizational Choice: Capabilities of Groups at the Coal Face Under Changing Technologies.* London: Tavistock.

Trowell, J. (1994) 'Assessing Sexually Abused Children.' In M. Rustin and E. Quagliata (eds) (2004) *Assessment in Child Psychotherapy.* London: H. Karnac.

Tucci, J., Mitchell, J. and Goddard, C. (2010) *Response to National Standards for Out of Home Care.* Melbourne: Australian Childhood Foundation.

Turner, S.W., McFarlane, A.C. and van der Kolk, B.A. (2007) 'The Therapeutic Environment and New Explorations in the Treatment of Posttraumatic Stress.' In B.A. van der Kolk, A.C. McFarlane and L. Weisaeth (eds) *Traumatic Stress: The Effects of Overwhelming Experience on Mind, Body and Society.* New York: Guilford Press.

van der Kolk, B.A. and McFarlane, A.C. (2007) 'Conclusions and Future Directions.' In B.A. van der Kolk, A.C. McFarlane and L. Weisaeth (eds) *Traumatic Stress: The Effects of Overwhelming Experience on Mind, Body and Society.* New York: Guilford Press.

van der Kolk, B.A. and Newman, A.C. (2007) 'The Black Hole of Trauma.' In B.A. van der Kolk, A.C. McFarlane and L. Weisaeth (eds) *Traumatic Stress: The Effects of Overwhelming Experience on Mind, Body and Society.* New York: Guilford Press.

van der Kolk, B.A., McFarlane, A.C. and van der Hart, O. (2007) 'A General Approach to Posttraumatic Stress Disorder.' In B.A. van der Kolk, A.C. McFarlane and L. Weisaeth (eds) *Traumatic Stress: The Effects of Overwhelming Experience on Mind, Body and Society.* New York: Guilford Press.

van der Kolk, B.A., van der Hart, O. and Marmar, C.R. (2007) 'Dissociation and Information Processing in Posttraumatic Stress Disorder.' In B.A. van der Kolk, A.C. McFarlane and L. Weisaeth (eds) *Traumatic Stress: The Effects of Overwhelming Experience on Mind, Body and Society.* New York: Guilford Press.

Waddell, M. (1989) 'Living in two worlds: Psychodynamic theory and social work practice.' Available at http://human-nature.com/free-associations/waddell%20living_in_two_worlds.htm, accessed 4 April 2011.

Waddell, M. (2004) 'Attachment anxiety.' *Young Minds Magazine 72*, September/October.

Wadsworth, Y. (2011) *Everyday Evaluation on the Run.* Crows Nest, NSW: Allen & Unwin.

Ward, A. (1996) 'Never mind the theory, feel the guidelines. Practice, theory and official guidance in residential child care: The case of the therapeutic communities.' *Therapeutic Communities 17*, 1, 19–29.

Ward, A. (1998) 'On "Reflection".' In A. Ward, and L. McMahon (eds) *Intuition is not Enough.* London: Routledge.

Ward, A. (2004) 'Assessing and meeting children's emotional needs.' Lecture notes presented at the Therapeutic Childcare Study Day, University of Reading.

Ward, A. (2010) 'The Learning Relationship: Learning and Development for Relationship-Based Practice.' In G. Ruch, D. Turney and A. Ward (eds) *Relationship-Based Social Work: Getting to the Heart of Practice.* London and Philadelphia: Jessica Kingsley Publishers.

Wharf, B. (1993) 'Rethinking Child Welfare.' In B. Wharf (ed.) *Rethinking Child Welfare in Canada.* Toronto: McClelland and Stewart.

Whitwell, J. (1998a) 'Boundaries and parameters.' Available at www.johnwhitwell.co.uk/index.php/boundaries-and-parameters, accessed 6 May 2011.

Whitwell, J. (1998b) 'What is a therapeutic community?' *Emotional and Behavioural Difficulties 3*, 1, 12–19.

Whitwell, J. (2009) 'Why a therapeutic community approach? (or "What did I learn from my 27 years working in a therapeutic community that I have found to be useful in other settings?").' Making All the Difference: A Therapeutic Community Approach to Residential and Community Care conference, 9 March, Carlow College, Carlow, Eire.

Whitwell, J. (2010) 'Therapeutic communities and therapeutic fostering: Similarities and differences: My journey.' Paper presented at the conference Using High Quality Residential Care to Meet the Real Needs of Children: From Theory to Practice, 4 October 2010 at the Northern School of Child and Adolescent Psychotherapy, Leeds. Available at www.johnwhitwell.co.uk, accessed 4 April 2011.

WHO (World Health Organisation) (1986) *Ottawa Charter.* Ottawa: WHO.

Willis, M. (2001) 'Outcomes in Social Care: Conceptual Confusion and Practical Impossibility?' In M. Willis (2005) *Leadership for Social Care Outcomes Module Handbook 2005.* University of Birmingham: INLOGOV.

Winnicott, C. (1968) 'The stress of residential living.' Paper presented at the Association of Workers for Maladjusted Children (AWMC) conference, St. Mary's College, Cheltenham.

Winnicott, D.W. (1947) 'Residential Management and Treatment for Delinquent Children.' In D.W. Winnicott (1984) *Deprivation and Delinquency.* London and New York: Tavistock Publications.

Winnicott, D.W. (1953) 'Transitional objects and transitional phenomena.' *International Journal of Psycho-Analysis 34,* 89–97.

Winnicott, D.W. (1955) 'Group Influences and the Maladjusted Child: The School Aspect.' In D.W. Winnicott (1984) *Deprivation and Delinquency.* London and New York: Tavistock Publications.

Winnicott, D.W. (1956a) 'Primary Maternal Preoccupation.' In D.W. Winnicott (1975) *Through Paediatrics to Psychoanalysis.* London: Hogarth Press and the Institute of Psychoanalysis.

Winnicott, D.W. (1956b) 'The Anti-Social Tendency.' In D.W. Winnicott (1984) Deprivation *and Delinquency.* London and New York: Tavistock Publications.

Winnicott, D.W. (1958) 'The capacity to be alone.' *The International Journal of Psycho-Analysis 39,* 416–420.

Winnicott, D.W. (1960) 'Ego Distortion in Terms of True and False Self.' In D.W. Winnicott (1972) *The Maturational Process and the Facilitating Environment.* London: Hogarth Press and the Institute of Psychoanalysis.

Winnicott, D.W. (1964) *The Child, The Family and The Outside* World. London: Penguin.

Winnicott, D.W. (1970) 'Residential Care as Therapy.' In D.W. Winnicott (1984) Deprivation *and Delinquency.* London and New York: Tavistock Publications.

Winnicott, D.W. (1971) *Playing and Reality.* London: Routledge.

Winnicott, D.W. (1986) *Home is Where We Start From.* Harmondsworth: Penguin.

Winnicott, D.W. (1990) *The Maturational Process and the Facilitating Environment.* London: Karnac Books.

Winnicott, D.W. (1992) 'Hate in the Countertransference.' In D.W. Winnicott (1975) *Through Paediatrics to Psychoanalysis.* London: Karnac Books.

Winter, D. (2006) 'Avoiding the Fate of the Dodo Bird: The Challenge of Evidence-Based Practice.' In D. Loewenthal and D. Winter (2006) *What is Psychotherapeutic Research?* London: Karnac Books.

Wise, S. (1999) *Research Report No.2 1999: The UK Looking After Children approach in Australia.* Available at www.aifs.gov.au/institute/pubs/resreport2/main.html, accessed 6 May 2011.

Wise, S. and Egger, S. (2010) *The Looking After Children Outcomes Data Project–Final Report.* Prepared for the Department of Human Services by the Australian Institute of Family Studies, Melbourne.

Witness Justice (2011) *Trauma is the Common Denominator, Healing is the Common Goal.* Rockville, MD: Witness Justice. Available at www.witnessjustice.org/health/trauma.cfm, accessed 4 April 2011.

Woods, J. (2003) *Boys Who Have Abused: Psychoanalytic Psychotherapy with Victim/ Perpetrators of Sexual Abuse.* London and New York: Jessica Kingsley Publishers.

Worldwide Alternatives to Violence (2005) *The WAVE Report 2005: Violence and What to Do About It.* Croydon: The Wave Trust. Available at www.wavetrust.org/reports/wave_report_2005_1_0. pdf, accessed 4 April 2011.

Youth Coalition of the ACT (Australian Capital Territory) (2008) *The Big Red Book: A Handbook and Directory for People who Work with Young People in the ACT.* Available at www.youthcoalition. net, accessed 6 May 2011.

Youth on Board (2000) *Why and How to Involve Young People in Organizational Decision Making.* Washington, DC: National Center for Nonprofit Boards.

Subject Index

Author Index